BLUES &
BEATLES

BLUES & BEATLES

NEIL ROBERTS

Pitch Publishing Ltd
A2 Yeoman Gate, Yeoman Way, Durrington,
BN13 3QZ
Email: info@pitchpublishing.co.uk
Web: www.pitchpublishing.co.uk

Published by Pitch Publishing 2011
Paperback edition 2018
Text © 2011 Neil Roberts

A CIP catalogue record for this book is available from the British
Library.

13-digit ISBN: 978-1-78531-399-8

Typesetting and origination by Pitch Publishing.

Printed in India by Replika Press

Contents

For George and Liam

Foreword

by Bill Kenwright CBE

There are two questions I'm constantly asked, that really faze me. 'WHY do you love your football club so much? Not support it – love it?'And secondly: 'What was it about the music of 1956 that changed your life?'

Two questions that are probably impossible to answer. All I can say is: 'When you know – you know!'

I had worshipped Everton and in particular their centre-forward 'the Cannonball Kid' Dave Hickson for a few years before 1956, and the previous year I had written to every director telling them that the club was insane to have transferred him to Aston Villa. Similarly, I had enjoyed the few 78s of Frankie Laine, Johnnie Ray and Doris Day that my family owned. But until 1956, I didn't 'know'. Truly know!

Then on 20 October, 1956, the lowly-placed Blues travelled to high-flying Manchester United and with a young goalkeeper called Albert Dunlop making his debut, trounced the Red Devils 5-2 at Old Trafford. My life changed on that day. I knew!! The die had been cast and my whole life would be lived as a worshipper of the Merseyside team that played in blue. The following Saturday we smashed Arsenal 4-0, and if confirmation was needed (it wasn't!) my decision had been approved by those up above who smile on us!

On that same weekend, Elvis Presley's 'Hound Dog' went to number two in the charts (alongside Frankie Laine, Johnnie Ray, and Doris Day!). I had never heard anything like it. A rhythm, a beat, and a singer that got to me like no other had ever come close.

So my love affair started – and continues to this very day. And undoubtedly will for every day of the rest of my life.

When Neil sent me his wonderful book, long before it had been published, it reminded me so much of my own journey. The boys' pen, the half-time gate, bunking in behind the church, queuing all night for a derby ticket, seeing 'the lights' at Goodison for the first time at a Lancashire Senior Cup tie, and crying all night after a defeat by lowly Bradford City. Just like Neil, I could try and tell you what it all meant to me – but I wouldn't come close. I could tell you about the goals against the Reds; Bally's from the by-line; Kingie's drive which restored our pride; Sharpie's strike at their place; TC's unbelievable double reprieve, and probably the most famous of all – the one that Clive Thomas robbed us of in 1977. I could try to explain what they meant to me – but I wouldn't come close. What I do know, though, is that hundreds of thousands of Evertonians all over the world would understand. As would Neil. And that matters.

They might also understand that 'Don't Be Cruel' (the B-side of the aforementioned 'Hound Dog'!) and 'Let It Be Me' by the Everly Brothers are as close to musical perfection as I probably ever want to get. But that's more personal!

The author of this book found his particular musical heaven in the music of the Beatles, and Paul McCartney in particular. Of course I understand that. But it's an odd thing in that when you go to school with someone (I met Paul on my first day at 'big' school when I was 11 at the Liverpool Institute and we have been mates since), they probably somehow can't have the same kind of legendary status for you that they do for others. Although undoubtedly Macca is a legend and a musical genius – and he too is devoted to Elvis and the Evs. (But I am not too sure he is a Blue!)

And now there is George – Neil's very own addition to the 'People's Club'. Like his dad, and like myself, George will relive time and time again those magical moments that seem to shape our lives. Not just our 'Blue' lives, but simply our lives. If I spent time with him I would tell him, as I will undoubtedly tell my new young grandson Finn, my stories of Wembley in 1966 with half an hour to go; Oxford in 1984 with nine minutes to go;

and probably the most joyful and painful of them all for me, Wimbledon in 1994 with an hour left. And maybe, maybe, if it was a good day, I would just give myself a thought towards my overwhelming pride as I stood and watched us celebrate in 2009, through teary eyes, from the chairman's seat, as we secured our first Wembley final in a decade.

It's been my privilege over the last decade to be in a position where I could hopefully help shape the future of the club, not only for the hundreds of thousands of Evertonians who are out there right now – but also those who have yet to find their moment of decision. Like me, like Neil and like George, it will be a decision they will never regret. At that moment they will become a member of the greatest family in football. And more than my shareholdings, my chairmanship, and my place in the directors' box, it's being a member of the Everton family that makes me proudest of all. Neil will understand. George will understand. If you have bought this book you will probably understand. That matters.

Respect, Neil.

Bill Kenwright, 16 February, 2011

Prologue

It's been a hard winter in England. More snow than we've had in twenty years, sheet ice and biting temperatures. But in mid-February, the edge has come off the chill, a mild breeze has replaced the shivers and I have a distinct feeling of spring in the air. It's not natural for an Everton supporter to be this optimistic. And it's not normal for my state of mind to be so full of hope. But I'll repeat it. Spring is definitely in the air.

Perhaps it's because my team has just reached the quarter-finals of the FA Cup for the first time in seven years. We beat Aston Villa yesterday. Not only that, but a 3-1 win against a team currently third in the league. What's more, that followed a heart-thumping victory over Liverpool in the fourth-round replay. I was at the 1-all draw at Anfield. I was at the return at Goodison Park. And I was part of that picture. Part of the scenes of jubilation. I've had some high points since I started watching Everton. League championships. FA Cup wins. European triumphs. But victories over our arch-enemies are always sweet – and savoured. When Dan Gosling turned the cold night air blue in the 118th minute ... let's just say it was ecstasy the like of which I have rarely experienced.

Perhaps it's not really spring in the air but that tantalising whiff of Wembley? We've had our first home draw of this season's competition. And we play West Ham or Middlesbrough in the next round. Victory in that tie, and we're into the semi-finals.

Or perhaps it's because I've been thinking about my four-year-old son. Thinking about our time together. Thinking about the things we already share. Thinking about our future together. Dreaming about the day when I'll take him to Goodison Park. It's a simple dream, but I dream of that day.

A while ago, I went for a stroll. Two minutes later, I became conscious of a dream-like sound. A sound from my past. From everybody's past. One of the soundtracks to all of our lives. But most certainly, one of the soundtracks to mine. An unmistakable guitar solo. A melody which has been etched into my soul since before my seventh birthday. I was walking past a house when I heard that raw, emotional piano. That electrifying, heart-tugging guitar. From a workman's radio. 'Let It Be'. That song was released on 6 March 1970. Eighteen months before I was even born. Thirty-four years before my son was born.

At time of writing, I have been to 320 Everton matches and I have more than 600 CDs. Music and football are my passions. They have brought me unbridled joy and unrelenting despair. They have brought me both comfort and sadness. They have provided me with direction when I have needed it and diversion at some of the lowest points in my life. They have given me something to share with my father. And now I want to share them with my own son.

Words of wisdom, as Paul McCartney once wrote. Whether or not we win the cup this year, Let It Be. Evertonians are brought up to be philosophical. And I will bring my son up to be an Evertonian. Let It Be.

The School Of Science

'Evertonians are born, not manufactured.
We do not choose, we are chosen.
Those who understand need no explanation.
Those who don't, don't matter.'

Young, Labone and Beamish

I was born with Everton in my blood. It is a source of great pride to me. And it forges my identity more than anything else. In fact, there is a saying in Goodison Park folklore:

Evertonians are born, not manufactured.
We do not choose, we are chosen.
Those who understand need no explanation.
Those who don't, don't matter.

They are four sentences which have a particular resonance for me as I was born 200 miles from Liverpool. And for long periods of my early awareness, I resented the fact that I was not a natural born Scouser – so proud was I to be a True Blue. My connection to the club, and to Merseyside, comes from my father. He was born and bred in Bromborough, a village on the Wirral peninsula. And it is in Bromborough that my genetic love for Everton, my birthright, was nurtured and reinforced.

I have never really thought of myself as having a 'home town', another source of early resentment. But my geographical home town is St Albans, Hertfordshire. The problem is that I have no fondness for that area, no real knowledge of it and no connection with it apart from the fact that I was born there and it was my home for the first six years of my life, before I emigrated to Bermuda with my family. So a geographical home town it may be. But an emotional home town it is not.

Throughout my early years moving home was a common occurrence for me, my younger sister and my parents. So it is perhaps only natural that I found the most comfort in my grandparents' house at 48 Valley Road, Bromborough. It was always 'my home'.

I remember the click of the gate before heading up the garden path. The front door. The shrill bell. The 1970s wallpaper. I remember the sideboard. I remember the ticking clock in the warm living room. The old-fashioned telly always on in the corner. I remember the smell of my nanna's bacon butties. I remember her kitchen. Her pantry. Her 'hand-washer'. I remember our drives up the M1 and M6 in my dad's orange Morris Marina, usually on a Friday night after my dad had got home from work. I remember waking from a deep, car-induced sleep. Three years old and in my father's arms, being carried across the threshold of the small council house into the warmest of Cheshire welcomes.

I remember the card games. The bowl on the table, always full of sweets. The carpet. The cuckoo clock on the wall. The barometer from the hallway, which I salvaged and still keep now, in my grandparents' memory. I remember old-fashioned furniture. The old mirror, getting frayed around the edges, already probably fifty years old in the early seventies. The Victorian photograph of my great-grandmother. The cosy, homely smell of the place, the feel of it, the sense that here was all my family's history.

I remember the back garden. The smell of freshly-cut grass. I remember kicking a cheap plastic ball in the side alley and in the backyard, for hours on end, to the annoyance of the neighbours and staying out there until the sun had gone down. Practising my headers. Deck chairs my nanna used to sunbathe in. Clothes pegs on the line. Cut flowers. The hedge. Even the pigeon loft just over the other side of the fence at the bottom of the garden. My memory of 48 Valley Road, Bromborough, is so vivid I could probably draw a diagram pinpointing the drains. And of course, I'll never forget the unfinished Brian Labone that my dad Colin had painted on to the shed door as a teenager. Some of my earliest memories are locked up in that house. And as my love of Everton grew and grew, that painting of Labone – with no right arm – was imprinted as much on my mind as it was on those old wood panels.

Colin Roberts showed promise as a footballer from an early age, in boys' brigade and school teams. One of his boyhood friends, Kenny Beamish, forged his own professional career. Kenny graduated from Bromborough to Tranmere Rovers, Blackburn Rovers and Brighton under Brian Clough. He played more than 500 times in the Football League, scoring more than 150 goals. And he made my dad insanely jealous. Colin and Kenny were pals. Born ten days apart, they were as thick as thieves from their early days together at Woodslee Primary School. Classmates. Team-mates. Just mates. Both of them had talent with a ball at their feet. Only one of them had the required dedication to make it.

My dad still has the letter he wrote to his idol, Alex Young, at the age of 13. 'How do I improve my ball skills?' 'How can I work on my dribbling?' 'How can I be good enough to play for Everton, like you?' It seems almost incredible now, half a century later, to think that a top-flight footballer, a superstar, would write back. But he did.

Young was known as the 'Golden Vision'. An Everton hero, a legend in the truest sense. A talisman for the entire club. Someone with sublime skills. A footballer ANYONE would pay to watch. Just to see him with the ball glued to his foot, outrageously humiliating defenders and deftly jinking through the opposition before planting the ball into the Gwladys Street net. And in some style. Sadly for me, the Golden Vision finished at Everton three years before I was born and 12 years before my own 'debut' as a spectator at Goodison Park. But I feel I grew up with him all the same. Dad has shown me the letter he got back from Young, several times. I've asked him the stories, several times. I've watched the BBC play about him directed by Ken Loach, several times. I even fulfilled one of my father's own ambitions – I met him and interviewed him in 1995. To this day, I kick myself that my dad wasn't with me. That I didn't get an autograph, or some personal message from the Golden Vision to the erstwhile 13-year- old schoolboy he'd written to back in the early 1960s.

When dad penned that letter, little did he know that one day he'd forego the chance of his own football career. At 16, he was given a trial by Liverpool and he failed the test. Played out of position, perhaps. Overcome by the occasion, perhaps. Heart not really in it in a red shirt, perhaps. But so devastated was he by this failure, that he didn't even turn up for his trial at Everton only weeks later. Now that's what you call a missed opportunity for a dyed-in-the-wool Evertonian. Instead, dad was a spectator, five years later, when Ken Beamish played for Tranmere against Everton. He felt what it was like to play on the pitch at Goodison Park. To cross those thick white lines at the 'School of Science'. He felt what it was like to play in front of 60,000 people.

So dad never played professionally but he did at least grow up supporting Everton and watching some glorious football. The fifties was a particularly low period for the club but when he started watching, at least Liverpool were in the Second Division. And Everton still had heroes like Dave Hickson and Brian Labone, the man my dad carved and painted into the shed.

By the time he did that, the doldrums of the fifties had passed and there was a bright blue new era at Goodison Park. Dad got his paints out in the school holidays of 1963. Everton were the champions of England and Labone was a blue-blooded hero. An England international, a classy defender and a proper Evertonian. And Everton's love for Labone was matched by Labone's love for Everton. At the end of his interview for the BBC's official history of the club, he clarified the relationship in his own words:

> Don't forget, lads – one Evertonian is worth 20 Liverpudlians.

And so it is. Brian Labone is another of those 'School of Science' icons I had the privilege to meet in my later life as a journalist. 'Footballer, Gentleman, Evertonian' is a moniker applied to the greatest Everton legend of all, Dixie Dean. But it could equally be applied to Labone, a one-club man, a loyal servant and a graceful footballer. Like me, Everton's chairman Bill Kenwright drew that comparison between those two giants of Goodison Park. Our most successful captain, Kevin Ratcliffe, gave BBC News another fitting tribute to Brian after his death in 2006:

> Brian was Everton. If you could put together a team of every player that has ever captained Everton, every one of us would turn to Brian to lead us out. He will always be known as the captain of Everton.

Years after Labone was immortalised on that common garden shed in Bromborough, dad and I were at Goodison Park for the first Everton home match after he died. It also happened to be the last match in a royal blue shirt for Duncan Ferguson, who was captain for the occasion. And he capped the occasion. He scored a last-minute equaliser against West Brom, tapping in the follow-up after poetically missing from the penalty spot in front of the Gwladys Street End. There wasn't a dry eye in the house when Duncan took that final lap of honour, his children in tow, around the Goodison Park pitch. But there hadn't been a dry eye in the house all day. Most notably from my dad, a man I have seldom seen give shows of emotion. The prolonged, loud applause in tribute to Labby before kick-off summed up all that is great about Everton – all that is great about Evertonians– all that makes us proud. As we like to say, 'We know our history'. For my father, that match on 7 May 2006 was the end of an era. The closing of a chapter in his own life. His tears at the start, and at the end, were for Brian Labone.

Band on the Run

My dad never finished painting Brian Labone on to the shed door, he said, because he didn't know how to. He didn't want to ruin that statuesque, imposing figure. So there he was, Everton's captain, resplendent in his royal blue jersey, with his crop of jet black hair. Long white shorts with a blue stripe down the side. White socks almost to the knee. And one arm. It was nearly perfect, this image of football from a bygone era. This painting that so embodied Everton. Almost perfect, but not quite. The letters *E V E R T O N*, in italic, had been transferred and painted on to the door, to go with the portrait. I loved looking at it. Kicking that plastic ball against it, imagining Brian was passing back to me. But still, Labone had the air of a broken Subbuteo player. Just one arm. Dad didn't know how to finish it so why spoil it trying? It was an image of beautiful football. Don't paint a player scuffing the ball into the net off his shin. Paint style. Paint grace. Paint 'School of Science' football, the Everton way. And that's what he did. But teenage Colin didn't finish it. He didn't want anything to spoil the aesthetic.

There's no getting away from it, though. As much as my dad was besotted with Everton, he was just short of his 16th birthday and it was the summer of 1963. Beatlemania had swept the country and the origin of it all, the city of Liverpool, was just seven miles away to the north. So never mind any fear that completion may have led to a blemish. Dad probably didn't finish that painting because he was too busy wearing out his copy of *Please Please Me*.

Just as I inherited football and Everton from my father, I inherited music and the Beatles. From a very early age, I had a fascination for music. I remember the record player at 48 Valley Road. My grandad gave it to me on one of my birthdays, probably my sixth. It was like a small, red box and I was captivated by it. By how it worked. By the needle, the crackle, the fact that the turntable went at 45 revolutions per minute unless you flipped a lever to make it go slower. Bigger records had to be played at 33 rpm. They said so on the back. And I read every single word on a record sleeve.

Jack Roberts wasn't a pop music man. But he was a music man. He'd been a bandsman in the Royal Marines, and there were pictures all over the house to prove his past life as a drummer and bugler, after which he was a boys' brigade leader. He was the man who taught my father to play the bugle. But it was that image of my grandad the Royal Marine that I loved. He looked handsome in his uniform, I always thought. His medals from both world wars were around somewhere and there was a big photograph of him on board HMS *Repulse* in 1925. It was a group photo of everyone on deck, around the time of the royal tour when the Prince of Wales was also on board. My grandad met the future king. And my family were proud royalists, just as most people were back then. In fact, all round, he was a proud man, my grandad. And we were all proud of him. So it was with real pride that I accepted his gift of a record player.

That wasn't the only musical present he gave me, either. A while later, my grandad bought me my first guitar from a shop in Liverpool. He took me on the bus, one of the old, green Crosville buses, and we sat upstairs, right at the front, as we used to do. Buses stand out in my memory from those early days on the Wirral. The rattle of the conductor's ticket machine. The paper tickets themselves, with HALF written across the middle. The smell of stale ash and smoke as soon as you boarded, and cigarette butts trodden into the wooden decking. The spiral staircase leading up from just behind the driver's cabin. The torn seating with foam poking through the tears. The graffiti, either in felt pen on the seats themselves or scratched into the back of the seat in front. The cold metal bars across the tops of the seating. (I don't know why, but I always used to lean forward and bite it.) The mirror right in the corner which not only allowed the driver to see the top deck, but allowed you to see the top of his head. Not always something you'd want to see, but you'd have to look anyway.

I remember the journey that day we went to get my guitar. Well, the bus part of it anyway. Turn right on to Bromborough Rake, past Bromborough Cross, left on to the New Chester Road on the A41 into Birkenhead. Past Port Sunlight. Past New Ferry and Rock Ferry until those dark, dominating, haunting sheds of Cammell Laird shipyard appear in the distance. Past the broken road sign that says TRANMERE, right outside the yard. And up Argyle Street until you get to Hamilton Square. That immaculately manicured lawn. The war memorial and the wreaths. The grid pattern of streets like a mini-Manhattan. Nearby Birkenhead Park, which itself was the model for New York's Central Park. Nanna and Grandad Roberts, me and my sister. School holidays and bus rides. We must have done that route dozens and dozens of times. And sitting right at the front on the top deck meant you could map the route perfectly, and plot every landmark along the way. Us, these two kids from the south of England, with our genial northern grandparents who said hello to everybody en route. Said 'ta ra' to everybody en route. Seemed to KNOW everybody en route, even though they didn't of course. They were just friendly. And so were the people.

This particular day, though, it was just me and my grandad who made the trip. I can't remember whether we got the train or the ferry from Birkenhead into Liverpool. But let's say it was the boat, because ferry rides across that brown choppy water were also very much a part of my childhood. Us Evertonians call it the Royal Blue Mersey. But it's only Royal Blue in spirit, I promise you. The world's greatest river, yes. Blue, no.

We'd walk down the wide gangplank at Woodside ferry terminal and wait to see if it was the *Mountwood*, the *Woodchurch* or the *Overchurch* which pulled up against the tyres. Stand outside the main cabin, feel the air in our faces. Watch as the Liverpool waterfront pulled nearer and nearer, loomed larger and larger, until we banged against the dock wall at Pier Head. My present that day was a Fender acoustic, model F-65, and it cost a lot of money even then. Certainly more than a hundred pounds. Sadly I never became as proficient as my grandad's generosity would have deserved. But nevertheless, it was one of those key moments in my life. My first guitar, bought by my grandad in the latter years of his life. A rare moment between just me and him. He died when I was nine, so there weren't many.

I know we went to a music shop in Whitechapel but I don't remember what it was called. Was it Hessy's, where John Lennon's Aunt Mimi famously bought him a guitar? Was it the old NEMS shop at number 12, which had been owned by the Beatles manager Brian Epstein? Or was it just an ordinary music shop with no claims to fame? Rushworth & Dreapers, perhaps. My grandad's favourite. I can't actually remember. I don't know for sure and I'll never know now, because my grandad isn't around to ask and neither is my nanna. Of course it doesn't matter. But just as football allows you to dream impossible dreams, so too does music. And as much as I'll always love Kevin Sheedy, the foremost of several Everton heroes, I've only really ever idolised two people – John Lennon and Paul McCartney. If my guitar had come from the same shop as John's ... Well. Somehow I'd be proud of that. Perhaps it's best not to know.

When nanna and grandad weren't taking us on bus rides or ferry trips, we'd be walking around parks, eating ice creams, sitting on benches. They were such simple pleasures when I think back to them. But they were always glorious days. And they were also the days when bandstands in public parks weren't just relics or architectural anachronisms. This was still only one generation after the Second World War and bandstands were still used, mostly for the military music which my grandad had played and always loved so much. It was on one such trip to the park, to hear a band playing, that my precocious love of music first became evident to my grandparents. And I think I was only three years old.

'Band on the Run, Band on the Run,' I said in some state of heightened excitement. The kind you can only get from a toddler. Grandad was perplexed. 'What the bloody hell's he talking about, Band on the Run,' he asked my nanna. She didn't have the answer.

But even back then, when I'd only just started forming the language and stringing my first sentences together, I knew which music I liked. And I recognised the non-military arrangement that brass band was playing. Now, jailer man and sailor Sam and rabbits on the run would all have been lyrics I'd have been able to associate with at three years old. But it was more than that. I loved the jangly intro, the electric guitar. The organ bit, the handclaps; the acoustic bit and the orchestral bit. It seemed like several songs in one and I could relate to it. I'm sure it wasn't written for such young ears. Maybe Paul McCartney was hoping for a more musically-educated appreciation. But the song has stayed with me all my life. And it took me years to work out that Paul wasn't really talking about milk when he sang that all he needed was a pint a day.

Edgar Chadwick

It's not just buses and ferries, bandstands and ice creams that I remember from the early part of my childhood. I remember sounds. Sayings. Mannerisms and clothing. Like the way my grandad always prodded his false teeth out, halfway out of his mouth, just to make me laugh. Like the royal blue V-neck jumper that he always wore, in honour of Everton.

He'd been born in the shadow of the Royal Marines barracks at Eastney, Portsmouth in 1904 and his life was a hard one. His father, Charles, was a colour sergeant and a notoriously tough man with a devilish look and a neatly-trimmed, Victorian-style moustache. A man who meant business.

But he was also a football man. He was the trainer at Portsmouth FC, in the days when a 'trainer' was a coach, a kit-man, a guy who did the paperwork and who ran on with a bucket. My grandad was a regular mascot at Fratton Park. And Charles Roberts, my great-grandfather, would take him along – regularly – to the matches. For some reason, Portsmouth's rivals – the Southampton players – were regular visitors to the family home on Highland Road. Charles obviously knew more than just how to handle a bucket. He was connected in footballing circles. And he could obviously handle a team, too. Because three months before my grandad was born, Sgt Chas Roberts trained the Royal Marine Artillery team which won the Army Cup Final against the Royal Engineers at Aldershot.

It was a big day. More than 10,000 people were there. And, as befits a team playing in blue like the Royal Marines did that day, there was a grandstand finish. The match report from the *Globe & Laurel*, dated 4 April 1904, summed up the drama in the dying seconds. It even sounded like a flukey winner:

> Then the Marines got up on the right, and Maclean made a capital centre, but it was not utilised, a throw-in only resulting. There was a pretty dash in the centre of the field, and Smith sent the ball outside. There was a scrimmage in the Engineers' goal during the last minute of the game, and Maclean scored with a cross shot. There was only time for his colleagues to congratulate him and time was called.

Even though he was enlisted as a Royal Marine, Charles Roberts began to become involved in even more serious football. Portsmouth had only been founded in 1898 and they were scratching around in the Southern League. But back in the early part of the 20th century, the Southern League was almost equivalent to the Football League, except that it was in the south of the country. Portsmouth's league battles would see them lock horns with their bitter south coast neighbours Southampton, as well as modern-day Premier Leaguers like Fulham, West Ham and even Tottenham Hotspur. They also knocked Manchester United out of the FA Cup. So, more than a hundred years ago, grandad Jack and great-grandad Charles would have been party to some fascinating football occasions.

It also explains why my grandad grew up supporting Portsmouth and continued that, even after becoming estranged from his father. Sadly, it was a rift that was never healed and even now, the family does not know when or where Charles Roberts died.

They'd both moved to Merseyside, my grandfather had his own Royal Marines career and their lives took different directions. Grandad's brother Leo played football for Tranmere Rovers while Leo's son, also Leo, was on the books at Liverpool. A dreaded Red, who had the audacity to marry Dixie Dean's niece and even convert her to the dark side. He was a tall man who also boasted the less than graceful nickname of 'Dirty Leo' in amateur football circles. No wonder he was a Red not a Blue. My grandad had already been a true convert to the blue cause, though. And his Everton commitment was confirmed when he took my father to Goodison Park for the first time in 1958, to see a game against Portsmouth. Everton 2-0 down, but eventual 4-2 winners. Now that's a proper introduction to Evertonia.

They were still the days of Lonnie Donegan and Buddy Holly, of Frankie Laine and the Everly Brothers. Elvis was the main man on the scene but the Beatles were still the Quarrymen, just over the Mersey. And on Saturdays, father and son would make the trip to Goodison (always leaving a few minutes early to get the 44D bus back to Pier Head, ready to catch the ferry across the Mersey). Then, a few years later, dad would start going on his own. Think about painting the shed door. Start buying his Beatles records. And eventually I came along.

A few years later, in 1976, grandad, Leo Snr and my dad were lounging around, passing the time by chatting football at home in Bromborough. The FA Cup Final, between Southampton and

Manchester United, was just a few weeks away. As it turned out, a famous final and a famous upset with Second Division Southampton winning the cup. But for my family, it was the beginning of a journey.

'Colin, have you got a bet on the cup final?'

The question came from Leo Snr. My dad didn't gamble. Never really has. Not because of some kind of moral stance, but just because it's not his thing.

'No. Why would I have a bet on the cup final?' he asked. After all, Everton hadn't been in it for eight years.

'Because the last time Southampton were in the cup final, your grandfather played.'

My dad was stunned. It couldn't be true. His grandad played in a cup final? He went away. He pored over his *Rothmans Football Yearbook*. He returned to confront Leo.

'You're wrong,'he said. 'I've checked. No one called Roberts played in that final.'

Great Uncle Leo simply smiled and shook his head. He remembered his time at Tranmere, while being in the Navy. Servicemen were not allowed to play professional football. He, himself, had been spotted, disciplined and stopped.

'Your grandfather didn't play under his real name,' he said. 'He played under an assumed name. Chadwick.'

Dad went back to his *Rothmans*. Sure enough, in the 1902 FA Cup Final, Edgar Chadwick had played for Southampton against Sheffield United. He played in the first game at Crystal Palace, in front of nearly 77,000 fans. He played in the replay, too, which Southampton lost 2-1.

Stunned silence. Amazement. Charles Roberts, dad's granddad and my great grandfather, played in the FA Cup Final. He must have been a good player, all right. Played under an assumed name. Forget the bucket.

Further research revealed just what a good player Edgar Chadwick was. An inside-forward who had played for Everton in the 1890s and won the league championship as well as appearing in two FA Cup Finals. A dazzling striker who was an England international and once held the record for scoring England's fastest ever goal. A man who was a household name, like some of those other Everton names such as Young, Latchford and Lineker. A player who was famous the length and breadth of the country, even in the days when news was delivered via telegrams or steam trains.

In 2009, *The Times* published their list of Everton's 50 greatest players. Edgar Chadwick, with 110 goals in 300 Everton appearances, was listed at number 17. He was ahead of Howard Kendall, Ray Wilson, Joe Royle, Trevor Steven and Andy Gray. And ahead of my own Everton hero, Kevin Sheedy. This is how they described him:

> A pipsqueak at 5ft 6in, Chadwick was a huge name in football. He joined Everton in the inaugural Football League season of 1888– 89, and went on to win the league in 1891 as Everton became the first champions to play at Anfield. Chadwick is also in the exclusive club of players to score over a century of goals for Everton. Seldom outfought by any opponent and a brilliant dribbler, his name proudly – and deservedly – sits high on this list.

Back in the late 1970s, dad still couldn't believe it. Too good to be true. And why hadn't his own father ever mentioned it? Everton's official history, published in the club's centenary year of 1978, shows a picture of Chadwick in an early Everton team. The team which won the first league championship for Everton, in the 1890–91 season. A season when Everton were still playing at Anfield, before setting up their proper home at Goodison Park. Dad got some paper and covered the names below the photo. He showed the open page to Leo and my grandad. And he asked them if they recognised anybody in the picture.

'There.'

They both pointed without hesitation, identifying the hard-looking man with an unmistakable Roberts face and that stern, Victorian moustache. So recognisable.

'That's my father.'

Well, that was it. Dad was convinced. Who wouldn't be able to identify their own father? So he set about assembling as much information about Edgar Chadwick as possible. Not all of it was easy to get – fires had destroyed records, clubs and the Royal Marines had incomplete archives – the whole process was painstaking and laborious.

But Chadwick WAS a star footballer – a superstar, if such a person existed in the early 1900s – and Charles Roberts was not. Service records are easy to come by, though. And slowly, but surely, the penny dropped. Charles Roberts was out of the country half the time he was supposed to have been playing for Everton. Or England. Or any of the other teams Chadwick played for. And Edgar Chadwick was born in Blackburn, not Wrexham. In 1869, not 1868. He had his own life. His own relatives and ancestors, doubtless immensely proud of him.

Who knows what the mistake was. How could such an error have been made? Where did the story come from? My dad almost didn't want to know. He didn't know how or where Charles Roberts had died. His own father had become estranged from him, and told tales of a cruel, heartless man. What was the connection between Charles Roberts and Edgar Chadwick? We'll never know. Perhaps they were doubles for each other. Perhaps it was Charles' nickname at Portsmouth with the Royal Marines Artillery team. Maybe they joked and called him Edgar. Ribbed him that he might look like Chadwick but he'd never be as good as Chadwick. Who knows? It's all guesswork.

Leo said my great-grandfather played in Southampton's last FA Cup Final before 1976 under the assumed name of Chadwick. The 1902 final, Southampton's last for 74 years, did feature Edgar Chadwick. But he was no relative of mine.

Two years earlier, in 1900, Southampton lost 4-0 to Bury in the FA Cup Final. Arthur Chadwick, born in 1875 and from Church in Lancashire, played at centre-half for Southampton. Interestingly, he'd also played for Portsmouth between 1901 and 1904. And England. Could it be THIS Chadwick? Who knows. Doubt it. Don't think so. No. Can't have been. This Chadwick died in Exeter in 1936. So no, not him – definitely not. No way. No, no, no. But then, just like the music shop and John Lennon's guitar ... sometimes it's just better not to know.

Starting Over

Double Fantasy

When everything seemed to be pointing AGAINST Edgar Chadwick and Charles Roberts being one and the same person, the research was given up. Investigations had moved from Chadwick (one of them, anyway) 'probably'being my great-grandfather to Chadwick 'probably not' being my great-grandfather. And that was enough for my dad to call it a day and preserve the family anecdote.

It was a crushing blow but not so crushing that we needed to move 3,000 miles to the mid-Atlantic to rehabilitate ourselves as a family. Instead, we made the move to Bermuda because cracks had already begun to appear in my parents' relationship. And an adventure on a sub-tropical island with a young family in tow was their attempt at real rehabilitation.

At that time, I was blissfully unaware of those cracks. Tensions and infidelity were not something I could understand at six years old. And when we arrived on the tarmac outside Bermuda Airport, my family was a picture of domestic bliss. Dad's smile softening his 1970s moustache. My mum Sheila looking genuinely delighted at this 'new start'. My sister Caroline sucking her thumb without a care in the world. Me just looking knackered. We looked every inch the perfect family.

Within a year, we'd settled into our new home. Notwithstanding cockroaches, mildew and humidity, we were happy. We had a lovely house. The sun was always shining. Dad was the sports editor on the local paper, the *Royal Gazette*. And mum had continued her career there in telesales. Caroline was in nursery and I was beginning to make friends at school. Just another one of the khaki-shorted brigade drinking chocolate milk at playtime and wondering why, all of a sudden, my class wasn't just full of white kids.

But for all its pink sandy beaches, crystal clear waters and carefree lifestyle, Bermuda wasn't quite the fresh start my parents had been hoping for. It certainly wasn't paradise. In Easter 1979 came a day that will always be stamped in my memory. And not for the right reasons. Not an FA Cup Final, a famous victory, a pop concert or meeting one of my sporting or musical idols, but a day which will traumatise me forever.

It was a hot day and as we often did, Caroline and I were playing 'it' in the front garden. Dad was chopping back trees with his machete. Mum was in the kitchen. And then there was this van, which was clearly busting Bermuda's 20 mph speed limit, tearing past our house and up the road to our landlord's place on the hilltop. The fact that I was chasing my little sister around the garden has always led me to feel responsible for the accident which was to follow. But when I saw her run into the road, right into the path of that speeding, returning vehicle, my mind just shut down. Blind panic. My little sister … into the road, into the path of the van. I remember it still like camera shutters. Freeze frames. As if my memory became broken at that very point in my life. First, the point of impact. Then beginning to fall. Getting lower and lower to the ground. Then lying there, motionless, under the van. My sister, four years old, unconscious under some kind of oily, creaking death machine. Unconscious in the gravel. Blood matted in her beautiful dark hair.

Suddenly, as if someone had just switched the lights back on, my brain gets back into gear. And all hell is breaking loose. The driver gets out. And I'm terrified. Shouting for my parents. 'Mum, dad, Caroline's been run over!' Looking back now, I can laugh at what happened next. My mum came out of the kitchen, shrieking. The man over the road, a policeman, heard my cries and rushed over to help. My dad, ever my hero, had the driver up against the wall. At least he'd tossed his machete away.

Of course none of this was helping poor Caroline. But the neighbourly copper, a British expatriate like us, knew what he was doing. And he probably saved her life. He knew it was pointless to call an ambulance because of the time one would take to navigate those narrow and windy Bermuda roads. He knew Caroline needed to be pulled clear from under the van and driven straight to hospital. He knew there was no point trying to kill the van driver and that it was my little sister who needed all our energies.

They say never to move accident victims but in Caroline's case, thank God he did. He pulled her out from under that van, into his car and drove her straight to casualty. My parents followed him there. I think someone living nearby must have been assigned to look after me, although I can't remember for sure. But after one night in hospital (it being Easter and everything) and large and constant doses of jelly and ice cream, Caroline was already on a far better road than the one she'd been lying on. She'd suffered a fractured skull. But she was on her way to recovery.

From there, things couldn't really go from bad to worse but they almost did. Not long afterwards, I broke my arm during some playground high jinks and needed three operations to put it right. Worse though was the infection I collected in the surgery process – and the subsequent illness that caused, which required three further operations and plastic surgery on my hip. All right, not really my hip. My bum. But hey. Forget the traumas. We were in Bermuda and the sun was shining.

I do remember our days on the beach and learning to ride my bike. I remember drinking chocolate milkshakes and eating toasted cheese sandwiches. If nothing else, our regular trips to the hospital taught us that it had one of the best cafes on the island. But for a while, there seemed little to connect me back to Goodison Park, to Merseyside and to my spiritual home.

Then, when the dust began to settle, our accidents began to fade into the memory. I was doing well at school, sitting by my dad's desk in the newsroom and bashing away at his typewriter. Writing made- up stories and dreaming of being a journalist. Thinking about meeting famous people. But which famous people? Who would I want to meet? Who would I want to interview? Just 'Imagine' ...

I remember once thinking that I quite liked cricket, after hitting a ball or two in the garden. I remember asking my dad to name some famous England players. I knew what I liked, but I wasn't yet sure WHO I liked. But then, just as I was precociously planning my own career in journalism, I began to revert to what I inherently knew. Everton and the Beatles.

Now, one thing which really connected me to my dad was his record collection. They looked so impressive, vertically stored, packed tight, the array of colours given off by their spines when they were all bunched together. And when my mum bought him the entire set of Beatles albums, my interest took on a whole new dimension. Dad had the old mono originals from *Please Please Me* through to *Revolver* and, bizarrely, *Let It Be*. I have those albums in my own collection now but only later was I to realise how incomplete his original assortment was. No *Sergeant Pepper*. No *Abbey Road*. For years, my two favourite Beatles records – only later challenged by my changeable tastes and fascinations and flirtations with *Rubber Soul* and *Revolver*.

But this new collection of Beatles albums introduced me to the entire back catalogue. We played them all. Back to back. Time and time and time again. They came in a royal blue presentation box and I had already developed a keen personal association with royal blue, of course. And they were in stereo which, as my dad explained very carefully to those young ears of mine, was a real revolution in sound and meant some parts of the song would come through the left speaker and some would come through the right. It was fascinating, alternating the balance to left then right, then left again.

Dad ran me off a tape of each album and there were 14 of them in all. *Please Please Me. With The Beatles. A Hard Day's Night. Beatles For Sale. Help! Rubber Soul. Revolver. Sgt Pepper's Lonely Hearts Club Band. Magical Mystery Tour. The Beatles.* (Though I learned this was also called *The White Album*). *Yellow Submarine. Abbey Road. Let It Be.* And one called *Rarities.* The sound in glorious stereo. The album covers in glorious Technicolor. (Well, apart from the monochrome *Revolver* and *The White Album*). I played them over and over and over until I learned almost every word in every song. What's more, the lyrics were inserted in each album sleeve which was, indeed, a 'rarity' as only *Sgt Pepper* had the lyrics on the cover. And as well as in English, the words were in Japanese.

I didn't know so much about Yoko Ono. Only that John was married to this crazy Japanese lady who used to wail a lot. But I find it amusing and not a little ironic, now, that my proper in-depth introduction to the Fab Four came from a set of stereo records made in Japan, that country of great technological modernisers. The country which gave us the Sony Walkman so I could play those tapes my dad made. And the birthplace of Yoko Ono, the woman who, according to the Roberts household, broke up the Beatles.

As well as all the vinyl and all the tapes, the thrill I associated with the crackle of needle on record and the constant rehearsing of the lyrics, there was my guitar. My grandad's guitar from Liverpool. And on my guitar, I would play Beatles songs. Pretend to be Paul. Pretend to be John. In truth, although he may not quite admit the same level of hero worship, so did my dad. And we both had the opportunity to explore our own form of Beatlemaniac escapism in the summer of 1980, because John Lennon was in Bermuda.

Exactly how I came to learn that John was on the island, I'm not sure. But certainly, there was lots of chatter about it. And it was something which excited my parents, both of them. Not far from where we lived was an estate full of gated mansions. The playwright Terence Rattigan was rumoured to have once had a place there, as was Robert Stigwood, the erstwhile friend and business partner of Brian Epstein and one of the early candidates to replace Brian as the Beatles' manager. We walked around the estate, all four of us, as a little Fab Four of our own. We looked brazenly through windows while chatting loudly about the Beatles. We wondered whether John might be about. We went to the harbour in St George and found a yacht called *Strawberry Fields*. Unfortunately, almost unbelievably, it wasn't John's – even though his yacht WAS on the island. We searched high and low for my dad's favourite Beatle. A man whose music I grew up with. A legend. But we never found him. Frustrated, dad and I would sit on the porch, strumming our guitars and playing our favourite Beatles tunes, hoping the amateurish strains of 'Julia' or 'Across The Universe' would float off on the Bermudian breeze and find John's ears. Hoping he'd hear and want to come and jam with us.

Of course it never happened. But we were agonisingly close. My father soon realised just how close he came to meeting his idol. A colleague of his at the *Gazette* was out drinking one night when he got chatting to a long-haired guy who was some sort of free-spirited hippie character who had brought along his business associate. The peaceable drinking partner was good company and engaging, just chatting about life in general, and the only one who would buy any drinks. When dad's pal – the *Gazette*'s chief reporter, Gerry Hunt – would offer to buy a drink, the offer was rebuffed and one was bought for him instead. Ultimately, he protested. He wanted to buy a drink, to repay some kindness. But the business partner interjected. 'You do know who that is, don't you,' he said. 'That's John Lennon.'

Some weeks later, late one night, the phone rang in the *Gazette*'s office and my dad answered, having by now been promoted to deputy editor.

'Hey Gerry,' he called over. 'Got a guy here who says he's got John Lennon on the line. Wants to talk to you.'

Imagine the scene. There must have been a splashing of spilt coffee, a fume of billowing smoke and an array of strewn paper and flying notebooks in the panic. Gerry rushed to his desk and took the call. The result? The news that John, too, was 'Starting Over', just like my family. It was a worldwide exclusive. (The John part, not the 'my family' part). He was coming out of self-imposed retirement, giving up being a 'house husband' and returning to making music after several years of pop exile. The album would be called *Double Fantasy* after a flower he'd seen in the Bermuda Botanical Gardens – a place I would visit on a weekly basis at that time, as a cub scout. He'd written the songs during his stay in Bermuda that June, having learned to sail his 43- foot sloop to the island from New York City.

The album was a worldwide smash. So was Gerry's exclusive. And then tragedy. John Lennon was murdered by the end of the year. I remember being numb with shock when my mum woke me for school and told me the news. Even now, I feel guilty that I didn't cry about it. I have cried about it since. And cried about it often. But Paul was always my hero. And after his drugs bust in Japan, I DID shed tears. In fact, I threw myself on the bed, so devastated was I that my idol was in some jail. Talk about getting my Beatle priorities wrong.

The truth is I loved Paul and I loved John. And it wasn't just my dad who came within a whisker of meeting the man who'd written 'Strawberry Fields' and 'Imagine' ... In a parallel life, it could have been me, as I found out on a voyage of rediscovery I made many years later.

Debut daze

Just four weeks after John Lennon was killed, my grandad died. He'd been ill for a long time, and the cancer which had taken hold ultimately deprived him of all his senses. When my dad flew in from Bermuda, and bolted through the front door in Bromborough, he was only just in time. When the moment came, my grandad was reaching out to his mother – the beautiful woman in that Victorian photograph on the wall at 48 Valley Road. The image that was so haunting to us as children. And one that was always so poignant. The wife of Charles Roberts, not Edgar Chadwick. My grandad's mum Margaret Sophia, reaching out to him from beyond the grave, calling him to her. And then later, always keeping her eye on us children like some Roberts family *Mona Lisa*.

Almost like my reaction to John Lennon's death, my reaction to my own grandfather's was one of numbness. I loved him, wanted to know him more, missed him. But at nine years old, I was too young to understand the finality of death. And as sad as I was, as much as I missed my grieving dad back in England and as upset as I was to see my mum in tears at home in Bermuda, I was glad at least that this family 'event' had given me the opportunity of a day off school. Only much later, back in Bromborough, did I fully realise how much I'd like to have known him more, how I'd love to have gone to a match with him. How I'd loved to have talked football with him and to have become his friend as I grew up.

For my Fender acoustic guitar wasn't the only legacy my grandad left me. It was Everton too. He and my father made sure I'd be a Blue. And that ever-present memory of my grandad in his royal blue V-neck meant I could never escape that legacy. Mind you, I never wanted to.

'Going to the match, Colin?'I remember him asking my dad. 'How do you think they'll get on against West Ham? Lee's no bloody good, is he.'

Whether or not Everton's hapless seventies manager Gordon Lee ever did come into that particular conversation, I'm not sure. But it's that kind of dialogue I remember. Banter, chat, football talk. Bacon butties, the pink *Football Echo*, tea and telly. And Everton talk. I was yearning to be a part of it, to understand those conversations, to be part of the Roberts gang. Dad would always tell me how, when he was a boy, he and my grandad would go to Goodison Park together on the bus, sit in the Park End together and always leave five minutes before the end so they could catch the bus back. Even in the latter years of his life, my grandad could sprint for the bus, dad would say.

After he'd gone, I yearned to have been a part of all that with my grandad. It wasn't to be, but at least he was around when I made my own Goodison Park debut. The date was 5 April 1980 – nine months before my grandad died and the date of my parents' 11th wedding anniversary. It was probably a more significant date for me than for them, because although grandad was too ill to come to the match itself, he was at home in Bromborough when dad took me to watch Everton for the very first time during a family holiday back from Bermuda.

A few days before that debut day, on the Tuesday night, Liverpool were playing at home to Stoke City in a match they won 1-0. I'm almost too embarrassed to admit it now but THAT was actually my first football match. Dad, the philanthropic and proud exiled Merseysider, was never anti-Liverpool in the way I became. So we went to Anfield with his cousin – that real Red, 'Dirty Leo' Roberts (who'd married Dixie Dean's niece) and his son Lee. All I remember from the night was Liverpool goalkeeper Ray Clemence ponderously kicking the turf outside his penalty area while Liverpool were on constant attack 70 yards in front of him. Evidently Ray was as bored as I was. I think Kenny Dalglish scored the winner and, even then, I remember feeling a little bit sick when the goal went in. As I saw the Liverpool supporters around me celebrating, I just got the sense that these really weren't my kind of people. There was something odd about them. Some kind of artificial superiority, even then. Even though they didn't know they had a born Blue in their midst. Apart from that, my only memory of Anfield that night was my cousin Lee boasting about how he always found pennies in the stand. Big deal, I thought.

So on the Saturday, when we took Lee with us to see Everton play Bolton, guess what he found inside the Bullens Road Stand? A nice, crisp tenner. All right, it made him richer. But at least it proved to me that everything Everton had to offer was better than ANYTHING Liverpool could. I was proved right, too. We had a better ground. The people around us seemed a bit classier. And we won 3-1, which was a lot better than 1-0 as far as I was concerned (then). I jumped up and joined in the roars as the goals went in instead of blankly looking round me in bemusement at gleeful, boastful faces. And I knew I'd found happiness. Just as Everton tried Anfield first and didn't like it much 90-odd years previously, so I had followed the same path. Anfield was crap. Goodison was great. We may not all have agreed but I certainly did. Everton were magic. Liverpool were tragic. Stick it up your jumper, Liverpool fans.

There's irony in there of course. Because Bolton were rock bottom that season, Everton only avoided relegation by one place and, yet again, Liverpool weren't just masters of Merseyside, they were masters of the whole country. They finished two points ahead of Manchester United to win the league, they were unbeaten at Anfield all season, and in Dalglish they seemed to have some kind of genius in the ranks, however unsavoury that was for me to consider. Like it or not, I already had the sense that Everton were in that shadow. And that shadow was dark.

But it was Everton that I was proud of, Everton that I loved. I had tracksuits. Scarves. Flags and pennants. And, of course, the garden shed at 48 Valley Road, with the unfinished Brian Labone to remind me. I loved Everton. I would dream about them. Talk to dad about them. Talk to nanna about them. Achingly, I don't remember talking to my grandad about them and I just don't know why, except perhaps he was too unwell.

I also knew that we were supposed to like Tranmere Rovers too because they were the 'local team'. This was PROPER crap, not like the way Liverpool were crap. Tranmere were Fourth Division rot.

'Okay dad,' I remember saying. 'I've seen Liverpool. I've seen Everton. Now I want you to take me to see some real rubbish.'

So on the following Friday night, he did. We went to watch Tranmere beat Hartlepool 1-0 at Prenton Park. I remember joining the patronising laughter. We wanted Tranmere to win, of course, but everyone seemed to be laughing as they aimlessly lumped the ball about. I realised many years later how disparaging it was. Tranmere themselves would remind Everton not to patronise them, in the cruellest possible fashion, on a day that would leave deep wounds in my Evertonian pride.

Still, that was years in the future, completely unknown to me then. Everton were way out in front. My only team. Tranmere were a dim and distant second, worthy of token support from afar. That's the way I saw it.

It was my formative period. I'd seen my first football matches and I was in something of a daze – three games in 11 days. Liverpool, Everton and Tranmere. The process confirmed me as a spiritual Merseysider despite the lack of accent, a dyed-in-the-wool Blue and a football fan for life. And I remember being jealous as HELL the day after the Tranmere game when dad went off from Bromborough to the FA Cup semi-final between Everton and West Ham ... without me.

Instead, I was left to look at my programme from Goodison Park the week before. Everton v Bolton Wanderers. Mike Lyons the warrior captain. The blond, dashing Andy King – my footballing hero now that Duncan McKenzie had departed the scene. Even perm- haired Trevor Ross. All of them early Everton icons who played in that match, chugging away on a minefield of a Goodison Park pitch. Not heady days in the club's history. I remember the game was no classic. But we won with goals from Peter Eastoe, Gary Megson and Brian Kidd. And little did I know it then but even the Bolton team had a player of interest in their ranks. The tenacious, bulldog-spirited powerhouse that was Peter Reid ... still two and a half years away from pulling on the royal blue jersey and becoming a True Blue Everton legend.

1982 and all that ...

On returning to Bermuda from that holiday, my status as a fully-fledged paid-up member of the Evertonian family was well and truly confirmed. And if I was already marvelling at my dad's record and my own tape collections, it was with real vigour that I took ownership of dad's football programmes,dating right back to his first Everton match against Portsmouth in 1958. I've never been one to shy away from geekiness. So they were all carefully arranged and looked after. Everton programmes, Tranmere programmes and Liverpool programmes (at the bottom of the pile, never looked at and always treated with a casual disdain but still ordered properly). Programmes from other clubs. A Man Utd v Everton programme with Matt Busby's autograph on it. Cup final programmes and international programmes. They were pristine. Arranged chronologically and alphabetically by club. And of course, the best one of all, Everton v Bolton Wanderers from 5 April 1980. The front cover shows Imre Varadi watching as Gary Megson bursts through midfield. Somehow Megson seemed more interesting back then than his latter-day persona as the dullest of dull managers with Bolton themselves. And there's a sea of expectant Evertonian faces in the background, urging the team on. That clamour, that collective willingness which is only portrayed by a photograph of a football crowd. Peter Reid, incidentally, is listed as Bolton's number 11 on the back.

Forget Lego. Forget *Star Wars*. When I busied myself at playtime, I'd get out my programmes. (Exciting, I know). My passions were football and music. And Everton, by now, were embedded. I was already learning about the Holy Trinity of Harvey, Kendall and Ball. About the legend that was Harry Catterick. And of course about the Golden Vision himself, Alex Young. More recently, Everton supporters had been idolising Bob Latchford for his 30 league goals in a season. He did 'half a Dixie Dean'. And Duncan McKenzie, too. McKenzie the mercurial striker, famous for doing things like jumping higher than a mini, throwing a golf ball the length of the pitch and rounding the keeper before stooping low to head the ball in from on the line. At least they're the stories I grew up with. I haven't really bothered to check those facts. But I DID meet the man in question. Duncan

McKenzie, once of Everton and Leeds, Chelsea and Nottingham Forest. He was the first of my heroes that I ever had a chance to meet. The genius who'd been unceremoniously dumped by Gordon Lee signed my autograph book when I saw him playing for Tulsa Roughnecks on tour in Bermuda in 1981. Dad took me into the dressing room, and Duncan obligingly made a young Everton supporter a very happy lad.

Around that time, Everton were playing Liverpool in an FA Cup match. And on the same day, Bermuda was hosting its annual international race weekend, an event dad and I used to watch because of his professional capacity at the *Gazette*. I remember this guy breaking the tape as the winner. A Scouser who collapsed over the line but instantly forgot about his marathon feat. He was an Everton supporter too, you see. And as dad congratulated him, all the runner could say was: 'Did we win?' The glorious answer was that we did. And as this guy stumbled a few steps forward before taking a drink and being wrapped in aluminium foil, he was able to savour a REAL moment of triumph in his life. Everton knocking Liverpool out of the FA Cup. Imre Varadi scored the winning goal and Everton had notched up only their third victory in Merseyside derbies in my lifetime. And that was in 23 attempts. Here was another reminder, as if I needed one, that Everton 'meant something'.

Football was playing an ever-bigger role in my life. And with FA Cup finals being broadcast live on TV in Bermuda, at least one day a year was devoted to that famous 'romance'. The first one I watched was West Ham beating Arsenal in 1980. Trevor Brooking's goal was probably one of the first – if not THE first – that I actually saw on telly. But we used to get *Match Of The Day* a week late in Bermuda, and I would sit up to watch that with my dad. Sadly, many of those programmes would concentrate on Liverpool. So it was all I could do to peep through my young fingers as I shielded my eyes. I had to remind myself it was FOOTBALL I was watching. Not Liverpool.

Education has always been important to me and I was learning more and more about all kinds of football teams and players, from all over the world. I was at school when my parents and sister went to meet the visiting New York Cosmos, with West

Germany's Franz Beckenbauer in their team – a veteran of a certain Wembley final in 1966. Not the important one, in which Everton came from two goals down to beat Sheffield Wednesday to win the FA Cup. The other one, when England won the Jules Rimet Trophy. So I missed meeting Beckenbauer, because unfortunately I needed to concentrate on my 'real' education. And, of course, I missed 1966 by five years.

But 1982 was a different story. England had qualified for their first World Cup finals since I was born. And for the first time, I would metaphorically wrap myself up in the England flag and immerse myself in the whole tournament. At ten years old, living away from your home country, you do develop a sense of national pride. And watching live on TV as Bryan Robson scored against France, practically straight from the kick-off, would be a moment that would always stick with me. But not quite as much as the final itself.

I've never forgotten 11 July 1982. It was gloriously hot with a beautiful blue sky. But forget the sunshine. I was glued to the World Cup Final being played in Madrid. I sat through a goalless first half between Italy and West Germany. But I was jumping up and down when Paolo Rossi etched his name into history. Yes, he won the Golden Boot, the Golden Ball AND became a world champion – the only player ever to win all three in the same tournament. But he was also now on my list of genuine football heroes and for me, of course, that was far more important. Rossi's goal lit up the match. And although it was Marco Tardelli who scored the brilliant goal in that final – and matched it with a celebration which was just as memorable – it was Rossi who I was trying to emulate with my football at full time. Once I'd seen Dino Zoff lifting the trophy amid all that confetti, it was time to get my Everton shirt and shorts on and get out in the sun. And I felt invigorated. We had a garden which encircled our house and I must have done dozens and dozens of laps, running as fast as I could with the ball at my feet and shouting Paolo Rossi's name to myself, occasionally thumping the ball against the wall in tribute to the goal he/I scored. It was the first time I sensed how football had the power to energise you, to make you feel elated. To dare you to dream, whatever your own shortcomings as a footballer. And I wasn't even watching Everton. At least Italy played in blue.

My soundtrack to 1982 was Paul McCartney's *Tug Of War* album, with its red and blue cover in digital computer-game style, showing Paul at the centre as a black-and-white figure in headphones. It was Paul's first album since John Lennon's assassination and I, for one, was eagerly awaiting it. I had recently begun my own vinyl collection when dad bought me a copy of Paul's 1971 album *Ram* as a reward for doing well at school. Straight B's, back then, constituted doing well – and that was my prize. But if I was in danger or wearing out that record, my tape of *Tug Of War* must have broken several times. It was a smash-hit album, as the world waited for Paul's response to John's death. And there was to be no disappointment even if the build-up, sadly, was dominated by Paul schmaltz. How two of my all-time favourite artists, Paul McCartney and Stevie Wonder, could come up with cheese like 'Ebony And Ivory' was beyond me even then. I was too young to stay up late to watch its debut airing on US TV but I asked my mum about it the next morning.

'Stevie sang better,' she said. 'But Paul looked better.' Dad was a touch more honest about the whole thing.

'It wasn't very good,' he said under his breath, as an aside.

That was enough for me. I took it as a given that Paul looked good. But if he hadn't performed well, that song had to be a write-off. All the same, *Tug Of War* had saving grace after saving grace. The album had so many redeeming features that it automatically became one of my all-time favourites and it still holds that position now. If not for the title track or 'Ballroom Dancing' or even 'Take It Away', then definitely for Paul's tribute to his old partner on 'Here Today'. If John was the guy who wrote meaningful words and Paul was the guy with an ear for a tune, then here was Paul writing right from the heart, just like John would have done. Even back then, I knew it. And besides, I was beginning to understand the process of grief after the death of my own grandfather.

Paul wrote of his love for John in 'Here Today'. It was written directly from the heart of one Beatle to another. One brother to another. And here was something which tugged at your emotions. Just like football, I was becoming aware that music was a power which could exhilarate you or knock you flat. It could instil euphoria or desperate sadness, make you think about your own life, your own dreams and your own heartbreak. Perhaps the age of ten is a bit early to be thinking about heartbreak but I was already having to get used to life's biggest letdowns. Two of my school friends, Alastair Smith and Harald Magelsen, died in tragedies less than a year apart. One from a brain haemorrhage and the other in an awful, horrifying speedboat accident. But if young minds and young hearts are resilient to these kinds of 'peripheral' losses, however sad both of them were, my heart was just steeling itself for its first real tear.

And that was being taken away from my father.

Mother

Hello, Goodbye

In September 1982, I hadn't been re-enrolled in my school and one day one of my classmates saw me in the street outside the Royal Gazette building, where my parents had been working for five years.

'Why aren't you in school?' he shouted. 'Coz I'm going back to England,' I replied.

And so I was. No more Bermuda sunshine for me but a new adventure, at age 11 (just turned). Going back to England, my homeland. Reclaiming my birthright. Standing up for myself in the real world. Going to the home of football and the Beatles.

But it wasn't at all the happy experience I had wanted it to be, because my father was staying behind.

I still remember his tears as we all waved him goodbye in the departure lounge at Bermuda Airport. And that's probably why I have ALWAYS associated airports with intolerable sadness. I know they can also be scenes of real joy, places where there are happy reunions. But for the Lennon in me as opposed to the McCartney, they are places of sadness. Places where people say goodbye, feel such painful loss and even lose a part of themselves. My dad was not someone I would often see crying and his tears that day served to underline just how momentous a day this was in my life. It's also why, in hindsight, the moments my dad and I shared at the end of that West Brom match – when tributes were paid to the late Brian Labone and we shared in Duncan Ferguson's emotional farewell – truly struck chords within me.

So that late September day was my own 'hello, goodbye'. Hello England. Goodbye dad.

But for me, the association has never been with that McCartneyesque joy of 'Hello, Goodbye', the psychedelic colour of the Beatles in their *Sgt Pepper* suits and upbeat, unbridled optimism of that lyric and tune. Instead, for me, this was my very own John Lennon childhood.

Unlike John, I wasn't forced, or even asked, to choose between my mother and father at six years old. Firstly, I was five years older and secondly, I had no option but to return. It was presented to me that my parents were separating and that was that. So those agonising lyrics of John's, when he wrote 'Mother' in his primal scream era, do not QUITE reflect my own experience. I didn't feel unwanted or unloved. But I understood John's pain only too well. John's mother had him – but he never had her. John wanted her – she didn't want him. John's father left him – but he never left his father. And John NEEDED his dad – but it wasn't the same in reverse. So John told them: 'Goodbye'.

The ominous tolling of the church bell in the intro to that song foretells the pain which is about to be recounted. For John, the pain was utterly unbearable. For me, his was a pain I could relate to in a very different way. My mother never left me, and nor would she. She loved me with every ounce of love she could possibly give. I never felt unloved. But it was suffocating, crushing, energy-sapping. I felt that I had to reciprocate it and if I didn't, I obviously didn't love her enough. I was disloyal. Her love was not entirely unconditional. It came with strings attached. And it came against the backdrop of a deeply unsettled family life.

My father couldn't have done more for me as a boy. Apart from the enormous gifts of football and music, he was generous with his time and attention. We played guitars together. We went running together from when I was seven years old. He taught me to ride a bike. He read all the instruction manuals to the most mind-numbing 'bored' [*sic*] games so he could play with me. We had kickabouts in the park. And he really made me laugh. But he was also distant. Unemotional. Unpraising. Sarcastic. Belittling. And there were times when he was bad to my mother. In later life, he was quite selfish and the sarcastic, condescending, distant dad was there – or rather wasn't there – all too often. Whereas my mother expected me to put her first and show her ALL the love she could clearly show me, my father made it seem as though my place was NOT at the top of his pecking order.

I was always a sensitive boy and I later grew into an overly-sensitive adult. My relationships were tumultuous roller-coaster rides. My behaviour, at times, was shameful. Like my mother, I could be incredibly loving but also emotionally exhausting. Like my father, I could step right away into the distance and appear uncaring. And as I bounced in between these two extremes, I would behave like some kind of human push-me-pull-you. Loving, then almost hating. Feeling totally affectionate, but then disdaining. Going out of my way to be affectionate but then withdrawing it. Sulking, having tantrums. Punishing my partner. I grew into a lost soul.

Counsellors say that your behaviour is based on your childhood experiences. What you saw, what you lived through. The examples you were set. And I know that is why I became a volatile individual – more volatile than 'Drunken' Duncan Ferguson at his best (or worst). But I also know that the way to move forward is not to apportion blame but to recognise the root of the problem; to face up to its effect on you and to moderate your behaviour. To grow up. Just like in 'Mother', and John Lennon's open letter to the children of the world. Not to do what he had done ... because instead of walking, he'd tried to run. And so he just had to tell them: 'Goodbye'.

My entire life has been a process of trying to say goodbye to my past. Trying to free myself from the shackles of my childhood. But more importantly, trying to recognise the nature of my relationship with both of my parents and how those relationships do NOT have to shape my own. I grew up without a proper understanding of what love really is. After many years of soul-searching, I have come to realise that truly unconditional love is a rare thing. We choose our partners. We fall in love with them based on what they're like, how they are with us, how we feel. Whether that love grows then depends on a number of factors. Many millions of people are in happy, fulfilling relationships. They are truly in love. But it is not unconditional love. It is a love which depends on their relationship with each other. Which survives because of how they are with each other.

For me, unconditional love is the love you feel for your child. And it's unconditional if you don't bruise them when it doesn't come back at you. For me, unconditional love is the love you feel for music. For your idols who make it. Who you grow up engrossed in. Whose lyrics and melodies you love so much that they become a part of your very soul.

And for me, unconditional love is the love you feel for your football team. The ecstasy you share with them when there is glory and the devastation you share with them when there is despair. The identity they forge for you.

And when we touched down at Gatwick in September 1982, I fell in love for the first time. I fell head over heels in love. With Everton.

Sheedy, Sheedy, Sheedy!

The pain I felt at missing my father was matched by this utter obsession I now developed with my football team. If before I had a burning passion for Everton, by now it was consuming my life. It was all I cared about and all I talked about. All I really thought about, apart from my dad. In 1982–83, Everton were an average side and to any of my classmates at school, there was no real reason for me to be supporting them. By now I was living in Chelmsford, Essex with my mum and sister. I didn't speak with the Merseyside accent anyone would have expected from an Everton supporter. I never went to any games. (I had been to one more match at home, with my dad, before the permanent move back to England.) And Everton were not one of those clubs that were likely to win anything, so they weren't popular in the schoolyard. To add to that, this was a season when Liverpool were successfully defending their league title and Manchester United would go on to win the FA Cup, as Tottenham (one of the favourite 'local' teams) had done for the two seasons before. It was also a season when even clubs like Luton Town and Notts County were considered established teams in the top flight of English football.

But I felt more committed than the most ardent of Everton fans could be. My obsession went far beyond my programmes and my Panini stickers. I ate, drank and slept Everton Football Club. Rebutted every single overture from my mum's family to turn me into an awful 'Tottenham' supporter. And I soaked up every single result, every scorer, every attendance figure, and wrote them down oh so neatly in a pristine notebook. And how I regretted goading my dad just before we'd left Bermuda, on the opening day of the season, when Everton were playing away at newly-promoted Watford. To my lasting shame, I told him I might consider supporting Watford, considering it was my local team (in the sense that it was 'local' to where I was born in St Albans). Of course, the thought of changing allegiance from Everton had never even remotely crossed my mind. But I said it to irk my father. And I'll never forget the colour draining from his face, the ashen shade it went, as he turned away in disgust. Everton lost that first ever match with Watford. And I felt enormous guilt for my footballing infidelity, however brief, artificial and transparent it was.

Watford had a brilliant first season in the top division, going on to finish second in the league behind Liverpool. Everton ended up down in seventh but that was of no real concern to me. It was Everton that gave me a sense of who I was. Gave me an identity. It was Everton that made me proud. Everton that drew me closer to my father, a man who I only had correspondence with via the odd letter, telephone conversation or taped message sent via airmail. On those tapes, we would post one-way conversations to each other. Talking about Everton. Talking about the latest records and perhaps playing the odd thing on guitar just to fill a bit of space. Maybe playing some kind of correspondence chess. I remember reacting with horror and desperately trying to self-elocute after I'd told my dad on tape how my new school was going to 'give me a good edu-cay-shun' in some kind of dreadful Essex accent, freshly adopted but stale in its delivery. In dad's tape which followed, that accent appeared to amuse and appal him in equal measure. It was a simple dose of Colin Roberts sarcasm which this sensitive boy took as a personal slight. I may not have sounded like a Scouser or had a Wirral accent like him, but I vowed internally NOT to grow up with anything remotely like an Essex twang. Besides, I had my Everton-supporting comrades to think about. And I was now identifying with them.

Around this time, we were lodging with my mum's sister and her husband Roger, a devoted Tottenham fan but a lovely, caring guy despite that devastating affliction. My mum was clearly aware of how much I was missing a dad. And during this period of his absence, Uncle Roger was the only father figure I had. He was a car mechanic who would bring me little motor industry mementoes from his work, as well as lots of avuncular attention. And he also gave me a really special early Christmas present – to this day, probably one of the most caring Christmas presents anyone has ever given me.

It was December 1982 and I was still acclimatising to the cold, to the fake frost on windows, to a British Christmas and to cheap decorations. I even remember the cheesy Abba songs that seemed to pipe out at any family party we went to around that time. But on 11 December, my Uncle Roger made my Christmas. He drove me the 40 miles from Chelmsford to Ipswich, so we could watch Everton playing at Portman Road. As far as I'm aware – and my mum no longer remembers – he bought the tickets, paid for the petrol, got me some lunch and saw me safely there and back. Of course he also bought me the obligatory match programme, which I was to file fastidiously. And he bought me my first ever Everton scarf, thick and woolly and so wide that I could fold it in two. He even showed me the different ways I could wear it. And throughout the match, he provided what some around us may have thought of as an annoying commentary but which I took as thoughtful analysis. 'I think it should go here next,' he'd say, pretty accurately predicting the passes in each passage of play. It was a truly touching early Christmas present but perhaps I should think of it more as a pre-Christmas cake, which was covered in delicious icing. Because Everton won the match. My first ever away match and Everton won it 2-0. There were only 17 and a half thousand fans inside Portman Road that day and any glance through the record books will show it as nothing other than an ordinary match. But to me, it was a special occasion.

The two Kevins were the match-winners. Kevin Richardson and Kevin Sheedy. The former Kevin was a versatile, underrated midfielder who was almost a fixture in the Everton side, despite never making it into any supporter's first-choice XI during what was to become the most decorated period in the club's history.

In modern football, when clubs use upwards of 30 players per season, he would have been invaluable. Back then, when teams used maybe 16 or 18 players, he was considered one of the also-rans. But Kevin Richardson played more often than he didn't despite never being a fans' favourite. He played in Everton's League Cup Final and replay of 1984, as well as the FA Cup Final win over Watford, in which he wore a protective strapping around a broken wrist at Wembley. He won league championship medals with both Everton and later Arsenal. And he popped up with some memorable goals, too, including one which took Everton to that League Cup Final in 1984, which we eventually lost to Liverpool in a replay.

The latter Kevin was also on the scoresheet in that League Cup semi-final against Aston Villa. But on this day at Portman Road, he was fast becoming my new favourite, en route to acquiring his later status as my all-time Everton hero. Kevin Sheedy is still the player who's awed me the most with his God-given talent, his sheer audacity and his supreme irreverence in delivering a two-fingered salute to the Kop, as he once did after thumping in one of his trademark free kicks. His ability to score from those dead-ball situations marked him out for me as some kind of Brazilian superstar, rather than an Irish international who'd arrived at Everton via the Welsh market town of Builth Wells and then Liverpool reserves. He'd long since confirmed his superstardom to me when he scored the equalising goal in the FA Cup semi-final against Luton at Villa Park in 1985. That was one of those free kicks he always scored from, and it was all the sweeter as there were only a few minutes remaining to chalk off Ricky Hill's early strike. Then, in extra time that day, he delivered another perfect free kick for Derek Mountfield to score the winner. My favourite number was number 11, in tribute to my idol. If we were in the playground I wanted to be Kevin Sheedy, despite the occasional switch to Trevor Steven. In school matches or in the park I wanted to play wide on the left, even though my best position was at right-back. And whenever I went to watch, it was Sheedy who would capture my imagination. If the ball was placed for an Everton free kick, almost ANYWHERE in the opposition half, a spontaneous, expectant chant would strike up of: 'SHEEDY, SHEEDY, SHEEDY!' Everyone knew the man was a magician. Journalists and commentators would talk of his 'cultured left foot', or even 'educated left foot', as if it was possible to teach something so bewitching to part of one's anatomy.

He couldn't tackle. Wouldn't get stuck in. Had no right foot. Couldn't head the ball, either. Liverpool fans thought he played like a girl. But he was a genius. Whether it was a pinpoint cross, a perfect through-ball or a devastating free kick, Kevin Sheedy was a master of his talent. David Beckham, eat your heart out. En route to Wembley in 1985, Sheedy well and truly established his status as my all-time Everton hero. It was in the quarter-final, ironically against Ipswich, that he wrote his name into folklore at Goodison Park.

I was at the match along with my dad and my nanna's brother, my Uncle Frank. Somewhere in the crowd, also, was the legendary manager of those dazzling Everton teams of the 1960s, Harry Catterick. It was a deep sadness to everyone at the club that Catterick died at that match. It was clearly a more significant event than the magic Kevin Sheedy was conjuring on the pitch that day. But that it was overshadowed by those mercurial talents began to speak portentously about the place Kevin Sheedy was creating for himself within the fabric of Everton Football Club.

The match finished 2-2 but it will forever be remembered for two things. The second is Catterick's death. The first is Everton's opening goal that day. Paul Cooper, in the Ipswich goal, was helpless when Sheedy struck the perfect free kick around the wall and into the top right-hand corner of the net. But that wasn't the drama. That came when the referee ordered the kick to be retaken, much to the Everton players' protests. But it's a moment frozen in time that I can recall so vividly, as Peter Reid placed the ball back on the spot from where Sheedy had hit it. I guess it was a little more than 20 yards out, just to the left of the goal at the Park End of the ground. Sheedy said he still fancied the kick, and promptly struck it hard and low, firing it into the bottom left-hand corner. Again, Cooper helpless. Again, Sheedy mesmeric. Again ... yet again, Everton fans in delirium. He'd scored from the same position, the exact same free kick, in the diagonally opposite corner of the goal. 'SHEEDY, SHEEDY, SHEEDY!' was ringing out around Goodison Park in tribute to an Everton god. And to think that he cost only £100,000 and he'd hardly had a look-in at Liverpool. How divine it was when he later gave his former employers that two-fingered salute, directed at the Kop, after firing the ball into their precious net. It was almost as if he was saying, 'Thank you very much for letting me move to your neighbours, where I've won just about everything in the game. Now screw you.' And I loved him for it.

Years later, when Everton's powers were on the wane and we were employing a more functional style of footballer, Sheedy and new signing Martin Keown were out with their team-mates on a 'team- building exercise' at a Chinese restaurant. According to urban myth, Sheedy's idea of team-building was to tell Keown he 'wasn't good enough' to play for Everton, and promptly get flattened for it. *Nil Satis Nisi Optimum*, and all that. 'Nothing But The Best Will Do'. Kevin Sheedy was the best. Full stop.

There were no real heroics back on that cold December day against Ipswich at Portman Road,my Uncle Roger for company. Kevin Sheedy was on the scoresheet but he was still vying for my hero worship with the swashbuckling Andy King who, for me, could do no wrong with his flowing blond locks and his cavalier skills and spirit. And it was another Kevin for whom that uneventful league match at Ipswich Town proved to be a real watershed.

Ratters Comes Of Age, Daddy Comes Home

When Uncle Roger and I walked towards Portman Road, me with programme in hand, I'd have scanned through my reading material. Then devoured it. One name which wouldn't have jumped out at me was that of Kevin Ratcliffe. Billy Wright, yes. Kevin Ratcliffe, no.

Billy Wright was a Liverpool lad, a stalwart at the heart of Everton's defence alongside the club captain, the imperious Mark Higgins. Ratcliffe was a bit-part player. A Welshman on the fringes. A defender without a great touch who was a little uncomfortable on the ball and only really kicked it with his left foot. Who only really scratched around the first team, mostly at left-back, and even then only usually when John Bailey was injured.

In fact, in December 1982, Ratcliffe was on the verge of leaving Everton and the dynasty which would soon follow at Goodison Park might never have been. Blackburn Rovers wanted him. Stoke City wanted him. Even that day's opponents, Ipswich Town, wanted him. All of them inferior clubs. But it was Ipswich who were the most persistent, under their manager Bobby Robson, and it was quite feasible that Kevin Ratcliffe might have been playing that day AGAINST Everton.

Bloody good job he wasn't.

This was the Everton line-up, as announced over the Portman Road tannoy at 2.55pm: Arnold, Stevens, Bailey, Ratcliffe, Higgins, McMahon, Curran, Heath, Johnson, Richardson, Sheedy. On the subs' bench, someone called Sharp.

So Kevin Ratcliffe was in the Everton team. No Billy Wright in central defence alongside Higgins. Ratcliffe instead. And it was a position which he made permanent. I can't remember if Kevin Ratcliffe was masterful in defence that day. I can't remember if he was the most dominant of our back players. I don't remember any of his trademark tackles, blocks, headers or clearances in that particular match. But I can guarantee you one thing. He would have been super-quick. That man could run ... FAST. He seemed to leave a trail of smoke behind his boots. He would just burn up the turf as he pursued an attacker. Even if the opponents had a few yards' advantage. Even if the opponent was his great rival – his Welsh team-mate and friend Ian Rush, of Liverpool FC. Ratcliffe was the quickest defender in the league. He was a brilliant athlete. And on that day, at just turned 22, he was beginning to acquire the experience and wisdom which would soon make him one of the best readers of the game in the whole land.

A run-of-the-mill league match it may have been for many. But not for me, of course. And not for Kevin Ratcliffe either. For both of us, it was a momentous occasion. I restarted my Everton watching career. Ratcliffe restarted his Everton playing career, in earnest. He'd claimed his place in the team and he would never give it up. From that day forward, Ratcliffe was an Everton regular. Within a year, he'd been appointed Everton's youngest ever club captain. Within another year, he was Everton's most successful captain of all time, at the age of 24.

Kevin Ratcliffe, under the tutelage of that magnificent manager Howard Kendall, led Everton through the most impressive period in their history. He won two league championships and also finished as a runner-up. He led us to three successive FA Cup finals, winning the first of those against Watford. He led us to the League Cup Final in 1984. Under Ratters, we won the European Cup Winners' Cup in 1985. And he led us back to the FA Cup Final in 1989, the year of the devastating Hillsborough tragedy. He also won 58 Wales caps and three and a half Charity Shields.

In fact, unpick all of that glory and focus just for a moment on the 1984–85 season. We'd won the FA Cup and finished runners-up in the League Cup in 1984. Then we embarked on the most remarkable season in Everton's history. We won the league by 13 points, setting a record points tally in the process. We beat Rapid Vienna to win that first ever European trophy for the club. We only missed out on an unprecedented treble when a future blue, Norman Whiteside, cruelly killed us off in extra time in the FA Cup Final, as Manchester United took that particular trophy from us. The season of 1984–85 was such a glorious success that it will always be remembered by Everton fans and non-Everton fans alike. It should also be remembered that 1984– 85 was, quite literally, the Year of the Rat.

Of the other players who made the pitch that day at Portman Road, only three of them played a major part in all of the success which was to follow. The three Kevins aside – Ratcliffe, Sheedy and Richardson – the match gave notable starts to Gary Stevens at right-back and Adrian Heath in attack, with Graeme Sharp coming off the bench for one of the more unremarkable appearances in a most remarkable Everton career which would see him end up as the club's post-war record goalscorer. Graeme Sharp hung up his Everton boots with 159 goals to his name. Only Dixie Dean had ever netted more for the Toffees. And the Sharp-shooter shared in every single one of those honours which Kevin Ratcliffe captained Everton to. Sharp was just another of those players who were jet-propelled into the footballing mainstream, practically from oblivion. And, ridiculous as it may seem, Everton weren't too far away from footballing oblivion in 1982 and 1983.

But Howard Kendall picked some special ingredients, threw in some of his intoxicating spells, and concocted the most magical potion ever to come out of Goodison Park.

He found Neville Southall, a former binman from Wales via Bury, and turned him into the best goalkeeper in the world. He found Gary Stevens, a supreme athlete, who became an England regular at right- back with power and pace in his locker. He got the best out of John Bailey and then replaced him with Pat Van Den Hauwe, Everton's left-back who strikes fear into me even now when I think back to how hard he was. He found Derek Mountfield, a tall central defender who almost doubled up as a striker, so prolific was he as a goalscorer. Dave Watson came later, another club legend in the Brian Labone mould. Big. Tough. Uncompromising. A Scouser who loved Everton (even though he had played in Liverpool's reserves). And he shared in that second league triumph alongside Ratcliffe at the heart of Everton's defence. Howard Kendall found Peter Reid from Bolton, the engine room, the heartbeat of the team, the midfield dynamo. The man who'd been playing on the day of my first match, even if not for Everton. He found the maestro Kevin Sheedy, the player every club wanted and the player Liverpool must have been kicking themselves to have released, and of course he found the all-rounder Kevin Richardson. Then came Paul Bracewell, a tactician, a midfield accomplice for Reid, a man who could play the ball all over the park. Kendall found Trevor Steven, paying the then substantial fee of £300,000 to Burnley for his services, and unearthing one of the most gifted goalscoring wingers ever to grace Goodison Park. Ever to grace England, in fact. He found Sharp and later Andy Gray, a superstar name already but a man whose frame, appetite and talismanic appeal meant he was built for the role of Everton centre-forward, and a man who was hero- worshipped by the Gwladys Street End not least for his dramatic diving headers and goals en route to Everton's first European trophy. It's a mark of how much Andy Gray was loved that the Gwladys Street Enders were only lukewarm to the man who replaced him, Gary Lineker, even though he scored an almost unbelievable 40 goals in his single season at the club. And of course Howard Kendall found Adrian 'Inchy' Heath, breaking Everton's transfer record by paying Stoke £700,000 for him. And it was the unsung Heath who started it all for Everton – around the time when Kendall's team were playing dire football, grinding out goalless draws at home like the one against Coventry in front of fewer than 14,000 fans at Goodison Park. And that on New Year's Eve.

But as the flyers flew around a windy Goodison, demanding Kendall's head; as his garage door was daubed with graffiti calling for him to be sacked; as the fans turned their ire on the man who was destined to overtake even Catterick as the club's most brilliant manager of all time, Adrian Heath wrote his name into history. In January 1984, Everton were losing to Oxford United of the Third Division in a League Cup match at the Manor Ground. With just a few minutes remaining, Oxford's defender Kevin Brock played what became known to both clubs as a quite infamous back pass. Heath ran in to intercept it, took the ball past the stranded goalkeeper and slotted it into an empty net. Everton had saved their skins. HEATH had saved Everton's skins. And the first step had been taken on the path to ultimate glory.

I spent a year with my mother as my only visible parent. When my dad showed up one day, to collect me from school, I abandoned any notion of 11-year-old fear that your mates might scorn at you for being affectionate to your family in front of them. I sprinted across that school playground and jumped into his arms. He swung me round and held me tight and I wanted to hold on to him forever.

Little did either of us know that, together, we were about to share the most joyful times of our footballing lives. And little did I know that, just a few years hence, I would be rubbing shoulders with Southall and Steven, Sharp and Stevens. I even met Kevin Sheedy. Gary Lineker. Even that Liverpool demi-god Ian Rush. I had begun to dream my dreams. One day, some of them would come true.

Help!

1984

And now our lives had changes in oh so many ways. My life had changed, and so had my sister's, because of the return to England of our father. Our parents' lives had changed because of their reconciliation. An end to their separation. I remember we'd been taken along on a 'date' when my mum organised a seaside trip with one of her work colleagues. I hated every single minute of it and I made it as plain as a 12-year-old could possibly make it. I'm sure the man in question would have gladly thrown me into the North Sea. And obviously, I missed my dad so terribly that I was just overjoyed at his return. I remember him taking me to the shop and I would refuse sweets, just for fear of overstepping the mark, or of ruining our reunion with some show of pre-teenage greed or ingratitude.

Dad and I had a couple of adventures. We drove in a van up to Bromborough so he could store some of his stuff. It was a rickety old rust-bucket we'd hired, and it could scarcely do more than about 50 miles an hour. The journey itself took eight or nine hours, we got to my nanna's house in the early hours of the morning and I loved every minute of the trip. It was just like the old days when dad would carry me across the threshold of the house, and my dozing senses would slowly take it in that I'd arrived in the comfort and warmth of 48 Valley Road. Dad was variously staying at my nanna's or staying in hotels while shifting on newspapers. I remember asking him one time if he'd be getting back together with my mum. 'I'm working on it,' he said. I was thrilled.

1984 was George Orwell's vision of a Utopian society. Just look at what happened there. It all went a bit pear-shaped. If leaving Bermuda had been Paradise Lost, this would surely be Paradise Rediscovered. Except it wasn't. The bliss that I felt was soon overtaken by regret. Bitter recriminations swept through my family. And old habits died hard. Just like Howard Kendall's later attempts at re-establishing his love affair with Everton, these things never do work out, do they? When a love has gone, it has gone. Attempts at re-energising it after a period of absence almost inevitably fail. And so it was to prove with my parents. Not immediately, but four years down the line, after the original cracks in their relationship resurfaced, deepened and eventually caused earthquakes.

They got back together for the kids. And the one good thing which came out of their re-emergence as two parents *in situ* was that I was about to spend a lot of yearned-for time with my father. We became regular watchers of Everton together, going to seven matches between his return to England and the end of the 1983–84 season.

In all of those games though, we didn't go up to Goodison. We went to five away matches, then the FA Cup semi-final and final. What a way to develop my relationship with both my father and my football club. Watching them win their first trophy since before I was born. And all that BEFORE I returned to see them at Goodison Park.

What I had no conception of was that I wasn't the only one who'd needed help, who needed reconnection with his family and his football. My dad did too, desperately. And in later years, I came to realise that all of those Saturdays out of the house with me in tow helped constitute his therapy. They provided him with what he loved, in Everton. They helped him establish a bond with the son who, hopefully, he'd also been missing. But they also got him out of the house and away from my mother.

Our first time back on the road together, apart from that van journey up to the Wirral, was an away trip to Leicester in October 1983. It was icy cold. Freezing. I remember that as we parked our car amid the Victorian terraced houses, strewn newspapers and multi- racial urchins, my knuckles went white. I was entering a new chapter in my life now. Experiencing new things. Going to places where kids asked you for money, just so they wouldn't smash your car in. This was the real world. And it was bloody cold out there.

The match itself was a 2-0 defeat and I remember at least one of Leicester's goals was a thunderbolt from distance. 'We haven't got anyone who can do that,' said dad, bemoaning the lack of a match- winner in our team. Steven and Sheedy WERE in our line-up that day. And both of them were lethal from distance. But we didn't quite realise their powers just yet. The game was also notable for being the only match we ever left before the final whistle. There were about ten minutes to go when dad took me out, as a horde of Leicester fans appeared to be sweeping towards us through the stand we were sitting in. There can't have been many of them, mind. The attendance was only 10,953. But these were the dark days of hooliganism and dad was having none of it. He protected me.

Our annual defeat at Queens Park Rangers followed that one – we were on the wrong side of another 2-0 scoreline – and things didn't seem to be getting any better for Everton. In fact, my hero Andy King finally lost that status with me when he missed a penalty. There was a sour atmosphere among the Everton supporters who'd travelled. It was around this time that those anti-Kendall flyers were littering the Goodison Park turf, covering almost every blade of grass just as the confetti had done when Argentina played Holland in the 1978 World Cup Final. Except this time, the paperwork was threatening rather than celebratory. Everton stood on the edge of the abyss, at least as a top-flight football club, and a famous one at that.

Paul McCartney was number one at Christmas. The video to his single, 'Pipes Of Peace', visualised the front-line truce in the First World War between British and German troops, when comrades on both sides of no-man's-land joined in the middle to share cigarettes, photographs of loved ones and a friendly game of football. With Paul's accompanying words, it was a reinforcement to me that football brought hope and joy. Most of all, football brought people together.

Paul sang about songs of joy and playing the pipes of peace. And as peace temporarily descended on my family that Christmas, so the unusually rebellious Everton masses were appeased. Within weeks of the New Year came Adrian Heath's date with destiny at Oxford. I remember listening on the radio while my parents were out. And it's the first time I remember leaping around the room like some kind of monkey on acid, at the sound of an Everton goal.

Dad and I went to two more away matches and instead of losing, Everton were drawing, 1-1 at West Brom and 4-4 at Watford, in what turned out to be the most memorable match of that league season. Then in April, we went to Luton and won 3-0. Ironically and depressingly for the young Neil, it was without Kevin Sheedy, who was already suffering one of his customary injury curses. But it was the most impressive Everton victory I had yet witnessed. Adrian Heath scored twice including one from the penalty spot, thus achieving what Andy King couldn't. Derek Mountfield got the other. Neville Southall had now replaced Jim Arnold as our regular goalkeeper and a great team was taking shape before our very eyes.

At the same time, Everton were performing heroics in the FA Cup, despatching Stoke, Gillingham, Shrewsbury Town and Notts County en route to the semi-finals. Gillingham could have derailed the new-look Everton Express, though. A young Tony Cascarino ought to have killed us off in the last minute at Goodison, before we romped through the replay. Rumour has it that Cascarino was sold to Gillingham from the non-league for a job lot of corrugated iron. Good job he wasn't worth more precious metal or history would have been rewritten.

The semi-final against Southampton was at Highbury, so dad and I went down to the Arsenal Stadium for a match we felt was destined to deliver us from the doldrums. Everton hadn't been in the FA Cup Final since 1968 and if they could get past Southampton, that old cup-winning club of the Chadwicks, they would play either Watford or Third Division Plymouth Argyle at Wembley. We knew it wouldn't be Plymouth, as their fairy-tale run had to come to an end. But even if the final was to be against Watford, we knew that a win in the semis and our name would be on the cup. But it was far from a foregone conclusion. This was a Southampton managed by Lawrie McMenemy. A Southampton which finished a club record second in the league that season. (To Liverpool, of course). And a Southampton just as keen on lifting the cup at Wembley. Somehow, using some kind of ingenuity he was able to display to get rare match tickets, dad got us seats in the executive box at Highbury, right on the halfway line. We had a perfect view of the pitch and were ideally placed throughout the 90 minutes of a frustrating 0-0 draw. Since the start of 1984, Everton fans had come up with a new ditty to sing to the tune of 'Que Sera Sera'. It was a song which stuck with the club forever more, words which belonged to the faithful fans who followed Everton all the way to both the League Cup and FA Cup finals in 1984.

> Tell me ma, me ma.
> To put the champagne on ice.
> We're going to Wembley twice.
> Tell me ma, me ma.

Later it was adapted to 'Tell me ma, me ma. I don't want no tea, no tea. We're going to Wembley. Tell me ma, me ma', before reverting to its original form 25 years later, when Everton went to Wembley to play Manchester United in another cup semi-final. But in 1984, I really did want to tell 'me ma' that we were going to Wembley. So when Adrian Heath scored with an unmarked header, three minutes before the end of extra time, all kinds of pandemonium broke out at Highbury. Everton fans invaded the pitch in sheer delirium, wanting to celebrate and wanting to mob their goalscoring hero. Unfortunately, Southampton fans invaded the pitch too, looking for a ruck. Remember, this was the heyday of hooliganism. For the last three minutes play continued with fans of both sides stood around the perimeter of the pitch, as some kind of more threatening throwback to the famous, overpopulated 'White Horse' final at Wembley in 1923. Cue the final whistle and cue more delirium from Everton fans, more aggression from Southampton fans and an invasion by police horses to separate those involved in the pitched battle. Our bourgeois seats, again, offered the perfect view as we drank in Everton's forthcoming trip to Wembley for the FA Cup Final and looked down at the gladiators whacking each other and being whacked by police officers on horseback. From this comparative position of safety, as opposed to our experience at Leicester, this sight of the Highbury horses seemed to amuse my dad. 'Arsenal will love that,' he said.

Dad scraped around for tickets to the final. He couldn't get them from Everton but thankfully, pulling some stunt which involved pretending to one of Watford's most senior officials that he was a lifelong visitor to Vicarage Road, he pulled two rabbits out of the hat – in the form of two tickets to what was then the 'Twin Towers'. Only problem was, of course, they were in the Watford end. But no matter. We were going to Wembley. On arrival, we decided to swap them and, these being the days when that sort of thing was no bother, there really was no bother. The tickets we got from Watford fans stranded in the Everton end had 'J. BUTLER'printed on them. So we took Mr Butler's tickets and we took our places on the deep bank of terracing for what was my – and even my dad's – first Wembley cup final with Everton.

I stood against some side railings so I could prop myself up, trying to get a better spec. The old Wembley had a wide running track round the pitch and you almost needed a telescope to get a decent view of the action. But it was all about the occasion for me. Comedian and Everton fan Freddie Starr laughing and joking with Andy Gray on the pitch beforehand. Elton John, the Watford chairman, wiping tears from his eyes when 100,000 people sang 'Abide With Me'. And the huge banner which said: 'I'm sorry Elton, I guess that's why they call us the Blues', which simultaneously respected and disrespected both Elton and his current hit single, while proclaiming the Everton victory which was about to follow.

Watford had future Red John Barnes and future Blue Mo Johnston in a decent-looking team but that Everton Express was just beginning to puff. Graeme Sharp scored the opener, controlling, turning and shooting in off the post. Andy Gray scored the closer, using his head (what else) and bundling in a pinpoint Trevor Steven cross. And bundling in the hapless and hopeless goalkeeper, too. It was as if Steve Sherwood had been attacked by Nat Lofthouse himself. It would prove to be one of the most talked-about goals in FA Cup Final history, but it happened at the other end of the pitch to us, so probably more than 150 yards away, and we didn't care.

'What happened?' I asked my dad, seeing him cheering and laughing.

'Sherwood made a terrible mistake,' he replied.

So Sharp and Gray won the cup for Everton. It was bedecked in blue and white ribbons for Kevin Ratcliffe to proudly show it off. Kevin Sheedy didn't play because of his injury, so Kevin Richardson was the usual, able understudy. And the nucleus of what was to become the best team in Europe was far too strong for Watford. We went home to Chelmsford, bought some lagers in the offy and bumped into some exiled Scousers ... Evertonians all of them. Oh, and I told me ma. It was a truly wonderful day.

Champions of England, Champions of Europe?

That initial trophy in the cabinet for Howard Kendall's Everton was the first piece in a set of silverware so sumptuous it would have graced Buckingham Palace's dining room. But this being Everton we're talking about, their rise to national and even continental domination wasn't without the odd hiccup.

Every school holiday, my sister Caroline and I would stay in Bromborough, being looked after by our ever-devoted nanna. That summer we did our bus trips, our ferry rides, played crazy golf in Southport and visited the International Garden Festival in Liverpool, complete with 'Yellow Submarine'. We would go to the 'Toffee Shop' (as my nanna would call it) on Goodison Road, almost always in search of a new tracksuit (for me, not my nanna). We would visit Mathew Street and the Beatles Shop, so I could pay homage to the Cavern en route. And we would return to Bromborough for card games and chocolate eclairs, usually having plenty of music or football-related souvenirs to while away the hours, days and weeks at Valley Road. That's when I wasn't passing a ball to Brian Labone on the garden shed door, of course.

On the first day of the 1984–85 season, it was from that 'home' that I made my first trip back to Goodison Park with my father. Everton were playing Tottenham that day, the team of my mum's family, and accompanying us to the match was her brother-in-law Steve. Dad's age-old family friend Taff would always come with us to matches and for years hence would be one of my main partners in Evertonia at Goodison Park. But on this day, it was Steve who I was revelling in sitting alongside.

Now I always liked my Uncle Steve. He was wealthy, entrepreneurial, gave me a lift in his white Porsche and was an 'all right' Cockney geezer in a very matey sense. So when Adrian Heath drove a penalty into the middle of the Park End goal to open the scoring for Everton, I was thrilled. Delighted. Even going so far as to roll up my precious programme so I could obnoxiously tap him on the head with it, in mocking delirium. This was going to be a good time for Everton, I could feel it. They'd paraded the FA Cup before kick-off and there was a wave of optimism erupting within the ground. But it wasn't plain sailing. Not that day, anyway. By half- time, Everton were 2-1 down. Steve had relished his opportunity to repay the favour and took some glee in playfully slapping me about the head with my own programme. And I was in tears. Not because of his revenge. But I was in tears. How could Everton let me down like this? I remember my dad and Steve laughing, telling me it was only half-time and there was a long way to go yet. They were right. We lost 4-1. How could Everton do this to me? After winning the FA Cup and promising so much?

Everton were thumped by Tottenham. They didn't look like a team that would run away with the league championship. Tottenham did though. And in fact, though the final league table shows that Spurs slipped away to third, they were our closest title rivals. I went to 12 matches that season, the most significant of which was the 11th. I'd already seen another 'Vicarage thriller' at Watford, where this time, we won 5-4. I'd seen defeats at Arsenal and Norwich, when Southall, all in white, bizarrely and completely uncharacteristically let one of the goals through his legs. I saw a rare point at Queens Park Rangers. And I saw victories at West Ham, Ipswich and Leicester. We weren't singing 'Tell me ma' this year. What I remember, instead, were the overjoyed Evertonians at West Ham.

> We're gonna win the league,
> We're gonna win the league,
> And now you're gonna believe us,
> And now you're gonna believe us,
> And now you're gonna believe us,
> We're gonna win the league.

They were right, too. And Everton gave me some outstanding memories, not least the 3-0 home win over Telford in the FA Cup. The non-leaguers, who brought the whole town with them in support, were loving their day in the Goodison sun, whatever the scoreline. But this was MY day in the Goodison sun. How dare they be enjoying themselves so much! I just didn't understand it back then. But the game is notable as the second-largest attendance I've ever been a part of at Goodison Park: 47,402. Ultimately more significant memories were of that victory at West Ham, and the fans joyfully predicting a league championship win. Andy Gray's 99th and 100th league goals, banged in during the match at Leicester. The home FA Cup quarter-final against Ipswich, which featured Kevin Sheedy's twice-taken, twice-scored free kick. And the anonymous photographer who took my picture during the preceding league win AT Ipswich, and made me the 'Face In The Crowd' in *Match* magazine. My school pal Robert Edge, an Arsenal fan, came to me one morning. 'Oi,'he said. 'You're in my *Match* magazine.'And there I was. My face encircled in white, as if in a halo. Me with my scarf and hat, all thumbs-up Paul McCartney style. I won a £5 postal order for that.

But the biggest joy that season, even more than the Sheedy-inspired semi-final win over Luton, was the return league fixture with our title rivals Tottenham. It was a white-hot night at White Hart Lane with 48,000 crammed in to watch the best two teams in the country. Everton and Spurs were first and second in the league. Neck and neck for the title. We knew we had to win. Anything else and we'd be handing the momentum to our rivals from north London. Our rivals from my mum's side of the family. Thankfully, we didn't have to wait long to get on top and Andy Gray scored in the ninth minute. The goal I really remember though was Trevor Steven's, which made it 2-0 and seemed to put the game beyond doubt on the hour mark. I remember him rounding Ray Clemence, that guy I'd seen kicking his heels apparently with the same boredom as I was feeling in the Liverpool–Stoke match five years earlier. Trevor Steven, always the coolest of Everton players, tucked the ball into the net right in front of us. Always one for the understatement, he just jogged away, wagging his right index finger as he was about to be mobbed by his team-mates. Tottenham pulled a goal back through Graham Roberts, as he reminded me when I met him almost a quarter of a century later. I was wearing a retro Everton shirt from that season on transfer deadline day in January 2009.

'How could you wear that,' he said, disgusted. 'How could you?' 'Easy,' came my reply. 'It was a brilliant season.'

And so it was. Roberts' goal didn't rescue Tottenham. But Everton still needed some injury-time heroics from Neville Southall to deny Mark Falco from point-blank range. It was one of the best saves of the big man's career. Probably one of the best saves of all time. And effectively it clinched the title, so valuable were the three points that night. Hoddle, Ardiles, Perryman, Galvin and Crooks were beaten. And they didn't recover, either. Liverpool pipped them to the runners'- up spot. And Everton simply romped away. We were champions by a clear 13 points. The fact that we lost the FA Cup Final to Manchester United hardly seemed to matter at all.

I didn't get to any European matches that season and what a shame that turned out to be. Everton beat Rapid Vienna 3-1 to win the European Cup Winners'Cup in Rotterdam, thanks to goals from Gray, Steven and Sheedy. But the most memorable night in Goodison Park history had come in the semi-final. Everton had drawn the first leg with Bayern Munich 0-0 but in the return, they were supreme in the extreme. Almost 50,000 crammed into Goodison making a noise so deafening it seems you can still hear some of the roars echoing around the streets of Liverpool 4 even now. Everton were 1-0 down at half-time and seemingly on their way out. But Sharp, Gray and Steven completed the rescue act on a night of Royal Blue ultra-glory. I was listening on the radio while playing snooker in our garage.

The reason why I'll always regret not going to any of those European matches, and that Bayern Munich game in particular, is because of what happened only a few weeks later, not that far from Rotterdam, where the well-behaved Everton supporters were practically given the freedom of the city by the local police. Of course I was a teenager at school in the south of England and there was no way I could make it to Goodison for night games. But the enormity of what I'd missed out on hit me on 29 May 1985. And the enormity of the futility of hooliganism hit me, also.

I was watching *Wogan*, the BBC1 chat show, waiting for the European Cup Final to start. Not in Holland but in Belgium. Liverpool were playing Juventus. I would be supporting Juventus. But there wasn't just a football match at the Heysel Stadium. There was a football match and the most awful, criminal disaster. Some Liverpool supporters charged at a crumbling old wall, knocked it over and killed 39 football fans, almost all of them Italians. The match, shamefully, went ahead anyway, with Juventus winning. But I was numbed with shock. The sense of injustice deepened in the days which followed. English clubs were banned from European competition. That meant that Everton, the league winners, European Cup Winners' Cup champions and FA Cup finalists, would NOT be playing in the European Cup. Everton, officially ranked the number one team in Europe, would not be in Europe's premier competition. And this was in the days when only the champions could play in it. Steaua Bucharest, who beat Barcelona on penalties after a boring goalless draw in the 1986 final, were vastly inferior to Everton. I know nothing can be proven. But I know this. Everton would have been champions of Europe in 1986, but for the Heysel disaster and the part those Liverpool fans played in it.

As it was, Everton seemed to begin the 1985–86 season where they had left off. We went to seven matches that season, taking in wins at Ipswich, Watford and an all-too-rare victory at Arsenal. I remember our win that day getting right up the nose of one Arsenal fan we were sat by.

'Handball!' my dad shouted.

'It wasn't his hand, it was his foot,' came the grump's reply.

'Funny place to have a foot,' said dad.

For much of the season, we looked to be on course for the double. 'And that's something Liverpool can't match,' said dad. 'That's something they've never done.'

But guess what? It wasn't just the stupid white 'bib' on Everton's new-design shirts that was a letdown. It was their efforts to get across the finish line. This was the 40-goal season of old golden boots himself, Gary Lineker. Gray had gone and Gary had come. Everton were in pole position, albeit with Liverpool breathing down their necks, when they went for an evening kick-off at Oxford, the place where it had all started to go right. But on the night when Lineker needed his shooting boots the most, he left them at home. Quite literally.

He later admitted to my *Liverpool Echo* colleague Dave Prentice that he'd been scoring with his pair of lucky boots – a pair so tattered that they'd been repaired about three times. But for some reason, those boots didn't grace the turf that night at Oxford. Lineker wore new boots instead. Chances went begging. And we lost 1-0.

We still had a chance of winning the title on the last day of the season, if Liverpool lost at Chelsea. I was at Goodison Park that day to see Everton demolish Southampton 6-1. Gary Lineker had found his old boots. And while he was scoring the first hat-trick I saw from an Everton player, Liverpool were winning at Chelsea even though the Chinese whispers sweeping the ground told a different story. Liverpool were the champions by two points. And they beat us in the FA Cup Final, even though Lineker had put us in the lead. To rub salt into the wound, there was a press camera right in the corner of one of the nets at Wembley and Ian Rush's final goal sent it flying. The image has always scarred me. Everton had now lost FA Cup finals for two seasons running, since that victory over Watford. We were the best team in the country. We'd been the champions, won the Cup Winners' Cup and SHOULD have won the European Cup. But it was Liverpool who were celebrating the double. Not us.

The 1986–87 season was another without European football for Everton and all the other English clubs who would have qualified. No Uefa Cup for us, although we would equally have been able to choose the Cup Winners' Cup given that

Liverpool would have been back in the European Cup. There was a European tour for my family, though. We went to France, wandered the towns and villages of Normandy, strolled around the battlefields and sleepy hamlets of the Somme. At nearly 15, my senses were awakened if I walked past a girl's bedroom. So it was in France one evening. A girl getting ready for a night out. Paul McCartney's 'No More Lonely Nights' drifting out of her window on to the breeze.

Paul's words were about the thrill of being near to the girl that he loved. The lyric didn't just apply to my teenage notions of romanticism with a mystery French girl getting ready for a night out. They could equally apply to the Everton team longing to test itself against the best Europe had to offer. And that applied to the manager, too. Inferior, substitute cup competitions were never going to fill the void left by the absence of elite European competition.

Despite the heartache, Everton were champions for the second time in three seasons. Twelve times I watched them weave their magic, a new-look Howard Kendall team now shorn of Gary Lineker but with Dave Watson, Ian Snodin, Paul Power, Wayne Clarke and Neil Pointon as new additions. It was our ninth league championship- winning season. And the dozen times I saw them included home wins over Brian Clough's Nottingham Forest and Dave Bassett's Wimbledon, a Wayne Clarke hat-trick in a 3-0 home demolition of Newcastle, and away wins over Chelsea, Aston Villa and (almost incredibly) our bogey side Queens Park Rangers. Even on their dodgy synthetic pitch, which so alienated Everton and their passing football, Graeme Sharp was able to notch us a winner.

It is my fault that we missed the moment we clinched the championship in a 1-0 win at Norwich. We didn't have tickets and I told my dad I didn't want to sit with the Norwich fans. We had a row about it and I had a big teenage sulk. Cutting my nose off to spite my face, as I was always wont to do. I wish we had gone, but we didn't. So we didn't see Pat Van Den Hauwe's goal giving the league championship trophy back to Everton. 'Hand it over Liverpool,' as we used to sing, and I wasn't there for the handover. I was there, however, to see it paraded around

Goodison Park after a 3-1 win over Luton on the final day of the season. I remember Peter Reid triumphantly thrusting it forward on the parade lap, presenting it to the fans. I remember the Gwladys Street End basked in sunlight, 14,000 supporters on that terrace saluting the champions as one. It's a memory which has always stuck with me. It's an image which I hope I will one day see again.

Revolution

Howard Kendall left Everton in the summer of 1987 and thus began a long, slow, steady decline in the fortunes of the club. He quit Goodison Park for Athletic Bilbao, and left behind him a trophy cabinet full of gleaming silverware. An FA Cup, two league championships, a European Cup Winners' Cup and three Charity Shields. Kendall had missed the challenge of Europe more than anyone so he left the club he loved, the club he had served so magnificently as both player and manager, and went to manage in Spain. The man who replaced him was his assistant Colin Harvey, Everton's first-team coach and another member of that Catterick Holy Trinity of the 1960s – Harvey, Kendall and Ball.

It seemed a natural progression for Harvey to become Everton manager and he was certainly everyone's natural choice. He'd been a brilliant player, a hugely inspirational and influential coach and now here he was with his hands on the tiller. But his time in charge of the good ship Everton was not to be plain sailing. Instead, he steered us through stormy waters, and Everton began to founder on the rocks.

Everton finished fourth in 1987–88, which was certainly no disaster. Nowadays it would be considered a triumph. But we were the defending champions. We had been champions for two of the previous three seasons. And while Everton's fall wasn't immediately spectacular, it was certainly obvious. Liverpool took the league championship trophy from us but worse than that, we lost our place at the top table. Manchester United and Cloughie's Forest now finished higher than us in the table. QPR and Arsenal were breathing down our necks. I saw 11 matches in that season, and we won six of those and only lost three. But in the previous, championship-winning year, I'd seen us win eight, draw two and lose two, and that was with seven away games. Before my eyes and away from my eyes, Everton were on the wane.

Even our return to Wembley for the pre-season Charity Shield seemed to have a sense of foreboding for me and dad. Our tickets were in the Coventry end. But this time, unlike for the Watford cup final, we didn't bother to swap them. We were present to see a League Cup semi-final defeat to Arsenal. Well, the first leg of that tie anyway, at Goodison Park, in which Trevor Steven inexplicably blazed a penalty over the bar. It all seemed to be going wrong. The only real highlights were Portsmouth's visit to Goodison, under Alan Ball (which my dad insisted on taking me to on account of my grandad's boyhood association with Pompey), and what still ranks as one of my favourite derbies of all time.

Liverpool came to Everton on the back of 29 unbeaten matches. It was a joint record with Leeds United, so avoiding defeat at Goodison Park would have given those loveable Reds just one more reason to crow over us. Wayne Clarke saw to it that their unbeaten run stopped right then and there. For years afterwards, I would say it was the loudest I had ever cheered when I saw him sweep the ball in from close range at the Park End of the ground to give us a 1-0 win. It was one in the eye for the Liverpool fans who were burning Everton scarves that day. One in the eye for Liverpool, who I blamed for depriving Everton of playing in (and winning) the European Cup. It was one of those poetic justices, too. Wayne's older brother Allan 'Sniffer' Clarke was part of the Leeds team whose record Wayne helped preserve. The papers the next day had a picture of Allan kissing his younger brother in gratitude. It's a great shame that Clarke didn't play enough matches to earn a championship medal in 1987. Because this was his last meaningful contribution to the club. Many years later, the next Wayne to play for Everton would also leave an all-too-temporary mark on the club.

As Everton were disintegrating, so was my parents' marriage and in the summer of 1988 they decided to call it quits. There was a revolution happening at home and within my football club and I was 16 years old and doing the new GCSE exams, with it being the first year post-'O' levels. This time I did get a John Lennon 'choice'. But I wasn't six years old and, at that time, I mistakenly felt that all the hurt and heartache would be behind me. I said I wanted to live with my father. My sister went to live with my mother. And my family was torn in two, when it really should have separated naturally back in 1982. It really was like destruction – but you know I wanted to be counted out.

The words John Lennon sang in 'Revolution' reflected a sentiment that I felt now. I wanted no more part of the arguments, of the tension, of the toing and froing, of being piggy-in-the-middle between two warring parents. Before dad and I moved into a little two-bedroom house together, we had the second of our Chelmsford–Bromborough adventures. But instead of going in a rickety old hire van, this time we cycled. We did 192,000 'revolutions', or 257.6 miles, mostly navigated along B roads using Ordnance Survey maps, in four days. Our bikes broke, my rainsuit broke, our patience broke and our legs almost broke. Well, they felt like they did. I got wet through, I was saddle sore and there were times when I felt I just wouldn't be able to make it. But we did, in partnership. It was the closest I would ever feel to my dad.

When we cycled down Valley Road and pulled up outside number 48, there was a sense of euphoria. Of optimism. The new season was starting that weekend and Everton were at home to Newcastle, so of course we would go. Tony Cottee, the club's new British record signing, would be one of four players making his debut as Colin Harvey sought to remodel the team. And Cottee began repaying his

£2.2m fee immediately. He scored a hat-trick, his first goal coming after 34 seconds, as Everton swept Newcastle aside 4-0 with Graeme Sharp also on the scoresheet.

The geek in me was alive and well, as it always would be. I'd diligently kept records of every single Everton match I'd been to and upon returning to my nanna's, I filled in the details for that season- opening game against Newcastle. 41,560 inside Goodison Park. 4-0 the impressive victory margin. Stuart McCall and Pat Nevin new additions to the team. Match number 53. It was bound to signal a great new season for Everton. Things were bound to get much better now it was just me and my dad and all the family rioting was over. Except it wasn't a great season. And my family life was just about to get worse.

Real Love

Hillsborough

That thrilling, hope-inspiring match against Newcastle signalled the start of another prolific season of Everton-watching for me and my dad. But it was to be the last season we would go so regularly together as father and son.

Dad was in the throes of a new relationship (so was my mum, incidentally). And soon, so was I. Just as the Beatles had once poured renewed vigour into recording *Abbey Road*, so dad and I made renewed efforts to watch Everton. Just as the Beatles had once sung 'The End' knowing it would finish their last record together, so dad and I seemed to be reaching a similar denouement.

We got to 12 matches that season. Five of them were away games in London. But thrown into the mix were matches in two ridiculous competitions, pointlessly devised by the FA to fill the void left by the European football ban. I made my first trip to Old Trafford to watch Manchester United beat us 1-0 in the Mercantile Credit Centenary Classic, supposedly to celebrate 100 years of league football. The 16,000 present was testimony to the general apathy which greeted the tournament. And we went to Wembley to watch Everton lose to Nottingham Forest in the Full Members' (or Simod) Cup Final. It was such a worthless trophy that there were only 46,000 at the Twin Towers. And I remember nothing about the match except that we lost 4-3 after extra time. My immaculate record-keeping does fill in some of the blanks though. Tony Cottee scored twice and Graeme Sharp once.

That said, 1988–89 was a season that will go down in history for all Merseyside football fans, and sadly not for the right reasons. At 17 years old, I was standing on the terraces. Bedecked in blue, bobble hat and scarf.

I remember going to Coventry early in the season. We were shepherded by mounted police officers, driven into a pen like cattle. Having to peer through the gaps in thick barbed wire just to get a glimpse of the pitch. It was an absurd way to treat genuine football supporters. I remember getting chips at the end of the match and watching the Everton coach driving past us through the Coventry streets after we'd won 1-0. I made eye contact with Stuart McCall and shouted his name in admiration. He responded with a beam and a thumbs-up at this teenage adolescent so thrilled to get a little piece of one of his idols. It was still years before I would meet him. And it's a mark of my innocence back then that that is what I remember most about that match, rather than the appalling view, the treatment by the police and the constant sense of being shoved into an overcrowded box.

Our second trip to the Midlands that season was for a match at West Brom in the third round of the FA Cup. I remember Kevin Sheedy's penalty getting us a late equaliser. But what I remember most was being swept off my feet as thousands of Evertonians spilled out of the Hawthorns on to a long ramp behind the terrace, and tried to get through an all-too-small gap for the mass of humanity travelling downwards. I was literally being carried along by the tide of people. No hope at all of regaining my footing. And if I had, I'd most likely have been trampled underfoot. I was genuinely frightened. And, I think, so was my dad.

Two months later, we made our second and last visit to Goodison Park that season. Dad had his new squeeze in tow and I knew that watching football with her was only likely to ruin my experience of that match against Millwall. So, perhaps in a fit of childishness, perhaps in resentment at my soon-to-be stepmother or perhaps in my first strike at independence, I decided not to sit with my dad for the first time. Instead, I stood on the Gwladys Street terrace for the first time. Standing was my new ritual. It was the way I wanted to watch Everton. With the masses. With the faithful.

It's remarkable that we got to so many matches considering my sixth form work placement had given me my first taste of journalism in the form of a Saturday job at BBC Essex. At weekends, I'd help to write and produce their sports bulletins. And that is precisely what I was doing on the afternoon of Saturday 15 April, 1989. Everton were playing Norwich City in an FA Cup semi-final at Villa Park. Liverpool were playing Nottingham Forest in the other semi, at Sheffield Wednesday's Hillsborough ground.

It began as a normal day for me. I can remember the excitement, the pre-match nerves. Absorbing the headlines on teletext. Dressing in nothing but blue and white ... again. A matchday ritual even though I wasn't at the match. Could we make it to Wembley? Would we be playing Liverpool in the final again? How could I concentrate on 'work' when Everton were in such an important match? How I wished I was there. Wished I was watching Everton in the FA Cup semi-final.

It was normal at work too. The calm before the storm which always blows through a sports newsroom early on a Saturday afternoon before all the action begins. Before the goals come in and the headlines begin to form. But it wasn't a storm, exactly. It was a maelstrom. A whirlwind which ripped through football. Ripped through humanity. Ripped through people's lives. The like of which we had never known, however old we were.

I can still remember the nausea I felt as I watched the television images from Hillsborough in the comfort of that local radio newsroom. I could have been at Villa Park that day. I knew what it was to watch your team in an FA Cup semi-final. I hated Liverpool as a football team; for the rivalry they represented, for lording it over us, for their seemingly unending success. I was bitter about the Heysel Stadium disaster which was the responsibility of hooligans – whether or not they were genuine Liverpool fans – and which killed not only 39 innocent people but also killed Everton's meteoric rise in European football.

But this. This was different. This was numbing. This was sickening. This was television capturing the deaths of 96 totally innocent people. Genuine football supporters who wanted to watch Liverpool in the FA Cup semi-final. Many of those who died were killed as they stood. Suffocated. Crushed. That is how tightly they were packed into those pens in the Leppings Lane End. They were people like me. The only difference was that they wore red, not blue. But they were people like me. People I might have rubbed shoulders with at Wembley. People who might have teased me. Bantered with me. Shared jokes with me. The friendly rivalry and all that. People who left their homes in the morning to watch a football match. People who said goodbye to their mums. To their sisters. People who didn't come back in the evening. People who went with their sons. People who went with their dads.

It was utter shock. I knew that Everton were winning their match. Then I knew that Everton had won their match. The Evertonians at Villa Park would have cheered Pat Nevin's winner and ridden a wave of triumph as they watched their team win through to Wembley yet again. Sheer joy. Then when they switched on their car radios and headed back up the M6, the pointlessness of it all would have hit them like a head-on collision in the fast lane.

Everton 1 Norwich 0. Pat Nevin the scorer. Everton into the cup final. Who cares. It was a bloody football match. So what. Not so far away, there was another bloody football match. People had died. Innocent people had died. People who many of those Everton fans would have known. Friends. Neighbours. Brothers. Fathers. Sons. Liverpool – the city – collapsed into grief and it was a grief I shared. Then came the anger. The senselessness of it all. The barbed wire, the high steel fences which penned us in. The mounted police who would shepherd us into an enclosed space. That experience I had at Coventry. That experience dad and I had at West Brom when I realised we could have been seconds away from a tragedy. Well, here WAS the tragedy. It was an accident waiting to happen. Except it wasn't an accident, was it? Football supporters were treated like the lowest of the low. By the police, by the Thatcher government. By the football authorities. As long as we were contained behind fences, we couldn't cause any trouble. The Chelsea chairman Ken Bates had even proposed electric fences at Stamford Bridge. Just imagine that ...

The underlying brotherhood between Everton and Liverpool is all too easily hidden in the present day. But it is there, beneath the surface. Beneath the chants of 'murderers' reminding

Liverpool supporters about Heysel. Beneath the hatred that went on to invade derby matches. Everton were Liverpool's first opponents after Hillsborough, almost three weeks later. It was an opportunity for two halves of the same city to grieve together. It is a shame that it is grief which brings people together. But no city can pull together like the city of Liverpool and the red and blue scarves which connected Anfield and Goodison Park showed the world's greatest city at its best. And that was in its lowest moment.

In football terms, I have always hated Liverpool. Like an overshadowed younger sibling, I revel in their misfortune (on the rare occasions they ARE unlucky). I hate watching them win. For me, their failures are only second in rank to Everton's triumphs. But in life, I love Liverpool. The city, all of it. And on 15 April 1989, I too was in mourning. For the city. For football. Even for Liverpool Football Club. And I was proud to be a Blue. I was proud to be part of the Merseyside football family.

There was a lot of talk about cancelling that season's FA Cup. If the final had been between anyone other than Liverpool and Everton, perhaps it WOULD have been cancelled. But this was the most fitting final of all, just five weeks after Hillsborough. I was stricken with the 'kissing disease'glandular fever in the weeks building up to the match. But nothing would have stopped me from going. I'd have found a way of getting to Wembley even if I had two broken legs.

I'm not normally one for whistling any national anthem, least of all our own. And my throat wasn't exactly in prime condition for whistling anyway. But the whistles which rang around Wembley on 20 May 1989 seemed to me to be the perfect riposte to the establishment – to those who had somehow allowed watching football to be some kind of criminal activity. To those who thought it was okay to treat football supporters – families – in that way. To bundle them into pens and cattle-march them with police horses. To treat them like hooligans.

What followed was a memorable cup final. Not the first 90 minutes so much, but the extra time certainly. Stuart McCall's late equaliser took the game into the added period. And that was also the first time I was kissed by a random supporter in a moment of euphoria. Sadly, it was premature ecstasy. McCall's second equaliser in extra time made him the first cup final substitute to score twice. But then Ian Rush became the second player to do it. And his second goal put the seal on a 3-2 win for Liverpool. Ronnie Whelan lifted the cup, not Kevin Ratcliffe. Liverpool had beaten us again. No one could argue they didn't deserve their victory. But, on so many levels, I was heartbroken.

A New Dawn

To a non-football supporter, it would be hard to describe such heartbreak. Yes, I'm sure many football atheists have suffered the anguish of their parents breaking up. Yes, many non-believers (well, some of them) have probably been through the trauma of adolescent love – the glowing rush of a new relationship; the desperate, lonely ache of that relationship's first fractures. And yes, the commonality of the human spirit unites us, as it did on Merseyside, when there is a tragedy like Hillsborough. But the anguish of a family breaking up, the pain of teenage love, the horrors of a human catastrophe ... dealing with all those things AND the disintegration of your beloved football team ... well, only a true football fan can understand that kind of heartbreak.

It all seemed to get too much for me. I was in my last year of school. Dawn, the head girl, was challenging Everton to be the love of my life. And Colin Harvey was proving that without Howard Kendall, he couldn't recreate that spark that so ignited Goodison Park just a few seasons before. So it was no surprise that I was far less frequent a visitor to Goodison, especially given that my father was now well and truly 'loved-up' himself.

Nevertheless, I was still eating, sleeping and breathing Everton. And I didn't completely starve myself of Everton oxygen. Three times I watched them play in the 1989–90 season. Each time I went, I went with Dawn. Looking back, that must have been the first sign that my relationship with Everton was changing. I still loved them. But I wanted to share them. I wanted to show off my pride. For someone else to smell the matchday atmosphere, to look at the rafters in the Bullens Road Stand and imagine Dixie Dean. For someone else to squeeze between those rows of wooden seating, to see the giant letters J, K, L on the far wall. To temporarily transport themselves back 60 years, imagining the stadium as it was then, deserted after a match, a cloth-capped figure slamming all the seats shut into an upright position as the crowds dwindled away reflecting on those dazzling displays from the men in royal blue. The men from the Dixie Dean era. To think that my dad's cousin, 'Dirty Leo' the Red, had the bare-faced cheek to marry Dixie's niece.

I was always proud of Everton. Always would be. From the traditions of the Toffee Lady to the 'Grand Old Lady' of Goodison Park herself. From the first, shrill notes of *Z-Cars* announcing the team's arrival to the departure of the masses – in all weathers – through Stanley Park and into the great beyond. From the guy on Bullens Road yelling 'Golden goal, 20 pence', to the guy on Goodison Road standing outside his stall and shouting, 'Hat, cap, scarf and yer badge!' It had always been a ritual to me and it always would be. I may not have been going so often, but my heart was always in L4.

Apart from a couple of Goodison trips that season, my only other match was a League Cup tie at Leyton Orient. Of course, I drove Dawn to Brisbane Road so we could go together in my banged-up Ford Fiesta. Banged up, you understand, not because it was an old car but because, just like Pat Van Den Hauwe, I would clatter into anything that moved. Or even didn't move. Still, we safely navigated our way to north-east London that cold September night to watch a 2-0 victory for Everton. Notable only, perhaps, for the inclusion in the team that day of Stefan Rehn. It was one of only two starts he ever made for Everton. Some kind of superstar from Sweden who went on to figure prominently in the 1994 World Cup but who wasn't good enough for Goodison. Where, let's face it, 'Nothing But The Best Will Do'. I remember telling Dawn about our *Nil Satis* motto. I remember being proud even of a workaday win over Third Division Orient. I remember holding her tight at half-time and being ridiculed by the guy four rows behind us for kissing her at a football match.

I was an 18-year-old man with romance on his mind. But even as I juggled A-level studies with seeing Dawn, I'd always find time for Everton. Usually in the constant monitoring of teletext ... gazing at the black screen with primitive digital text.

Just waiting to see if Whiteside had got us an equaliser yet. And if that 0 changed to a 1, nothing in the living room would be safe as I danced around it like I was on the Gwladys Street terrace. Usually, if I wasn't with Dawn, I was on my own. Home was now a little two-bed house with my dad on the outskirts of Chelmsford, but it was always clear to me that it was nothing more than a temporary crash-pad. His girlfriend was a natural born Londoner who considered anywhere outside the M25 to be 'the sticks'. And dad was clearly yearning for a younger, more urban lifestyle now he was free from the clutches of marriage to my mother.

It wasn't long before we moved to a tiny, pokey flat in Harold Wood ... itself a grotty, polluted part of grotty, dismal Romford. The only thing to say about Harold Wood is that the A12 goes right through it, as does the train line. And the quicker you can get away from it, the better. Besides, it's West Ham's heartland. Not an Evertonian in sight.

Of course, Harold Wood wasn't without its memorable moments. Like the time when Dawn and I had the flat to ourselves late one night and thought it would be a good idea to watch *The Shining*. Just as Jack Nicholson slammed an axe into the bathroom door, all the lights went out in the flat and a pneumatic drill fired up right outside our front door. Thank you so much, British Gas. I nearly died of a heart attack before I'd even turned 19. And then of course there was that mid-coital moment enjoyed by so many boys of my age. The moment when, just as it's getting really interesting, your dad walks in on you. 'Errr, sorry.'

Bizarrely, it was about as much communication as it seemed my father and I would come to enjoy as he moved on with his life, and I moved on with mine. If it wasn't 'what's the score', it was next to nothing. Thank goodness for Everton. Because without Everton, we'd have had nothing to talk about.

Not that my relationship with my mum was galloping forwards either. She had a new man in her life. She was living with my sister (that is, when my sister wasn't at boarding school). And there were lasting fissures driven right through my family life – just as there were lasting cracks getting ever wider and wider within the Everton team.

Flowers In The Dirt

My family would forever bear the scars. The tremors which broke out following my parents' divorce left chasms which wouldn't be filled. For evermore, a long-distance relationship between me and my parents. Long distance literally. Long distance emotionally. I did move into my dad's new house in Finchley very briefly. But within weeks, I was off to university. And I was off to find my own future ... and my own future with Everton.

In my last year of school, Paul McCartney released his best solo album for years. In truth, he'd dwindled in the wilderness and allowed himself to live off past glories. I might have been loath to accept that at the time, but as a teenager I was more into Simple Minds, U2, Pink Floyd and REM than anything Macca could muster. Until *Flowers In The Dirt*.

Paul's song 'Put It There' is about the relationship between father and son. About a common bond. And it was the relationship I longed for with my own father. Two friends who'd support each other through thick and thin. Who'd respect each other and be there for each other. Who'd enjoy watching Everton together. But who'd share all of life's ups and downs with each other. At 19, I knew I didn't have that. Don't get me wrong, my father loved me in his own way and that was something I would have to come to accept. It would be in his own way. And I would have to grow up. But, like I said, if we didn't have football to talk about, we'd have had nothing.

Another Paul song from *Flowers In The Dirt* is called 'Distractions' – like a conversation with himself, questioning why he was spending time away from the things that he loved. My fractious relationship with my dad – and his own reticence to go to watch Everton – meant that I, too, was staying away from the things that I loved. I had my teletext obsessions. I had my collection of programmes. My heart would still pound if I heard Bryon Butler or Peter Jones describing an Everton match on the radio. But, as explained by Paul McCartney, my life simply had too many 'Distractions' for me to make more room for Everton in 1990.

I'll never forget the day I got my A-level results. Dawn and I walked down to the school to collect our brown envelopes. And my stomach was in knots. I knew I needed two Bs and a C to be accepted into the University of York. Dawn, above everything else, wanted an A in art. To be the first student at our school to achieve that for many years. My results? A, A and B. Dawn's? A, B and B. Except the A wasn't in art. Cue an argument. Cue my path to York. Cue Dawn's to the Chelsea School of Art. Cue the beginning of the end of our relationship.

Of course, like any relationship, it was a slow death. Just like Everton's slow decline. The summer of 1990 was a good one. And it was hot. There was plenty of hope. And there was plenty of excitement. There's nothing like the excitement of going to watch Everton for the first time in ages. So when they played Fulham in a pre-season friendly at Craven Cottage, I decided to go. Dad didn't fancy it, of course. So instead, I left his house in Finchley on my own – in that beaten-up Fiesta. Finchley to Fulham? How hard can that be to drive? Well, I got there at half-time.

Still, my passion for going to watch Everton had been reawakened. I'd been stirred back to my senses. Everton had new signings – Andy Hinchcliffe and Martin Keown. Paul McCartney had a well- received new album. And I was heading off to university. How I needed somewhere to belong again. Somewhere like Bromborough. Somewhere that would be a home to me. When my dad and I went up to York for the university open day, just before his move to Finchley, we were given a tour of one of the colleges.

'And where are you from?' asked our helpful young guide.

I paused for a moment. How to answer this? Liverpool? No. Bromborough? Hmmmm ... maybe, but not quite. St Albans? Not now. Chelmsford? Not likely. Bermuda? Errrrrr ...

'Romford,' I said. And immediately regretted it. 'Romford? You poor sod. Five Star and Steve Davis.'

Quite. I wouldn't have minded but I wasn't even from Romford. Why on earth did I say that!?

When I arrived at York train station some months later, I plonked my case down like Paddington Bear. I looked out at the Roman city wall and I knew it was time to draw some boundaries. Time to put my childhood behind me and embrace the future. Time to re-establish my own identity. And time to re-evaluate my relationship with Everton Football Club.

Mind Games

'With Manchester City, it was a love affair.
With Everton, it is a marriage.'

'You are going to die.'

The 6ft 4in university radio geek who'd just burst into the two-foot wide corridor of Goodricke C block seemed to mean it.

'You are going to die.'

He said it again and began taking giant strides with his giant legs and his giant hands outstretched before him.

'You are going to die.'

Oh dear. This was getting serious. And suddenly his hands began to throttle me, gripping my throat, forcing me backwards against the breeze block wall.

'What have I done?'

It was all I could muster through my squeezed windpipe but I just about managed to get the words out. Then came his reply.

'Howard Kendall is going back to Everton.'

All of a sudden, I had a new-found burst of energy. I was free and his grip was suddenly feeble, even if he was 6 foot 4. And I was bouncing off those breeze block walls. My assailant was a friend. A colleague on the university radio station. A fellow player in our university 5-a-side team, the Totty Rumpers. A Manchester City supporter. Poor lad.

'You what? You're joking?' I said.

'I'm not,' he shouted. Cue door slamming and comic capers as I sprinted out of C block to be chased by this gangly buffoon, Benny Hill-style. But I had the power surge. The energy. That thrill of having scored a goal. Our hero. The man who brought us all our glory. Was back. Howard Kendall. The best, most successful manager in Everton's history. Was back. The betrayal that my Sky Blue beanpole pal was feeling was summed up by Kendall himself in his press conference.

'With Manchester City, it was a love affair,'he said. 'With Everton, it is a marriage.'

Quite. I understood the sentiment. Everton was a tie which bound him. But hang on. Was I entirely happy with this? What about the passion, the intensity, the surging sense of being head over heels in love? Was this something that Everton would lack under Howard Kendall second time around?

Howard Kendall had left Everton during the European ban on English clubs, thanks to Liverpool 'supporters' who had killed 39 Italians in the 1985 European Cup Final at Heysel. Everton had won the European Cup Winners'Cuponlydaysbeforeinnearby Rotterdam, with glowing tributes ringing in the ears of their supporters from the local constabulary, full of praise for their behaviour. Everton went on to be double runners-up the following season ... to Liverpool. And even winning the league back in 1986–87 wasn't enough to keep Kendall and several of his key players at Goodison Park. So Howard went to ply his trade in Spain. He came back to England shortly afterwards by way of the number one job at Manchester City, taking the Citizens to fifth place in the league. He re-established himself as one of England's best managers. And within months, he was out of the revolving door at Maine Road. Their chairman, Peter Swales, spoke of his broken heart.

'After all this time, it takes a lot to devastate me,' he was quoted as saying. 'But I am shattered. This is the biggest disappointment I have known in soccer – especially as I thought Howard would be here for life.'

Of course Howard was a True Blue. But he was a True Royal Blue, not a true Sky Blue. A hero of Harry Catterick's teams of the 1960s, he was part of the Holy Trinity – the triumvirate of Harvey, Kendall and Ball which became the best midfield in the country and obliterated all-comers, including our nearest rivals Leeds United ... Don Revie's Leeds United ...to win the league championship in 1970. Kendall was also the man who'd shrugged off the leaflets. Shrugged off the 'Kendall Out' graffiti on his garage door and the campaign of the same name back in 1983. Shrugged off the catcalls and the whistles floating on the wind at Goodison, when just 14,000 were turning up as Margaret Thatcher's government squeezed the life out of Liverpool and Everton squeezed the hope out of their supporters. He was the man who knew how to profit from that Kevin Brock back pass at Oxford. The man who turned Everton around. Made the most of what we had, found some genius footballers. And made Wembley Everton's second home. Who brought a string of trophies to Goodison Park. Who made us the best team in the country. The best team in Europe.

Colin Harvey was the man who'd replaced Kendall as Everton manager in 1987. He'd already provided the club with more than 25 years of distinguished service as a player and coach. But he became the man who presided over a dismal slump in the Toffees' fortunes. The man who dismantled a glorious and star-studded championship- winning team and who'd overseen a demoralising depth-charge down the league. The man who'd successfully understudied Howard during Kendall's first spell as manager. But the man who'd failed miserably once he was given the keys to the manager's office and his own name on the desk. And, in an extraordinary twist, now he was the man who'd be the understudy again. Sacked by Everton one day, re-employed the next. Sacked to make way for Kendall, hired again by his old boss as Everton's number two. This was the dream scenario for an Evertonian. An Evertonian like Colin. An Evertonian like Howard. An Evertonian like me.

For one of Colin Harvey's last matches as Everton manager, I'd taken the train from York to Sheffield with one of my college pals. We suffered a 2-1 defeat at Bramall Lane; Sheffield United knocked us out of the League Cup. I remember standing behind the goal and thinking: 'This team is crap.' And no, I wasn't thinking about the Blades but about the Toffees. But here, in Colin Harvey, was a man who the Evertonians simply couldn't dislike. A man who'd made his debut in the San Siro against AC Milan. A man who became 'the white Pelé'. Who thrilled the crowds with his abilities with a football. Who inspired our young players during his time behind the scenes coaching in the 1970s and 1980s. But the latter part of that latter decade wasn't kind to Colin Harvey. The 1990s would hardly be kind to him either. But with Howard in charge and Colin the coach at number two, Evertonians couldn't have been happier.

This was a reunion for Howard Kendall. Not only with Colin Harvey but also with Neville Southall and Kevin Ratcliffe. With Graeme Sharp and Kevin Sheedy. Although his title-winning team had largely been broken up, several of the key players were still there. And with Howard's magnetic management, I was buoyant. Sure that Everton would challenge once again. Optimistic. Oblivious to being chased by a 6ft 4in university radio monster.

But history has a tendency to write its own stories. And this one, ultimately, wasn't to have a happy ending. But while Kendall's love affair with Everton (or was that a marriage!) was only just being rekindled, my own love affair with Paul McCartney and the Beatles was entering something of a decline. At our college 'bops', it was all about the Stone Roses or Oasis. Blur or the Soup Dragons. The Charlatans or EMF. Jesus Jones or the Happy Mondays. James or even, dare I say it, the Rolling Stones. I lost count of the number of times I asked for Jumping Jack Flash after just a couple of pints had left me three sheets to the wind. In my room, on my shelf, a clutch of CDs. REM. B52s. U2. And one token memento from my muse McCartney. *Band On The Run*. The only 'respectable' album I dared flash in front of the noses of friends. Of course now I regret that my 'love affair' was temporarily on hold. But where Macca's music was concerned, it really was a marriage. It's just that 'Hope Of Deliverance' didn't exactly give me any. Hope of deliverance, that is. So he and I had a separation.

A few months after Howard Kendall's reappointment, my 'real' love affair was on the rocks. Dawn and I were in the process of breaking up. She had a new liaison at Chelsea School Of Art. I had not been unfaithful in deed, but certainly had been in thought. My first love (apart from Everton and the Beatles) had fizzled out in a way they never could. Even a 'coolness'doubt about Paul McCartney in the early 1990s couldn't totally kill my affection for the man or his music.

And so what of Everton? What of the first tiffs I'd inevitably have with the Toffeemen as they tried to feel their way under Howard Kendall's new stewardship? Well, the early stages went smoothly enough. The first three matches I saw under HK II (that's Howard Kendall Mark 2) were a draw with Tottenham, a win away at Charlton and an FA Cup victory over non-leaguers Woking at Goodison Park, which was memorable only for a venue swap to help Woking's finances ... and a Kevin Sheedy penalty.

Just a few weeks after that Woking match, Everton had the next round of the FA Cup to navigate. It was a fifth-round tie. And in accordance with the cruelty and irony that accompanies football fate, we drew Liverpool at Anfield. We'd just lost 3-1 to our bitter old rivals in a league game on their cabbage patch. And then days later – that ironic football fate again – we were back on the same soggy turf for a match against the old enemy in the FA Cup. The game finished 0-0. Everyone prepared to rock up again at Goodison Park for the replay. And this time, I had a ticket.

Travelling from York to Merseyside in the winters of the early nineties was never an easy trek. Sometimes I'd drive. Sometimes I'd get the train. Most times I'd be back in Bromborough, staying over at my nanna's with the warmth of an electric blanket, a game of cards, a cup of tea and a bacon sandwich to comfort me. But this time, I had to do something different. Ever the conscious student (yeah, right), I was reluctant to miss important lectures and seminars. My politics tutorials were rare enough in the course of a week, so to miss them didn't seem to me like much of a good idea. After all, when you're only doing two or four hours a week, should you really miss two or four hours of work? Probably not. But it meant a trickier trek to Goodison. So on 20 February 1991, I booked myself a return coach journey with National Express from York railway station to Liverpool Lime Street. This would allow me to hop on a bus in the afternoon, get to the game and then make the weary return journey across the Pennines to allow me to make relevant classes the next morning. The downside was it meant I wouldn't see my nanna. But it was, perhaps, the most memorable upside I can remember. The most memorable night of football I've ever seen at Goodison Park.

Four-four

It was a freezing night. My relationship with Dawn was dying. But with *Band On The Run* on my CD player, I had that air of optimism again. That football optimism, so often misplaced. But that optimism which always gave me a lift when I travelled to Goodison Park. On this occasion – and it's been repeated in floodlit FA Cup derby matches at Goodison Park – my optimism was not misplaced.

The bitterness in the air at Goodison only seemed to add to the occasion. But it was hardly a confident start by Everton. And a mistake by Ray Atteveld led to Liverpool's opening goal. He failed to clear from his right-back position. Ian Rush raced into the clear and, in turn, his shot was cleared off the Gwladys Street goal line by Andy Hinchcliffe – but only as far as Peter Beardsley, who tucked the ball into the net. Everton 0 Liverpool 1.

That was the score until half-time but to coin a cliché with some old football journalese, Everton were quicker out of the blocks in the second half. Everton, traditionally a second-half team, were now attacking the traditional home end. And it was often said that kicking towards the Gwladys Street End was worth a goal to Everton, with the collective 'sucking' of 14,000 souls on that famous old terrace drawing the ball into the net. Just a minute into the half, and the Toffees were level. Everton attacked through Pat Nevin on the right and when Liverpool failed to clear, Hinchcliffe swung in a fierce, curling cross from the left. Everton's record post-war goalscorer, Graham Sharp, was on the far post to nod into the net to send those 14,000 Blues into delirium. I was one of them. Everton 1 Liverpool 1.

The next 20 or so minutes were typical derby fare. Blood. Thunder. Guts. Bad tackles. Throw-ins cheered like goals. But then came an actual goal. And again, our heads were in our hands. On 71 minutes, Beardsley collected the ball 30 yards out and went on one of his jinking runs. Nobody got close to him and he unleashed a fierce, left-foot drive into the top left-hand corner of the Park End goal. Everton 1 Liverpool 2.

Thankfully, those Liverpool scarves and burning Everton scarves were soon out of sight. Because those loveable Reds had to put away their cigarette lighters just two minutes later.

Mike Newell, a boyhood Red but now a Blue, nodded the ball forward and Steve Nicol and Bruce Grobbelaar got into one of their customary mix-ups. The result was that Sharp could steal in and slide the ball home. It's lucky for Nicol that the ball did end up in the Gwladys Street net. Because in his attempts to chase Sharp down, he slid into him from behind in what would surely otherwise have meant a penalty – and a red card. Everton 2 Liverpool 2.

Cue more heart-stopping action. Cue another Liverpool goal. This time just four minutes after Everton's second equaliser. This time from our old nemesis Ian Rush. Molby crossed. Rush outjumped the Everton defence. The ball nestled into the corner of the Park End goal. We were destined not to win this one. Yet more heartbreak at the hands of our neighbours. Everton 2 Liverpool 3.

Howard Kendall was getting desperate. As the clock ticked down, he threw on Stuart McCall for Ray Atteveld and Tony Cottee for Pat Nevin. And it paid dividends. As the game entered the 90th minute, Goodison Park was shaking again. The 'Grand Old Lady', as she's known, is never better than when she's rocking to the sound of that tumultuous roar. The roar which greets a goal by the 'Grand Old Team'. Neville Southall punted the ball long. It found its way to McCall on the edge of the box and he prodded forwards. Cottee sprang the Liverpool line and his toe-poke just beat the advancing Grobbelaar. Everton 3 Liverpool 3.

Cottee's histrionics, celebrating in front of the Gwladys Street faithful, seemed to sum it up perfectly. There was real belief now. Real excitement. But again, as is Everton's way, we shot ourselves in the foot. Collectively shot ourselves in 22 feet. The game was into extra time now and as the first half of the added 30 minutes drew to a close, Liverpool were in front once more. John Barnes was pinned to the touchline when he received the ball. But he collected it, controlled it, ran (or rather, jogged) ten yards and slammed the ball in off the angle of crossbar and post. If it was a shot, it was brilliant. If it was a cross, he was just a jammy sod. Jammy sod, then. Everton 3 Liverpool 4.

But we weren't finished. It was our night, this one. With a few minutes left, Everton had a throw-in just 20 yards back from where Barnes had collected the ball. Ratcliffe took it, got the ball back and then played it forwards. Hinchcliffe collected it, turned and threaded it through to Cottee in the box. And his left-footed shot sealed a replay. Everton 4 Liverpool 4.

Eight goals. Four equalisers. Liverpool ahead four times, Everton level four times. Whichever way you looked at it, it was magnificent. It was called the 'Game Of The Century'by the iconic ITV commentator Brian Moore. I'm not sure about that. But it was the Game Of The Decade, all right. And it was the best game I'd ever seen. And I'd seen 4-all before. AND 5-4. But never like this. Never in such drama. Never against Liverpool.

I repeated my bus journey for the second replay. The momentum was obviously with us that night at Goodison because Kevin Ratcliffe won the toss at the end of the game and we'd be at home again for the second replay – the third match of the tie. So back I went on the bus. *Band On The Run* back in the CD Walkman. Back to Lime Street for the Merseyrail up to Kirkdale station and the walk to Gwladys Street. Back to the chippy on Goodison Road for sausage and chips. Back behind the goal for a good spec. And back behind the Blues.

This time Everton won. In truth, it was memorable only for the victory over our arch-rivals. Dave Watson got the goal, and we were through. But nothing could match that 4-4 for sheer drama, raw emotion and absolute quality in the toughest of circumstances. It was the game which cost Kenny Dalglish his job. He quit the next morning. We'd obviously piled on more pressure than he could handle, poor fella. Everton pushed. Kenny cracked. So he was gone and Everton were through to the quarter-finals of the FA Cup.

Where we promptly lost to West Ham.

Three-two

Sadly, that kind of typified Everton. And Everton under HK II. Brilliant one minute, hopeless the next. Perhaps it was always inevitable that after beating Liverpool in such an epic tie, we would go and lose to West Ham. Or perhaps it was just Everton. We were back at Wembley that year. Dad and I watched Everton play Crystal Palace in the Zenith Data Systems Cup Final. Enough said. We lost 4-1 after extra time. But it was indicative of how our stock had fallen. And indicative of how we were continuing to struggle because of the European ban. The next two seasons were unmemorable. Without wishing to write off large chunks of history, there seems little point in writing much about 1-0 away defeats at Oldham except that the Latics were managed by Joe Royle, still Everton's youngest ever goalscorer before a certain W. Rooney came along years later. Or indeed writing about 5-3 home defeats to Queens Park Rangers. Or 5-2 away wins at Manchester City. Everton were going nowhere, fast. One step forwards, two back.

Even the introduction of Peter Beardsley, in one of those few genuinely surprising transfers, failed to sharpen the Everton senses. The man had gone from zero to hero in my eyes. But before I hear the cries of 'fickle!', in truth he was never a real zero for me. A genuinely exceptional talent, he was a footballer I admired for England and even (yes, erm hrm) for Liverpool. Six months after he scored those devastating goals on that incredible, epic night, playing a full part in that 4-4 draw, Beardsley had swapped a red shirt for a blue one. One wonders how he felt about that. He swapped John Barnes and Ian Rush for Paul Rideout and Tony Cottee. Plus Mo Johnston, of course. Hmmmm. Still, he was ours now. And he was every bit as hero-worshipped in the Gwladys Street End as he was on the Kop. A true gentleman footballer, he's one of the few who crossed the great divide and – in footballing terms – lived to tell the tale.

Beardsley was only with us for two seasons before moving on to his boyhood club, Newcastle United. The Barcodes'gain was definitely our loss. And I can genuinely say that each of the ten goals I saw him score in 28 games was a pure moment of Royal Blue pleasure. In all, he scored 32 goals in 95 Everton matches. We bought him for £1 million. We sold him for £1.5 million. And he'll always hold a place in the hearts of Evertonians – not least for the fact that he scored the winning goal against Liverpool at Goodison Park in the league derby match of December 1992.

There was more upheaval at Goodison Park in the 1993–94 season. Howard Kendall fell out with the board when they wouldn't back him over the signing (that never was) of Dion

Dublin. So one Saturday evening, after we'd won a home match with Southampton, he announced to the world that he'd quit for a second time. The man to replace him was Mike Walker, the Norwich manager. To this day, one wonders why that decision was taken. Everton's most famous victory was a 3-1 win over Bayern Munich en route to winning our first European trophy in 1985. Norwich's most famous win was also against Bayern in the Uefa Cup, upon English sides' re-inclusion. That, plus a 5-1 win over Everton at Goodison. An utter humiliation, compounded by the four goals we gifted to Efan Ekoku, a local lad who had once played for Liverpool Schoolboys.

Either way, Walker was in soon after his Canaries had humbled us. With me watching on from the Gwladys Street End. By now, I'd finished at York and I was training to be a journalist at Preston, just 30 miles from Liverpool and within easy reach of Goodison. Plus, my new girlfriend was a York student who happened to be an avid Bolton Wanderers supporter, then in the third tier of English football. So it was with some trepidation that I endured a ten-match winless streak watching Everton, the last match of which was a 1-1 draw against Bolton at Burnden Park in the third round of the FA Cup. By now they were leading their division with an exciting brand of attacking football, fashioned by their manager and former Everton midfielder Bruce Rioch. Paul Rideout notched the goal at Burnden which spared my blushes after the match. And when we thumped Swindon 6-2 in the next match I saw, I was confident enough to take my girl's father to Goodison with me for the Bolton replay. Sadly, that turned out to be an error of judgement.

One of Everton's front line back then was a player called Stuart Barlow. A young, Liverpool-born striker. Or should I say 'Jigsaw', because he fell apart in the box. Sometimes also affectionately known as 'Barn Door', because he just couldn't hit one. But it was Stuart Barlow who seemed as though he'd be the match-winner for Everton against Bolton. His two strikes had seen Everton go 2-0 up just after half-time and both he – and the new manager – seemed as though they had the Midas touch. But all that glitters is not gold in football and Bolton came roaring back into the match with a vengeance. Their toothless, burly Scottish striker John McGinlay reduced the arrears only for future Blue (and True Blue) Alan Stubbs to draw them level. The match went into extra time and the winner was struck by Bolton's Owen Coyle. Everton had been dumped out of the FA Cup by a side two divisions below them. Me all blue with a lower case b – and red- faced in front of my girlfriend's father. Everton 2 Bolton 3 (AET). Final score.

The season continued and Everton drifted. Drifted down the league, that is. So that by the final game of the season, we HAD to win. Wimbledon were the visitors to Goodison Park and we simply had to win the match. However I write this now, I can't do the occasion justice. Everton. More seasons in the top flight than any other team. Founder members of the Football League, only relegated twice in their history. Only ever having spent four seasons away from the elite. In the top flight by now for 40 consecutive years. Stalwarts of the English game – one of the most famous names in English football. In world football. But now, the stakes were higher than you could imagine. We were in a desperate state. We needed to win to stay up. And even that wouldn't be enough if Sheffield United won at Chelsea. And these were the days before Chelsea were rich ... and good.

So I trekked to Goodison Park from my nanna's on the last day of the season. I'd been going of course. Been going a lot. Driving down from Preston for night matches. Staying over in Bromborough at weekends. Practising my T-line shorthand by drawing out the symbols for JOHN EBBRELL and ANDERS LIMPAR with a mate, and fellow Blue, also studying journalism. But now this. This was serious. And forget all that optimism I associate with going to Goodison. This was terrifying. No optimism. Not optimum. *Nil Satis Nisi Optimism*, in fact. Just foreboding. Lose – or draw – and we're down. Playing in the second tier for the first time since the 1950s. Relegation. That dirty word that you never associate with a great club like Everton. Swindon were rock bottom and already down. Oldham, just above them, were all but mathematically down. And we would be the team to follow them through the trap door, whatever happened, if we didn't win against Wimbledon. And even then, a win might not be enough to save us.

Goodison Park was undergoing major reconstruction work. The Park End had been demolished to make way for a new cantilevered, all-seater stand. The final piece in the Goodison jigsaw to give Everton a four-sided, all-seater home ... now five years after the tragedy of Hillsborough.

I reached Gwladys Street at 11am, four hours before kick-off. And I was already a long way back in the queue. But to guarantee my seat, that's what I had to do. And after those four hours, long before a ball had even been kicked, I didn't have much left in the way of fingernails. That's the optimism of Evertonians for you. As the game approached, the news came through. Somebody had set fire to the Wimbledon coach the night before. John Fashanu and Vinnie Jones, two of the hardest men in English football, had apparently woken up to the sight of a torched team bus. Now, I'd never be one to advocate arson, you understand. But did this, in some remote and obscene way, actually put the Dons at a psychological disadvantage for the match?

No. After four minutes, we were behind. Everton were defending a corner and – inexplicably – Anders Limpar thrust an arm out to connect with the innocuous cross that was floating over. Penalty. Dean Holdsworth stepped up right in front of us at the Gwladys Street End. Hush. The ground was so quiet you could hear the ripple of the net. Everton 0 Wimbledon 1.

Bad. Then worse. Twenty minutes on the clock and Everton were committing collective suicide on the football pitch. Sheer panic in the Everton defence. Dave Watson and David Unsworth bumped into each other. Gary Ablett sliced the ball into his own net. Silence. Everton 0 Wimbledon 2. Real silence.

You've heard of lying back and thinking of England. Well I sat back and thought of relegation. In all seriousness. We were dead and buried and we all knew it. But then came the lifeline. Limpar, perhaps atoning for his ridiculous handball, was guilty of a ridiculous dive. He tripped over a huge slice of thin air to win a penalty. Graham Stuart had only taken one penalty for Everton, and he'd missed it. But he must have nerves of steel, that man. How his heart must have been pounding, even though this spot kick was at the Park End (or Building Site End, whichever you prefer). No away fans behind the goal to distract him, at least. Bang. Everton 1 Wimbledon 2. Roar. And half-time.

Still,the gloom and despondency hung over the ground. No optimism here at Goodison Park. The 31,000 people crammed into every corner of a three-sided Goodison were thinking of nothing except the prospect of relegation. And it was more hope than reason which kept them in their seats. More desperation than anything else. Where would we get two goals from to win the match and save our skins?

Firstly, from Barry Horne. I didn't even know he could kick the ball 35 yards, let alone kick it into the corner of the net from 35 yards. An absolute screamer. Everton 2 Wimbledon 2. Deafening. And still more than 20 minutes left.

And then from Graham Stuart. By way of a helping hand from the Wimbledon keeper Hans Segers. When Cottee prodded the ball to Stuart, Stuart did little more than prod the ball to Segers. But bizarrely, it escaped his grasp and ended up in the net. P A N D E M O N I U M. Everton 3 Wimbledon 2. 'SAFE!' was the splash headline in the *Football Echo*. 'DOWN!', which had been prepared as I later discovered, was destined never to reach the news-stands. In 1966, we produced the greatest FA Cup Final comeback in history, coming from two goals down to beat Sheffield Wednesday 3-2. In January 1994, we were dumped out of the cup by the same score and the same comeback – by my girlfriend's beloved Bolton. And now, with our necks on the block and seemingly doomed, we produced one of the greatest Premier League comebacks of all time. If not THE greatest. With relegation lurking over Goodison Park like the biggest, blackest cloud, we came back from 2-0 down to win 3-2. Sheffield United had lost by the same score at Chelsea. And we were safe.

It was a remarkable turnaround. Within a year, I was in Graham Stuart's kitchen in Formby.

'What about that goal?' I asked him.

'I can't explain it,' he said. 'It was certainly very strange.'

The conspiracy theorists will have you believe that two members of the Wimbledon team threw the match. Hans Segers was later embroiled in the match-fixing allegations which, along with his team-mate John Fashanu and the Liverpool goalkeeper

Bruce Grobbelaar, saw him at the centre of the biggest scandal ever to grip our national sport. The three men, plus a Malaysian businessman said to have been behind the betting ring, were cleared at their trial at Winchester Crown Court. I know this because I covered it for the *Liverpool Echo*. But Segers and Grobbelaar were later found guilty by the Football Association of breaching betting regulations. I always hoped they were innocent of match-fixing. I hoped football fans – even Liverpool football fans – weren't taken in by star players 'taking a bung'. I hoped. Because it's more deceit than can be stomached. But the case against them was not proven.

And that day against Wimbledon – that 7 May 1994 – I hadn't dared to hope. I prayed. And my prayers were answered. 3-2.

Nil Satis Nisi Optimum

'Nothing but the best will do'

Bellefield

Everton's Latin motto is *Nil Satis Nisi Optimum*. Variously translated as 'Nothing But The Best Will Do'or Only The Best Is Good Enough'. Variations on the same theme. I grew up inspired by these lofty ideals. You could hardly blame Everton for lacking ambition. You could certainly blame them for not fulfilling those ambitions. Time and time and time again.

In late 1994, we had nine league titles, four FA Cups and one European Cup Winners' Cup locked away in the Goodison trophy cabinet. Aside from various glorious spells, which came in clusters in the 1920s and 1930s, the 1960s and 1980s, the history of Everton seems to have been littered with disappointments. More seasons, more matches, more wins, more points, more goals than anyone in top-flight football. But not more trophies. Yes, nine is a good clutch of league championships, bettered only by Liverpool, Manchester United and Arsenal. But still bettered by them.

Yes, four is a reasonable return of FA Cups. But from 11 finals? Yes, a European trophy was a historic triumph. But after years of trying? Now you get to see why us Evertonians are rarely optimistic. And my *joie de vivre* en route to Goodison Park is rarely symptomatic of the blue and white masses.

Beating Wimbledon. That amazing day in May. That glorious comeback. But was it so amazing? Was it so glorious? Was it *Nil Satis Nisi Optimum*? It wasn't. We survived by the skin of our teeth. We'd plumbed the depths and only just about managed to resurface without getting the bends. We'd been to hell and back. And we weren't going there again.

And if we were in any doubt, Peter Johnson, the new chairman, told us we weren't. Mind you, the fans knew him as Agent Johnson. A former Liverpool season ticket holder who'd made millions from Christmas hampers, bought Tranmere and now fancied a crack at the big time. We splashed the cash left, right and centre. He told us we'd win the European Cup. The most gullible believed him. The least gullible drew the Agent analogy.

Even so, Agent Johnson made one decisive call which turned 1994–5 into a remarkable season. We didn't get our first win until 1 November – a home victory over West Ham. The only goal was scored by Gary Ablett in front of just 28,000 at Goodison, and I was one of them. But after those precious three points, the reward for Mike Walker was the sack. His replacement was Joe Royle, the bustling centre-forward who made his name as a 16-year-old at Everton. If that sounds familiar now, Royle was no Rooney. He won trophies with Everton. He won the league title. He made his name for Everton and England. Only then did he drive down the M62 to Manchester. To City, not United. But Royle, like his old Everton team-mate Kendall before him, was bursting with Royal Blue blood, not Sky Blue. And Everton was his destiny both as a player and a manager.

Joe didn't bring us the league title we craved. Or the European Cup that Agent Johnson dangled like a giant, gleaming silver carrot. But he did whack something into our trophy cabinet. A gleaming silver FA Cup. Oh, and he saved us from relegation as well.

By November 1994, I had my own season ticket for the first time. I also had my own proper job for the first time – as a trainee reporter with the Liverpool Daily Post & Echo. The editor and sports editor were Blues. My news editor was a Red. My allegiances were well known too. And just after that Royle appointment, I was given my own Royal appointment, even if it actually involved me stashing that season ticket away inside my nanna's mantelpiece. I was asked to help launch a new magazine called *The Evertonian*. It was to be the official magazine of the club, published by the Post & Echo. One of my Red- leaning colleagues was asked to work on an equivalent publication called

The Kop. But I was in Blue heaven. And for the rest of the season, I rubbed shoulders with my heroes.

Bellefield has since been replaced as Everton's training ground by a huge super-complex of state-of-the-art football pitches, all-weather surfaces, indoor facilities and hi-tech gym, physio and medical equipment. By all accounts, the players want for nothing at Finch Farm and it's among the best training grounds in the country. Perhaps even THE best. That honour actually fell to Bellefield in the 1960s. It was made so by Harry Catterick, the master tactician who brought Everton two league titles and an FA Cup in those intoxicating years between 1963 and 1970. The years in which Everton became the Mersey Millionaires. The School Of Science. Perhaps the biggest club in the land. The years in which the Beatles made a succession of smash-hit records. As Everton took the football world by storm, so the Beatles took the music world by storm. But it was only the Beatles who made a lasting mark. Everton's mark came and went.

But Bellefield was the des res of training grounds. My father had been a visitor there while we were in Bermuda, famously (in our family) interviewing a young Steve McMahon, that graduate of the Goodison ball boy school and graduate of the Gwladys Street terrace, who went on to grace the royal blue shirt. Before turning to the dark side, that is. Dad mixed with the notorious joker who was John Bailey, who brought unique hilarity on to the training pitch. Sometimes on to the football pitch, too. He asked Bob Latchford for a word or two. He got two back, the second being 'off'. Such is life when you're a reporter at the training ground of a big football club. Sometimes they'll love you – and the chance to get their names in print. Sometimes the doors will be closed. Literally.

In fact, the gates were shut for my first visit to Bellefield. I got out of the taxi from Old Hall Street and surveyed the scene along Sandforth Road. It's in the heart of West Derby, a leafy suburb of lower-middle-class Liverpool. Terraced houses and football pitches. Tree-lined suburban roads and corner shops, in the hinterland of the Alder Hey Children's Hospital. And boasting two training grounds, Liverpool's Melwood and Everton's Bellefield.

I got out of the cab and breathed in the December air. Cold. Fresh. Life-giving. This was life. A clutch of kids hung around with autograph books or programmes they wanted to get signed. Then the giant blue gates. They could have led to a car body repair shop or a junkyard, such was their anonymity and their industrial façade. But they led to the home away from home of Everton Football Club. The place where the players came every day to train or to recover from injury. The place where the manager and coaches set the workouts and the drills. The place where they drew up the tactics for Saturday's match. Where they decided who's in and who's out. Where they inspired. This is the place where Alan Ball was told by Harry Catterick that he was going to sign for Arsenal, like it or not. This is the place of Colin Harvey and Howard Kendall, Joe Royle and Alex Young, Bob Latchford and Duncan McKenzie, Peter Reid and Trevor Steven. All of them. Where they honed their skills. Played football behind closed doors. Day after day after day.

Footsteps approached the gate from inside. An iron rod was pulled upwards and the gates swung open. Creaking, squeaking. A wizened old man peered out from behind them. Harry.

'Hello lads,' he said. 'Come on in.'

The gates revealed a long drive. A few cars already there but others still to roll in. Mercs, Porsches. BMWs. Tinted windows. Sparkling alloy wheels. All shiny and new. The players' cars. On the left of the drive, a giant sports hall. An indoor, synthetic football pitch. At the end of the drive, a two-story building with a royal blue front door. Changing rooms and giant baths downstairs. Offices for the assistant manager, the youth coaches, the visiting referees. Upstairs, a canteen. The manager's office, with a window peering out on acres and acres of lush green land. Football pitch after football pitch, lying side by side as if plotted using rulers and T-squares. Beautifully mown and manicured. The white lines marking them standing out like some mathematical example of immaculate geometry. This was where it all happened.

The pack began to arrive. Richard Tanner from the *Mirror*. Phil McNulty from the *Sun*. John Keith from the *Express*. Colin Wood from the *Mail*. Men with notepads and trench coats. I'd have to get one. I'd already got the notepad. We were invited in. Through the door. Into the corridor. The referees' office just to the left. A shuffling inside it. The sound of studs on polished floors. Out came a man. Willie Donachie. Former Scotland player. Former Manchester City defender. Current assistant manager of Everton Football Club.

'Morning lads ...'

More studs. Laughter. The sound of a group of young men taking the piss. Giving what's known in football circles as 'stick'. Some of them came by.

'Morning ...' 'Morning ...' 'Morning ...'

Wrapped up in each other. Hardly noticing us. But in fairness, my head was in a whirl. I hardly noticed them. At least for a moment.

Then another came by. Perhaps injured, as he wasn't wearing boots. Instead, flip-flops. And just a towel round his waist. Dave Watson. The Everton captain.

'All right fellas,' all Scouse smiles and cheery nature. 'Doin'all right today?'

Then the manager. Suited. Perhaps no training ground for him today. Perhaps the business of signing new players. Who knows? He appeared in the corridor and made a beeline for me.

'You must be the new fella,' said Joe Royle, offering me his hand. 'Yes. Neil Roberts. I write for *The Evertonian.*'

'Well we're very pleased to have you here.'

From one new boy to another, as it were. And so it went on. And on. And on. For seven months of seventh heaven. Royal Blue heaven. If I achieved nothing else in my career, I'd achieved this.

Living with legends

So Everton had won their first game of the season. A scrappy 1-0 win over West Ham. And despite the three points, the boss was told to clear his desk and M. WALKER, MANAGER was replaced with J. ROYLE, MANAGER on that door upstairs at Bellefield. Everton's next game would be Joe Royle's first. A home match. A night match. A match against Liverpool.

Mike Walker had secured the services of two young Scotsmen – the midfielder Ian Durrant and Duncan Ferguson, a striker –

both on loan from Rangers. In truth, neither had set the Goodison Park pitch alight during their holiday from Ibrox. A holiday is what it felt like, too. Because neither player seemed all that bothered to be playing for Mike Walker's Everton. But of the two, Evertonians initially took to Ian Durrant a little easier. 'He's blue, he's white, he's f****** dynamite, Ian Durrant, Ian Durrant,'was something you'd hear from the Gwladys Street End. There wasn't much endorsement for Duncan Ferguson though. He was a tall striker with a reputation for goals. Equally good in the air and on the ground, he was billed as the all-round footballer. Someone with a deft touch and a bullet header. Someone who, at 6ft 3in, could bully defences. Sadly he could bully cripples at taxi ranks too. Or so they said.

Duncan Ferguson had form. No form for Everton but form with the police. And when he headbutted John McStay when Rangers were playing Raith Rovers, Ferguson was heading out of the exit door at Ibrox and into the HM PRISON entrance at the notorious Barlinnie jail in Glasgow. A jail which still practised slopping out. A jail where there was no mucking about. Just mucking out. Only he had to be introduced to the school of hard knocks at Everton first.

Duncan Ferguson was hard. There was no doubt about that. He was the sort of player who'd clatter into Roy Keane of Manchester United. Keane would get up snarling. Frothing at the mouth. Looking for vengeance. Then he'd figure out that Ferguson was responsible and would walk away. To us Evertonians, everyone was terrified of Duncan. To coin the old Millwall phrase, nobody liked him. But we certainly didn't care.

When I went to see Everton play Liverpool that night, we won 2-0. Paul Rideout scored the first goal, Duncan Ferguson the second. A header. A header which switched Goodison Park into shaking mode. A header which encapsulated the imagination of the Gwladys Street End. A header which triggered the trademark fist-pumping of Duncan Ferguson, a man who was to become an Everton legend.

Duncan didn't do interviews. He was too wary of a press which he felt had stitched him up. Plus, at this time, he still had that stretch in Barlinnie to look forward to so he had other things on his mind. But after his 44 days in jail, Duncan Ferguson returned to Everton with the number 9 firmly stitched on to the back of his shirt. The shirt worn by Dean, by Lawton, by Hickson, by Royle, by Latchford, by Lineker, by Gray and by Sharp. It's the shirt which carries with it a legendary status. And it fitted him perfectly.

During my time on *The Evertonian*, I met all the players. Every weekday I would chat with Joe Royle and Dave Watson. And I'd do interviews with them every week. I sat down for official interviews with everyone from David Unsworth and Andy Hinchcliffe to Anders Limpar and Daniel Amokachi, Everton's breakthrough black player who helped eradicate the obnoxious chants of 'Everton are white'. Mind you, his German Shepherd almost eradicated my suit trousers when he mauled me at Amo's house in Woolton. 'If you're not careful,' he said. 'That dog will ruin your suit.' Yeah thanks Amo, I thought. Why don't you put him down!! (Didn't say that, obviously.)

I interviewed Joe Parkinson and Graham Stuart. Graham made me a cup of his tea in his kitchen on the north Merseyside seaside. That was when we mused over the 'what-might-have-happened' for his winning goal against Wimbledon. Then there was Gary Ablett and Stuart Barlow (him of Jigsaw and Barn Door infamy). Barry Horne and Earl Barrett, who I interviewed in his Liverpool hotel room. Paul Rideout and Matt Jackson. Peter Beagrie (at Maine Road) and John Bailey (in a pub). Ian Durrant and Stuart McCall, who gave me their time when I made a trip to Rangers. Even Dixie Dean's son Geoff, who ran a pub on London Road in Liverpool. And the Evertonian snooker world champion, John Parrott, who I met at a café on Penny Lane. He spent half the time telling me of his love for Everton, half the time telling me of his love for horse racing and half the time giving me snooker tips. Actually that's one and a half. Must have been thirds.

I met legends like our record post-war goalscorer Graeme Sharp. Like Johnny Morrissey. Like the Last of the Corinthians himself, Brian Labone, the man whose memory drew tears from my father when Goodison Park paid tribute to him after his death. The man who I respected and admired – even though

I saved my tears that day for Duncan Ferguson, who paraded on the pitch with his kids at the end of his emotional farewell match. I met stars of the sixties like John Hurst, who I even played against on that indoor pitch at Bellefield. Jimmy Gabriel and Alex Parker, who I met at his pub in Gretna. I sat in the chairman's office at his firm in Birkenhead, with the FA Cup bedecked in blue and white ribbons, just sitting there on his desk. I remember Agent Johnson tapping it with his fingertips as though it was a mug of tea while I looked on, awestruck, trying to find the name EVERTON engraved on it through the years. I interviewed 'Tricky' Trevor Steven on that trip I made up to Ibrox. I interviewed Neville Southall at Bellefield – the extraordinary story of Everton's record appearance-maker. And I interviewed Colin Harvey about his own extraordinary lifelong dedication to the club. This is not meant as an exercise in name-dropping. Well, it IS name-dropping, obviously. And I haven't even mentioned my boyhood hero Andy King. I interviewed him in his office when he was manager of Mansfield Town. The point is I was living a dream. And living with legends. Because the names I haven't yet dropped are the interviews which will follow – a famous five from the Everton history books. Duncan Ferguson, Alan Ball, Howard Kendall, Alex Young and Gary Lineker.

Duncan Ferguson

Duncan had been made a permanent Everton player by Joe Royle, for a then club record fee of £4 million. He knew there was no escaping his spell in jail that coming spring. He knew there was no escaping the fact that he had a point to prove. I knew there was no escaping that trench coat. 'Look at you, Inspector Gadget,' he would say as he strode past me in that Bellefield corridor. Duncan never shuffled, he strode. He was 23 years old. He had the world at his feet. 'Who's Alan Shearer?' he would say of the man plundering goals for fun at Blackburn. The man who would one day lead the line for Newcastle alongside Duncan Ferguson, in a thankfully brief spell before the prodigal son returned to Goodison ... and to Bellefield. 'He's not the top man,' said Duncan. 'I'm the top man.' And it would have taken a far bigger man than me to argue with him. Not least because I could barely understand what he was saying half the time, so thick was his Glaswegian brogue.

I interviewed Duncan twice. Both times under the proviso that I'd publicise his charity work. Laudable though it was – and genuinely admirable – I knew the readers were more interest in Duncan the man and Duncan the footballer than Duncan the fund-raiser for the Alder Hey Children's Hospital. Even so, I stuck to my word and I think Duncan respected me for it, which is why I was granted a second interview.

That first official chat he had with me hit the second issue of *The Evertonian* in January 1995. It was the first time he'd been interviewed by a member of Her Majesty's press corps in England. It was before he'd become a guest of Her Majesty's Prison at Barlinnie. And I sat with Duncan in his car in the Bellefield car park. Me twitching with my notebook in the passenger seat, Duncan vainly twitching with his curtains-style hair in the rear-view mirror.

NR: Mike Walker signed you on loan. But what made you decide to make the move permanent, once Joe Royle arrived?

Dunc: Joe had a big influence on me coming to the club because he was a striker and he wanted both me and the club to be successful. He pointed out, too, that he wanted me. And the fans have been absolutely brilliant. They will now see the best of me when I settle down and now that I'm an official Evertonian.

NR: It didn't really look like being made a permanent move, did it? You came down with Ian Durrant and it seemed like maybe you just needed a change of scenery after the incident with John McStay at Ibrox.

Dunc: Before, of course, I was just on loan and at first I just thought I would be here for three months. Rangers pointed out to me that I would be back and that was as far as I was thinking ahead. I was disappointed to be going out on loan but once I was into it with Everton, it wasn't a wrench to leave Rangers. I loved it as soon as I came. It didn't take me long to settle in after the first week or two.

NR: So what did you know of Everton before coming here?

Dunc: I knew that this was a big club and I was confident that I could settle here easily. The people of Everton and the city of Liverpool have been great to me. The fans have been brilliant and everything's ticking along nicely. I didn't need to leave Rangers if I didn't want to but I liked everything about Everton and it was an easy decision for me. It was also good that the team started to win but I always knew that things would improve for this team anyway. We are on the way up and I knew we would climb the league if the team worked hard.

Somehow when Duncan spoke, he commanded attention. Perhaps it was because he knew what he was talking about. Perhaps it was because he was spellbinding company. Perhaps it was because he was six foot three and sitting right next to me.

NR: You mentioned the fans. What about the atmosphere at Goodison? How does it compare to Rangers' home matches?

Dunc: The atmosphere was good at Ibrox. But in fact the atmosphere at Goodison is better because at Ibrox some of the fans are set in their ways about winning and they expect it, which takes the buzz out.

But the Everton fans are all fired up to help get the team out of the relegation scene. The gates have been exceptional, even in midweek. It's a lot of money to go to football nowadays, so it shows how much passion there is for the club.

He spoke with passion too. Genuine passion. And not just passion for his latest hairstyle and what he'd be doing in Liverpool city centre that night. Immediately, I was struck by how much Duncan loved it at Everton. And I was struck by how aware he was of Everton's rich history.

NR: So you're the number 9, which has a special feeling for Evertonians. How do you feel about following in the footsteps of your fellow Scotsmen Andy Gray and Graeme Sharp?

Dunc: I always knew Everton was no small club but I wasn't that aware of the history surrounding the place. Now I know about the long line of great number 9s they have had here and hopefully I can continue their reputation in some way. But I'm not an Andy Gray or a Graeme Sharp. I'm a Duncan Ferguson. They have been very successful at this club and obviously I now want to be just as successful. The club have shovelled out a lot of money for me and hopefully I can repay some of that with some good performances and the team will keep winning.

NR: But this Everton isn't the same as Andy Gray and Graeme Sharp's Everton ...

Dunc: I know what we won in the eighties but now we are obviously trying to survive first. We can't go down so we must work hard to keep ourselves up. Then we will think about winning trophies.

NR: And what about you? What kind of player are you?

Dunc: I have not really been known as a great goalscorer. There's a lot to my game and I never set goalscoring targets – except for the whole team. It doesn't matter if the keeper scores goals as long as we move up the table. Everybody must work hard together and Willie Donachie has been getting us to do just that. He knows his football and combined with the gaffer, the two of them make a good partnership.

NR: But there's pressure on you to score goals, isn't there? You're the club's record signing ...

Dunc: The way I see it, a club could pay £10 million for me and it would still be nothing to do with me. It doesn't put any extra pressure on. I'm still the same player that I was.

He had a swagger all right. He had an arrogance. But I liked him. I took to him instantly. And he was always good to me, be it banter in the Bellefield corridor or the proper time to sit down for a chat. The second time I interviewed Duncan was on a visit to Alder Hey. He was serving a suspension for elbowing a Leicester City player at the time. My interview appeared in April's edition of *The Evertonian*, around the same time as Duncan went off to jail. He was on the front cover, proudly clutching his Premier League player of the month trophy.

NR: Duncan, why don't you talk to the press?

Dunc: People say Liverpool and Glasgow are similar. Working-class cities with the docks and that may be but Glasgow was a wee bit of a goldfish bowl for myself and I had a lot of bad press up there. But I have changed and that's mainly down to the fans. Fans can make or break a player.

NR: So that's why you'll talk to me on the record?

Dunc: I'm doing this interview for *The Evertonian* because I want to get my view across to the fans. Hopefully they will all go out and buy the magazine. People think it's selfish of me not talking to the press. But that's the way I want it and I want a lower profile. But I think I'm settling in now. Living in a hotel doesn't help you to settle, but now I have found a nice home.

Duncan was an icon. Even then, he'd written his name into the club's folklore. He was a talisman. He was an enigma. A giant, bustling centre-forward. Strong, quick, powerful, aggressive. Oh … and he was a pigeon-fancier too.

> NR: What about away trips? Do they help you to settle in with your team-mates? And what's all this about you being a pigeon-racer?

> Dunc: I have got plenty of room-mates on away trips. They keep on swapping. Perhaps that's because I have been cooing in my sleep. I don't snore, I coo! I love my pigeons. Me and my dad started it together at home in Scotland and I really do love it. Everybody's got an interest outside their work and mine is just to race pigeons.

> NR: Getting back to football for a minute, what are your international ambitions?

> Dunc: Playing first-team football is a big boost for me and it's nice to be involved in the Scotland squad again. It's always good to be recognised by your country and it's not only a credit to myself but also to Everton that I'm back in the international spotlight. I was disappointed to miss the qualifying game in Russia last month and it's very frustrating because it was a big game for Scotland. We all want to be in the European Championships and play in England.

History will probably judge that Duncan was NOT an Everton legend. His record of one goal in every three games probably won't justify that tag when the generations have passed. Except he WAS a legend. He just didn't show it on the pitch as much as he could have done. For Everton OR for Scotland. His international career was hardly historic. His prison spell in Glasgow and his subsequent arguments with the Scottish FA put paid to that. But in Liverpool he'd found a home. At EVERTON he'd found a home.

NR: You mentioned earlier that Glasgow was a goldfish bowl but surely Liverpool is too?

Dunc: When I'm out and about in Liverpool, I do get recognised, especially being so big and good-looking. But the fans have taken to me and I think I have done reasonably well for them so far. Obviously there's a lot more to come from me. I'm really looking forward to getting back into it after my suspension. I feel in a way that I have let the team down, but you have got to go with the referee's decisions. I feel a bit aggrieved about the thing but you have got to respect what the ref says. So now I'm chomping at the bit to get back in and help us stay up.

NR: What do you make of the Duncan Ferguson song that the fans sing? They love you ...

Dunc: All this so-called Fergiemania is unbelievable. The fans have been great to me. What can I say? They have been treated to a good tradition of watching their number 9s, so if I can live up to some of their expectations I'll be more than happy. You cannot but have a good feeling for Everton. I want to do well for the team and everybody thinks that the club should be higher up in the table. But nobody's got a divine right and we have got to dig in.

NR: And what about winning trophies?

Dunc: Next season, you will see a big difference. The chairman and the manager want us to be successful and that aim is carried down to the players – so we will be successful. The Cup run has obviously been a good boost for the supporters because it's something to look forward to. But the main aim is to stay in the Premier

League. First Division football cannot be any good for Everton. But we were all so pleased to get through to the semi-finals and it is everybody's dream to win the FA Cup. I have played in two Scottish Cup finals and been runner-up twice so I would love to get a winners' medal with Everton. Obviously the Everton fans would love it too. We struggled at the start of the season and that's what's left us in trouble. If we hadn't had that poor start, we would have been up above the middle of the table.

NR: So you blame Mike Walker?

Dunc: We let ourselves down before Joe Royle arrived. It's no good blaming other people. And there have not actually been that many personnel changes in the team.

Duncan's prophecy of trophy-winning success would come sooner than he thought. But it wasn't just his heading ability that was graceful. His attitude to his former manager was, too. As was his appreciation of his current bosses – Joe Royle and 40,000 Evertonians.

NR: You're quickly developing a reputation for those dashing centre- forward headers. What's the art of scoring goals?

Dunc: For my part, I have got to be on the end of those crosses. But I also need the delivery. And Andy Hinchcliffe – or Brucie as we call him because he looks like Bruce Forsyth – really does know how to deliver the ball. He can whip the corners in.

NR: So you respect your team-mates. What about the manager?

Dunc: The gaffer has got a good reputation both as a manager and as a player. They tell me he was a centre-forward but that was a wee bit before my time! Seriously though, I have heard so much about him and obviously the boss was a quality player. I think he's hoping he can take something from his Everton football days to his Everton manager days. I think he would be made up if he could emulate that.

NR: And finally the supporters. What about them?

Dunc: So now my message to the fans is to keep on backing us, backing me and backing the club. Hopefully we can do the business on the park for you and we will all be trying 100 per cent for you. The tremendous support that we get just shows the potential of the club. And any charity work which I do, perhaps here at Alder Hey, is just to try to put a wee bit back into the community and show the fans that I really do appreciate them.

Duncan only played twice more for his country after that interview. He felt badly let down by the Scottish FA when they imposed a 12- match ban on him for the headbutt incident – on top of his prison sentence. At the same time, during those six weeks he spent in jail, Duncan was opening letters of support from Evertonians on a daily basis. He was flooded with them. He became one of us. And he became an overnight legend. Once you got to know him, it was hard not to like him. He was charming and generous. Generous with his time and generous with his answers. Apart from gazing into that rear-view mirror to check his hair every time I asked him a question. But we were a similar age. Professionally, we got on well. And I was proud to get those two interviews. I should mention that the second time I met him, he was even more generous. Generous with the children at Alder Hey. He responded to them so well, and they to him. Their eyes would light up when he walked in. So would his when he saw their smiles.

Of course, had I been more savvy, I'd have made plenty of money out of my interviews with Duncan, because all the national papers lifted quotes from them ... something which happened frequently during my time at Bellefield. I complained about this to Joe Royle once. 'Don't worry about them,' he said. 'They're jealous of you.'

Forget the money. My ego went through the roof, nestling at the top of the pigeon loft alongside Duncan Ferguson's.

Alan Ball

Duncan Ferguson scored 73 goals for Everton. He started almost 200 games and played in dozens more as a substitute. It is a respectable goalscoring record but not one which automatically lends itself to legendary status. It was the cult of Duncan Ferguson which elevated him to that level. His abilities as a talisman. His ability to inspire his team-mates and the supporters. What he represented to them. He WAS Everton for a while. Possibly in the same way as Dixie Dean was 70 years previously. Just without quite the same goalscoring prowess. But the goals he scored were almost all memorable. Ball in net. Duncan in net. Keeper in net. Winning goals against Liverpool and Manchester United. Goals which made him reveal his ripped torso and swirl his shirt around his head as he sprinted the full length of the touchline in front of the Main Stand.

Alan Ball was another showman. The first to wear white boots. A gifted midfield schemer who scored goals, mercilessly teased defenders and yet found himself an expert craftsman either out wide or in the middle of the park. Alan Ball really WAS the complete footballer. One of Everton's greatest ever. Someone the fans would pay to watch alone for his outrageous antics and his daring on the pitch. I was on holiday in the Caribbean when he died in 2007. I'll never forget receiving the news via text message. I'm proud I was at the next Everton match, against Manchester United, where his family felt the lasting adoration for Bally which flowed from all four sides of the ground. I'm also proud that I went to interview him when he was manager of Southampton in early 1995.

I drove down to their training ground, somewhere deep in the New Forest. I got lost. I got there. I watched the Saints train. Matt Le Tissier smiled at me. Alan Ball welcomed me into his office. He was all flat-capped and high-pitched, just as I imagined him to be. In the preliminaries, before getting my pad out, I asked what he made of his old team-mate Joe Royle being made manager of Everton.

'I rang him up,' he squeaked. 'I said: "You always were a lucky bastard."' He squeaked higher.

He was red-blooded and red-headed. But Alan Ball was a True Blue. A true gentleman and a true Evertonian. The quotes he gave me appeared in *The Evertonian* magazine in February and March, 1995.

> NR: Alan, you won the World Cup for England as a Blackpool player. Your next match was for Everton. How did it all come about?
>
> Bally: It was a typical thing that happens to young people. I got a World Cup winners' medal and then signed for Everton. I had to grow up very, very quickly from obscurity with Blackpool to breaking the British transfer record – £110,000 – within three months.

I had to pinch myself. Duncan Ferguson was a legend all right. But here – here across the desk from me, just a few feet away – here was a World Cup winner. A true legend of the game. A football god. An England legend. Above all though, an Everton legend.

> NR: So what was it like joining Everton at that time? You'd won the World Cup but they'd just won the FA Cup and it was a star-studded team ...
>
> Bally: The move to Everton came very quickly after the World Cup when I was still a young man and thank goodness, with the guidance of my dad, I took it all in my stride. I remember being in awe of the Everton situation at the time. I looked at the Everton stars and the names they had in the team and I can assure you I was nervous just walking into the Bellefield dressing room and seeing household names on the Tuesday before the season started.

The house at 48 Valley Road, Bromborough, which had been in the Roberts family since the 1930s. It was here that I developed my fascination with Everton. The door was always open, even to Liverpool supporters.

My father, Colin Roberts, was a talented young footballer and a devoted Evertonian. Here he is, aged 11, skipping a tackle while playing for the Woodslee School football team in Bromborough.

Alex Young, the famous "Golden Vision", celebrates the 1966 FA Cup win over Sheffield Wednesday with legendary Everton manager Harry Catterick. Young was my father's hero – and even wrote to him once.
(Courtesy of Liverpool Daily Post & Echo)

The myth of Edgar Chadwick. Chadwick, a superstar of the Victorian age, is pictured front-right in this picture of Everton's championship-winning team of 1891. But was he also a Roberts? My grandad once identified Chadwick in this very picture as his own father….

(Courtesy of Everton Collection Charitable Trust)

… but the real Chadwick connection was always an unresolved mystery – and probably didn't exist. My great-grandfather Charles Roberts may have played professional football under a pseudonym because he was an active serviceman. He was also trainer at Portsmouth FC and coached the victorious Royal Marine Artillery team in the 1904 Army Cup Final. Here he is top-left of picture. He seems to bear an uncanny resemblance to Chadwick, even though there are 13 years between the photographs. *(Courtesy of The Globe & Laurel)*

My grandad Jack inherited the Roberts flair for football but was clearly carrying an injury when this team photo was taken in 1917. Later that year he began serving in the First World War as a Royal Marine at the age of just 13.

Grandad in much later life, with my nanna. The baby is my younger sister Caroline. I am clearly too shy to look straight at the camera.

My dad looks proud as he holds me on my first birthday. It's a picture I've always cherished.
(Picture: Bob Vickers)

Two more pictures of my grandad. He died when I was only 9 but this is how I remember him.

Alan Ball with the league championship trophy at Goodison Park in 1970. Brian Labone is right behind him.
(Courtesy of Everton Collection Charitable Trust)

My nanna, Irene Roberts, was a devoted grandmother and a devoted Evertonian… because she was also devoted to her husband Jack, to her son Colin and – of course – to me.

Starting over. Colin and Sheila Roberts took their children Neil and Caroline for a new life in Bermuda in November 1977. This picture was taken as soon as we arrived at the airport. Just three years later, we'd be sharing the tiny island with John Lennon. *(Picture: Tony Cordeiro)*

Bermuda and Bromborough are separated by an ocean but that didn't stop the author showing his true colours at age 7.

At age 12, I had a cup final ticket. Dad and I managed to get in the Everton end at Wembley after swapping our tickets with a Watford fan called J. BUTLER, who we met outside the stadium. Five pounds proved incredible value.

WEMBLEY STADIUM

5

The Football Association
Challenge Cup Final Tie
SAT., 19 MAY, 1984
KICK-OFF 3.00p.m.
YOU ARE ADVISED TO TAKE UP
YOUR POSITION BY 2.30p.m.
1. This ticket is not transferable. 2. This counter-foil must be retained for at least 6 months.
STANDING   £5.00

TO BE RETAIN   ISSUED SUBJECT TO THE
CONDITIONS ON BACK

TURNSTILES
J or K
ENTRANCE
**51
WEST**
LOWER
STANDING
ENCLOSURE

214

It was one of the most joyous days of my life. Everton 2 Watford 0: the first time Everton had won a trophy in my lifetime. Seeing Kevin Ratcliffe lift the cup filled me with pride. *(Courtesy of Everton Collection Charitable Trust)*

I had plenty of heroes as a youngster. Most were Everton players. One was Paul McCartney. But there was also no disguising my admiration for Ian Botham.

(Picture: Paul Fender)

The 1980s was a period of unprecedented Everton glory. This is our most successful manager ever – Howard Kendall – with the league championship trophy in 1985. *(Courtesy of Everton Collection Charitable Trust)*

In 1994, I joined the Liverpool Daily Post & Echo
– and also the Daily Post football team. I am front-left of picture.

I was determined to succeed in journalism… and
as a rookie reporter, the Echo despatched me
to Liverpool's training ground to plead for an
interview with Nigel Clough about his father's
controversial comments over Hillsborough.
(Courtesy of Liverpool Daily Post & Echo)

The tunnel at Goodison Park.
I spent six months writing
The Evertonian magazine, in
Everton's cup-winning year of
1995. *(Courtesy of Liverpool Daily
Post & Echo)*

I still own the Everton scarf which I gave Alex Young for this picture. My only regret is that my dad wasn't with me. *(Picture: the author. Courtesy of Liverpool Daily Post & Echo)*

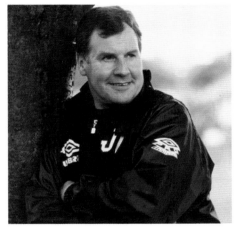

I met with Joe Royle practically every day for six months at Everton's old Bellefield training ground. I was in the background when this picture was taken. *(Courtesy of Everton Collection Charitable Trust)*

Compiling my notes after an interview with Joe Parkinson at Bellefield. And ear-wigging the quotes given to fellow press members Richard Tanner and Phil McNulty. *(Courtesy of Liverpool Daily Post & Echo)*

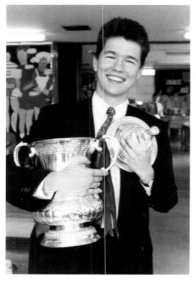

Getting my hands on the FA Cup, decked in Everton ribbons after Royle led us to our victory over Manchester United at Wembley in 1995. *(Courtesy of Liverpool Daily Post & Echo)*

Duncan Ferguson featured in that cup-winning team. He became an Everton talisman and gave me his first press interview since moving from Rangers. *(Courtesy of Everton Collection Charitable Trust)*

Perhaps Ian Rush knew I was an Evertonian. He seems to be suspiciously studying my shorthand as he gives me an exclusive interview on the day he announces that he's leaving Liverpool. *(Courtesy of Liverpool Daily Post & Echo)*

Above: In 1997, I left Liverpool and returned for a spell in Bermuda. I had a home in a sub-tropical paradise. But 3,000 miles from Goodison Park was just too far.

Below: Outside Goodison, after Alan Ball's death in 2007. Ball had told me how much he loved Everton. The tributes on the Dixie Dean statue showed that Evertonians loved him too. *(Picture: Mike Green)*

Above left: The pride of being a father for the first time. George Jack Roberts was born in 2004 on June 18th – Paul McCartney's birthday.

Above right: Dad tells George he's Everton's youngest fan. George cries…..

Below: It wasn't long before George was sporting Everton gear. Here he is, aged 2.

Aged 3 with his Beatles haircut….

And aged 4, learning football, the School Of Science way.

With Lizzie on matchday.
(Picture: Mike Green)

David Moyes transformed
Everton from a team
fighting relegation to a
team fighting in Europe.
*(Courtesy of Everton Collection
Charitable Trust)*

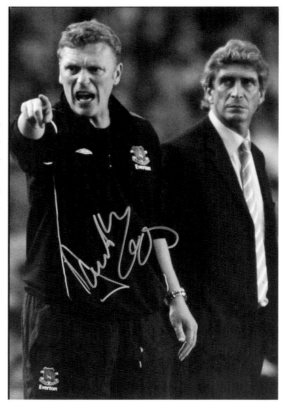

Let It Be. After years of trying, I finally got an interview with Paul McCartney, my lifelong musical hero. *(Picture: Craig Doyle)*

George's first match was Everton 2 Bolton 0 in March 2010. It was almost 30 years since my first match, which was also a home win against Bolton.

Three generations of Robertses: George, Neil and Colin.

Above: Daddy with the new arrival. Liam James Roberts was born on February 9th, 2011.

Left: My two sons… George and Liam.

I'd read up on Bally. I'd been through the cuttings library back at the *Echo*. I knew all about him. I'd done my homework. And so I started to delve into the detail.

NR: You scored on your debut at Fulham ...

Bally: I was so confident in my own ability that I just wanted to get on the pitch and earn the respect of those big stars. I was never overawed on the pitch but I was in the dressing room, to start with. Then I got two against Liverpool, so nobody could have had a better start to a career than I had at Everton. In the early days I was playing with Ray Wilson, Alex Young, Alex Scott, Derek Temple, Jimmy Gabriel, Fred Pickering and Roy Vernon. They were great players and it was a marvellous period in my life, playing and working with these super footballers. It was easy to gel in that team. They could all pass it and play. They were the best days of my life, football-wise. The most comfortable days of my life were at Blackpool but for competitive football, Everton gave me the best days of my life.

NR: What stands out for you when you look back? What are you most nostalgic about from that period?

Bally: There were highlights all the time I was at Everton. The affection and the passion from the people. Just going and playing at Goodison, against whoever, was special. It was magical to a young man. It suited me. I couldn't have been happier.

Alan Ball was so typical of Everton. He embodied the passion that is endemic in the club. He embodied the spirit of *Nil Satis Nisi Optimum*. Nothing but the best would do for Bally. He wasn't so much a student of the School Of Science – he was a master of it.

NR: So what about the School Of Science and the way Evertonians were brought up with stylish football?

Bally: I can always remember my father saying, the day I signed, that Everton fans wanted me to play football the way they supported it. That meant playing with everything I could possibly give and I would suit the crowd. Those words stuck with me. I tried to give the fans that total commitment to the cause. Dad knew what the Merseyside supporters demanded of players.

NR: You wanted to provide value for money?

Bally: Still to this day, I ask my players at Southampton to go out and win games but never forget that people work all week to spend money to watch them play. That's a big factor. If people manage to scrape up enough money to watch you play, you have got to entertain them somewhere along the line, as well as win football matches. And that's what I tried to do for Everton. If I did that, they would always pay to come and watch me again so I always had something up my sleeve, whether it be cheek, pure ability or sheer effort. I had to deliver for those fans.

NR: It wasn't just work-rate though, was it? You had an arrogance too. You played with flair. You had tricks ...

Bally: Sitting on the ball was just one of the tricks I used to get up to. It was just sheer arrogance at times. We were that good that we could do it. The atmosphere both in the dressing room and at the ground in those days was one of invincibility. The whole team was arrogant and there was a real swagger about the place. I just looked forward to going out there at Goodison. I thought to myself: 'This is what I want. I'm going to play for these people today.'

He was a superstar. The 1960s had Best, Law and Charlton. But it also had Ball. The multi-coloured boots sported by ordinary players in later years became symbols of how far the game had deteriorated in the commercial world. Gimmicks. But Bally had actually set the trend when he wore the first pair of white boots. Except for Bally, it wasn't about gimmicks. It was about glamour.

NR: So tell me about the white boots.

Bally: It was one of the first promotional things that started to creep into football and I had that little bit of arrogance about me to wear them. I just wanted to be different.

NR: Even under Harry Catterick?

Bally: Harry ruled by fear and it suited me at the time. He earned his respect and he was a marvellous manager. But he was a real disciplinarian in every way.

To dare to be different. That was Alan Ball. But he was a team player too. And who knows if he'd have had the same impact without those Goodison Park brothers in arms – Colin Harvey and Howard Kendall.

NR: And what of the Harvey–Kendall–Ball partnership? The holy trinity?

Bally: We used to say we could find each other in the dark. First of all, we were good pals. We respected each other tremendously. We were all individuals in our own way and we would do anything for each other on the pitch. That's what made it special.

NR: Colin Harvey played only once for England and Howard Kendall is often described as the best player never to have played for England. You won 72 caps for England. Still Everton's most-capped England international ...

Bally: That's a nice honour. But in the present day all three of us would have been picked for England. In the championship year, nobody could live with us in the middle of the pitch. Everything just came together. And we didn't do an awful lot of work on the training pitch, either.

NR: You lived in Formby. How did you get on with the Reds?

Bally: Actually I had a good rapport with the Liverpool fans. I had a good record scoring goals against them and I think I earned their respect. But I never experienced anything like Merseyside derbies again. The north London derby didn't really come close. That 1969– 70 season was the only time I won the title as a player or as a manager and I moved to Arsenal in December 1971, when they were already double champions.

NR: Tell me about how you came to leave Everton.

Bally: I got a call to pop up and see Harry Catterick and he told me there had been an approach from a top club, Everton had agreed the fee and I could speak to them. I told him I didn't want to go but I spoke to my father and I realised I had to go where I was wanted. I went for another British record fee but I was leaving a place I didn't want to leave.

NR: My dad told me your first game for Arsenal was against Everton at Highbury. He was there and said it wasn't very pleasant watching you play against us ...

Bally: That was a very emotional day for me. Everton left an indelible mark on me, without a shadow of a doubt.

Alan Ball spoke of an emotional day. But more than that, he spoke to me with true emotion about Everton. I reminded him that he was still president of the Jersey branch of the Everton Supporters' Club despite managing Southampton and having gone on to have a rich playing career, even after leaving Goodison Park. But it was Everton that was in his heart. And in his blood. 'I love that club,' he told me. And when I looked at him, looked into his eyes, I could see that it was true. There was a wistful air about Alan Ball as he sat back in his manager's chair at Southampton. Content with life, yes. But regretful about the way he left Everton. And perhaps a touch envious that his old pal now had the top job at the club he loved.

Alan Ball loved Everton. I wasn't old enough to have seen him play for Everton. But being part of the family, having spoken to the man himself and knowing precisely what he gave for us, I loved him too.

Howard Kendall

If I was to include every interview I ever did with every one of my heroes, this book would become as long as *War and Peace*. Duncan Ferguson earned his place as the man of the moment when I had my time at Bellefield. And of course as the living legend he became at Goodison Park. Alan Ball deserves his place as perhaps Everton's greatest ever England player; the gifted firebrand who dazzled with his skills but who would also die for the cause. My father's hero Alex Young is still to come. So too is old Golden Boots himself, Gary Lineker. A one-season wonder, signed for a record and sold for a record – to Barcelona. He came, he scored, he went. He won nothing. But he buried 40 goals.

But when Everton were marching to Wembley in that stunning cup run of 1995, when I was in my element as the launch writer for *The Evertonian* and when Joe Royle was meeting me every day at Bellefield – every single day while still galvanising those players – Howard Kendall was back on the managerial trail. After leaving Everton, he took over at Xanthi in Greece. But he didn't last long. And the following year – 1995 – he was appointed manager of the oldest professional football club in the world, lower division Notts County.

I rang him up from my office in the *Echo* building and he invited me down to Meadow Lane for an interview for *The Evertonian*. Now Howard was known to favour a drink or two. So it's perhaps appropriate that after giving me a quick tour of the

Magpies' ground, we sat in the corner of the club bar. Howard Kendall, the man who made my teenage years bearable. The man who restored Everton to their rightful place at the pinnacle of English football. The man who signed my heroes, who told them how to play, and inspired them time and time again. The man who inspired the supporters. Was now sitting with me, in a corner of the club bar at Notts County, telling me all about his time at Everton. And his time as a player. The interview appeared in the May issue of *The Evertonian* magazine.

NR: Let's start at the beginning. Everton are going to Wembley for the FA Cup Final. But you played at Wembley for Preston in 1964. And you weren't even 18. You were the youngest ever to play in an FA Cup Final ...

Howard: Playing in that final against West Ham was a real surprise to me. I can only have played about ten first-team games for Preston but I had played the previous weekend. One lad had told the manager he had to get to a funeral in Scotland and then something happened. He was disciplined and suspended and I found out in the midweek that I was in for the final at Wembley. It was a tremendous feeling but also one of disappointment for the other player because he had been in all season. It also meant that I was the youngest to have appeared in a cup final at that time.

NR: Silly question, but were you feeling the pressure?

Howard: In fact it eased the pressure on me because the other players in the team were all the more concerned about making sure I was all right. They didn't want to make a fuss of me but doing that helped their nerves too.

NR: You weren't at Everton in 1966 so your next crack at Wembley was the 1968 cup final, which we lost to West Brom.

Howard: I remember we were odds-on favourites because we had beaten them convincingly in the league, 6-2 at the Hawthorns. In the game itself, we had opportunities but just didn't take them. They scored one out of the blue and we lost it. That was an even bigger disappointment for me than 1964 because to play there not expecting to win and then losing wasn't so bad.

But the expectancy level at Everton was so high that it was a great disappointment to lose to West Brom. We played fairly well and had the chances to have won it. But we had been to the final, had the joy of a semi-final victory and given our supporters a day out. You must think that you have actually taken part in the spectacle of the season, which is the FA Cup Final.

Howard Kendall and the FA Cup seemed made for each other. In years to come, I felt privileged to have interviewed Everton's greatest ever manager.

But even more privileged to have done so around the time of another great FA Cup success for the club. But there was so much more to the man than football's most famous trophy. He was a born winner. And he took on all-comers ... as a manager AND a player.

NR: You got to the semi-finals the following year but Everton were really starting to build something and, of course, then came the league title in 1970.

Howard: We were starting to play our best football that year [1969]. People say it was Harvey–Kendall–Ball that did it. The three of us did have a tremendous working relationship and there was a good balance but when people try to talk about that midfield, I try to talk about the team. It was a very, very good team – not just a trio. Midfield is a vital area but when I look at the quality players I had around me, I know it was a team effort ... not just a midfield effort.

NR: And what about your Wembley experiences? They were rarities, obviously, because you never won that full England cap ...

Howard: The Charity Shields weren't at Wembley in those days, so that limited further appearances there. But when I went to Birmingham in 1974, I thought I had a chance of going back to Wembley. But Fulham beat us at Maine Road in a semi-final replay and that was a real sickener. I had even been an unused substitute there for an England match when I was an Everton player. And I'm obviously disappointed that I got so near to an England cap. But in my time there were a number of top-class midfield players, or wing-halves as they were then. Alf Ramsey was very loyal to the players he selected. But I made the bench at Wembley in 1972 against Yugoslavia and he said that if he could make a substitution, I would play. Joe Royle played and scored that night. Alan Ball also played but he had moved to Arsenal by then. But Alf didn't make any substitutions. It was a case of 'nearly'.

NR: Let's move from your playing career to your managerial career and fast-forward a bit. There was a crisis at Goodison Park in 1983, wasn't there. A campaign against you. Poor crowds. Boos and leaflets. Then of course came Kevin Brock's back pass at Oxford. Adrian Heath scored that goal and the rest is history ...

Howard: My answer to the press when they were talking about a crisis in the early part of the season was that if we were out of both cup competitions and near the bottom of the table in January or February, then I would admit there was a crisis. But of course we went to Wembley twice – the Milk Cup Final and the FA Cup Final. And the so-called turning point wasn't Adrian Heath's equaliser at Oxford. It helped and it was important we were involved in cups but it wasn't all down to one back pass.

NR: Well, something changed our fortunes in that time. We drew with Liverpool in the League Cup Final, only losing in the replay at Maine Road. But we beat Watford to win the FA Cup.

Howard: We needed three games to get past Gillingham in the FA Cup and we even had to go back to their ground for a second replay when the chairman lost the toss at Goodison. But nobody goes through to the final without having a narrow miss. Andy Gray was cup-tied in the Milk Cup but he was desperate to get to Wembley in the FA Cup. He was a brilliant influence, willing the lads on. There was an extra determination from him because he so wanted to get to the FA Cup Final.

NR: And that League Cup Final – the Milk Cup Final – was a historic day even if we didn't lift the trophy ...

Howard: The Milk Cup Final was unique because it was the first Wembley final with the red and blue of Merseyside travelling down together. On the day we felt we were unfortunate with a rejected handball decision which might have given us a penalty. But maybe 0-0 was the right result for all Merseyside. We showed the football world how two teams from the same city could behave.

NR: Still, we lost the replay! So how did that affect the determination to win the FA Cup?

Howard: When we played Watford, everybody expected us to win and that was an important factor. For us, it was all about winning the game and it was a way into Europe. It was so important for the fans and the club. They could look forward to European football. We had an amazing run after that and there was a lot of confidence in the side. And it had great balance. We went on to prove we were the best in the league. We had pace, aggression and good quality players who wanted to play for the club.

NR: It was probably Everton's best ever side, winning the league by 13 points and the European Cup Winners' Cup. But still we lost at Wembley that season ...

Howard: That 1984–5 team was by far the best I have ever managed and it would certainly take some beating. But the 1985 FA Cup Final against Manchester United came too quickly after the Cup Winners' Cup Final in Rotterdam, which was just days before. It was a very hot day as well and we just didn't have a lot more to give. Plus they had the catalyst when Kevin Moran was sent off.

NR: Let's not delve too deeply into the 1986 final, because Liverpool beat us. But we did make it to three finals on the trot ...

Howard: We had started well in the 1986 FA Cup Final against Liverpool and we were full of confidence. But we made defensive errors. We won three semi-finals on the trot in extra time: 1984, 1985 and 1986. To win each one showed tremendous character.

NR: And I was at two of those semi-finals. 1984 and 1985.
Howard: The game against Luton in 1985 was the most satisfying. But I'm sure all Evertonians will remember the first against Southampton at Highbury. We played Luton after just coming back from Munich in the Cup Winners' Cup and we looked a bit jaded in the first half when we went 1-0 down. But the players never believed they were going to be beaten.

Belief. So important for a football team. Belief and confidence; something to build your team spirit around. Someone to pin your hopes on. Someone like Duncan Ferguson.

NR: Well now we're going back to Wembley and one man who has made that possible is Duncan Ferguson ...

Howard: I tried to sign Duncan and now he's proving what a superb player he is. We made a massive offer for him when he was at Dundee United. Football transfers are all about available finances at a particular club at a particular time. Peter Johnson's millions might have helped. But a manager can't ask for more if his chairman and directors back him in his judgement and back it with money.

NR: And really now we're getting down to why you left Everton second time around. They didn't back you when you wanted to sign Dion Dublin.

Howard: The reasons why I left Everton have all been said. In fact, what I said in the previous paragraph says it all.

They have got to back your judgement and also work within the financial structure of the club. It was always going to be a risk, signing Dion. But that's the same with buying all players. Dion is a smashing lad who works hard. And he's improving. But Joe Royle's efforts so far have been superb.

With that, we shook hands and rose from the table. Howard Kendall had greeted me like a long-lost uncle. We parted on similar terms. There was a camaraderie. A warmth. A feeling of having shared something. Even though I only met him once, and his contribution to Everton's history was so huge, I felt like I had shared something with him. And not just a lager. Like I was important to him, if even for that short time. Perhaps that's why he was such a successful manager. It was the way he could make people feel important. Never again did I see Howard Kendall. But never again did I need to. It was a dream fulfilled.

Alex Young

When he was 13 years old, my father had his own dream. To be Alex Young. That artist who used the turf of Goodison Park as his canvas. As stylish a player as Everton would ever see. As stylish a player as any club would ever see. Alex Young. The Golden Vision.

That was also the name of a BBC play about Everton's most hero-worshipped footballer in the 1960s. It was directed by Ken Loach, co-written by the ITN newsreader Gordon Honeycombe and featured a load of actors who went on to star in the Liverpool soap opera *Brookside*. But this piece of television was no *Brooky*. There was no soap opera here. This was an epic. The story of a hero. An icon. A legend. The Golden Vision.

My father was a budding young footballer himself in 1961. So he wrote to Everton's new signing. The man who'd transferred from Hearts. The man whose arrival had prompted a surge in the Everton gate. And what's more, dad got a reply to his letter.

'How do I get better?'asked dad. 'How do I improve my ball skills?

My balance. My crossing. My control.'

'Just keep practising,' wrote the Golden Vision in his generous reply. 'Practise with a tennis ball in the yard. Practise and practise and practise.'

Well if practice made perfect,then Alex Young was the perfect example of practice. Dad would tell me about the Golden Vision's balance. How he would drop a shoulder and effortlessly ghost past a player. About his grace. About his ability to dribble as if that old lace-up leather ball was glued to his foot. How he could spring high into the air for headers despite not being a tall man. How he cut a dashing figure as he darted across the pitch,all golden-haired,fleet-footed and jaw-droppingly gifted. By all accounts, it's no exaggeration. Alex Young played in the days before every match was covered on TV. Before hardly any match was covered on TV. Few people travelled long distances to away games in those days. He was a celebrity figure on Merseyside. At Goodison. In the pubs around the ground. But he was hardly brought to wider audiences. Only the BBC play – *The Golden Vision* – brought him anything like the fame he deserved. Years later, dad told me the nearest player to Alex Young in the modern game was Paolo Di Canio. Now Di Canio was a talented footballer. But you can't help but think that even this comparison did a disservice to the gifts of the Golden Vision.

Dad would have loved to have met him. So it was with a mixture of excitement and guilt that I drove up to Scotland to have my own meeting with the man himself. I parked up in a cobbled side street in Leith, Edinburgh. I found an old merchants' warehouse. I knocked on the door and was summoned up. This was a soft furnishings business specialising in curtain poles, curtain rings and fabrics. The unassuming, slightly awkward, slightly nervous man who greeted me was a salesman in curtain rings. Years before, he had been the Golden Vision.

I sat with him. We drank tea. I took pictures of him around his shop. With the fabrics. Nervously wearing my own Everton scarf. I had to pinch myself. Here was I, face to face with my father's hero. Aside from John Lennon, there was probably nobody on Earth he would rather meet.

I sat with him for what seemed like an age. Certainly an hour, maybe two. I later sent the full transcript of my interview with him to my dad. There was so much of it, it was serialised in three issues of *The Evertonian*. When we began, we talked about how he'd been signed by Johnny Carey. The Everton manager famously sacked in a taxi so that Harry Catterick could take over. Alex Young had arrived from Hearts in November 1960. He'd been in the same team as Dave Mackay at Tynecastle and he'd been playing for the Army during his national service. But Carey still signed him despite various knee ligament injuries he had – and it took the Vision a full season before he got his sights perfectly right. According to the man himself.

Everton, West Brom and Preston North End had all wanted this rising young star from Hearts. But it was Goodison Park which swung the deal for Johnny Carey. Not Deepdale for Alex Young. That ground I'd played at myself while doing journalism training. That ground of Tom Finney. Not the Hawthorns either.

I had played once for the Scottish under-23s against England at Goodison. And I remembered the pitch, the ground, the stands.

Ah yes. That pitch. That ground. Those stands. That place of Joe Mercer. That place of Tommy Lawton. That place of Dixie Dean.

That place of Dave Hickson. Now that place of Alex Young.

> But it was the Hearts manager who guided me towards
> Everton. He said it would be better going to a bigger club
> like Everton. He had played for Chelsea and he said he
> would have chosen Everton. Personally, I think he was
> worried about getting his money and he knew Everton
> would pay up! But I'm glad that I took his advice!

Everton, a bigger club than Chelsea. Everton, the Mersey
Millionaires. You knew they would pay up. Ah, how times change
in football.

Alex started to get fit. Started to play to his peak. A peak that
he said lasted until he was 26. But then he got another knee
injury. And after the 1966 FA Cup Final, he felt he was limping
on in the last two years of his Everton career.

> I had to have a cartilage out and I was never the same
> again. I didn't have that same bounce or ability in the
> air. I always used to jump off my right leg but after the
> cartilage problem I couldn't bounce the same.

Alex Young went to Stockport County, by way of Irish League side
Glentoran. Why is it that football geniuses so often have a tragic
end to their football careers? Alex Young's genius was remarkable
in itself. All the more remarkable when you learn that he was
partially deaf. A secret he kept. And a little exclusive he gave me.

> NR: So your career seemed blighted by injuries ...

> Alex: Everton saw me at my best for about three years
> because of injuries. And then there was another reason
> why I struggled in the later stages of my Goodison
> career. I've never told this to anybody before ... I actually
> started to become deaf when I was about 25 or 26. I
> never mentioned it but if you speak to any pro they
> will tell you that one of the main things on the pitch
> is communication and shouting at each other. If your

marker is coming in, your own player will shout: 'Man on', or: 'Watch your back', but loads of times I didn't hear them.

Due to the deafness that was happening to me now and again I got caught in possession, whereas before, that never really happened. It's okay now because I have got a very tiny inside hearing aid. But all my family had this deafness. I obviously wasn't completely deaf but there was considerable loss in both ears and that honestly affected my game.

NR: So you could have been even better?

Alex: I never played those last five years as well as I would have liked although I had lots of good games and good spells. I never really played consistently well. Many players played well into their thirties. But they didn't have knee or ankle injuries and then of course there was my hearing problem as well. I didn't really tell any of the players about it at the time but they gradually found out. Like at half-time I would say to people that I didn't hear them shouting and it modified my performance. I am telling Everton supporters the truth. I knew they liked me and I liked them. I loved Liverpool and Liverpool people.

Alex Young had a genuine warmth for Everton and for the city of Liverpool. He never wanted to leave. Another to have his heart broken by Harry Catterick. Great manager. Heartbreaker. Alan Ball. Alex Young. Turfed on to the scrapheap by Mr Catterick.

I regret ever leaving the club and the area, but I came away and that's that.

Nostalgia was not something you'd necessarily associate with this modest man. But it was there. It was real. And his feeling for the city was a concept I readily bought in to.

You have to make your bed and I did. But Liverpool is my spiritual home. You go to certain places and you feel at home there, you are immediately accepted by the people and the crowd. And it was such a wonderful feeling to play at Goodison Park in those days. I don't think there was a better supported team in Britain then. I felt instantly accepted by the fans. Whenever I came on to the pitch, I knew they were with me. I sometimes used to go out and I could feel the goodwill emanating from the terraces. They wanted me to do the business, I could feel it.

Alex spoke about the 1962–3 championship season. About how Everton fans would pack behind both goals. About how huge Ds were cut behind the goal at each end after a 'hullabaloo' when something was thrown at the Tottenham goalkeeper. About how the electric atmosphere was slightly numbed by this. About how this helped bring an end to an unbeaten home run spanning two and a half years.

He talked about freezing on the international stage. About how he only won eight caps and constantly understudied Liverpool's Ian St John. It was nothing to do with Alex's abilities. But he was never a natural goalscorer ... if that sounds familiar. But where Duncan Ferguson was all power and talismanic spirit, the Golden Vision was all effortless grace. God-like. And STILL a talismanic spirit.

> Winning that championship was a terrific season for me. We bought one or two players and Tony Kay came to the club. He got kicked out of football for betting on matches at Sheffield Wednesday. But that decision was a sin – and I don't think Tony really did anything. He would have been a legendary player at Everton. He was one of the best players I ever played with. He was special.

Tony Kay. Banned for life from playing football because he gambled a hundred quid on Sheffield Wednesday to lose at Ipswich. Except he was man of the match in that game. Alex

Young regretted what happened to Tony Kay. Everyone at Everton did. Alex was right that Kay would have become a legend. Perhaps he already had become a legend. But the most powerful post-war legend at Goodison Park? Not Alan Ball. Not Howard Kendall. Not Harry Catterick. The Golden Vision. And 1962–3 was when he glittered at his most brilliant.

> There was a very harsh winter that season and Everton were one of the few clubs to have undersoil heating which helped us, because we had a game at least every fortnight. But we won the league on merit. Spurs were our championship rivals that season and one of the big games was when we beat Tottenham in front of a huge crowd at Goodison. That turned the league around. And I scored a goal with a header but I was always quite good in the air with timing my jumps.

> NR: You played at Wembley in 1966. That great comeback to beat Sheffield Wednesday and win the cup.

> Alex: We were shell-shocked at the start and we had a goal disallowed and penalty appeals turned down. But we got back into the game and winning it is what made it so memorable. I don't think any team had come back from 2-0 down in a cup final before then. Wednesday were a hard team and the feeling was unreal when Derek Temple put our third one in. And in the end we could have won it with one or two more goals.

> NR: So why did Everton start so slowly in that game?

> Alex: We didn't knock the ball around that well and a lot of players were under par that day. But I still think it's one of those days in Everton's history that will live forever. We came through some hard games and beat a very formidable Manchester United team in the semi-finals.

NR: And it was the Cornishman Mike Trebilcock who scored twice to get us back into it. Never heard of before. Hardly heard of again...

Alex: All he had was the ability to score goals and he could whack it in and sometimes seemed to get it on the spot. But he never played much after that even though he got two, might have had three and it was his final. We all battled and fought so well that season. We won the cup but we weren't a terrific side. And then I left in 1968.

Alex talked about leaving 'under a cloud'. How he missed the 1968 FA Cup Final. How he was forced to play wide right rather than up front in the latter stages of his Everton career. How playing with Alan Ball kept him going – one of the best players he ever played with – but how 'it was sad the way it finished for me at Everton'. Glentoran didn't work out. Stockport didn't work out.

NR: So what happened at Stockport?

Alex: The atmosphere at Stockport in the Third Division was never the same as the atmosphere at Goodison. I couldn't get geared up properly, even if it was a good enough wee club. You didn't get a proper ball given to you and you were getting 50-50s all the time. I had played at top-class sides so of course it was a come-down.

NR: But you have those memories of Everton. And they have those memories of you. As a showman.

Alex: I wasn't really a showman but if you are quite good at some things, you concentrate on them. When I was on top and really performing, I suppose I could be a showman. I always used to try to throw dummies. Some do it nowadays but it's harder to play in today's game. The ball gets laid up to front players and they keep their backs to goal and shield the ball. I would do that occasionally but I was always throwing a little dummy, then checking and going the other way to leave defenders standing.

NR: This is what inspired my father. What made him write to you for those tips. He wanted to get better. He wanted to improve his control and you were the man to ask.

Alex: You just had to have good, tight control and when I was a younger lad players had this control. I used to look at players like Stanley Matthews or Tom Finney who was my idol at Preston. He had real total control and used to drop his shoulders to beat a man. He held the ball in tight to him and never let the ball run away.

Like having the ball glued to his foot, as it were. Like the Golden Vision. After retiring from football, Alex Young retired from Merseyside. Packed up his things and left Ormskirk with his wife Nancy. He returned to Scotland to run pubs, as so many footballers do. Then he started his soft furnishings business in 1972, before I'd reached the grand old age of one. In the intervening period, he'd brought up his sons Alex and Jason to follow Hearts and Everton. 'I have brought them up right,' he said. And in years to come, I'd second that. Jason himself ploughed a footballing trade in the third division of the German Bundesliga. But Alex's heart was at Hearts ... and at Everton.

Nancy loved it in Merseyside and much preferred living in England. She never forgave me for two or three years for coming back. We were so happy down there. And Everton is very important to me. Please pass on my regards to everybody in Liverpool and I hope Everton do well.

NR: How often do you get back?

Alex: I don't really get the chance to go to many matches although I went a couple of years ago. But there's something about the club that makes it very special.

NR: Something about the club clearly got inside you when you played there.

Alex: I love it and I think the spectators help to make it what it is. They are great fans and then there are the Dixie Dean legends. It's as if the spirits of these great players like Dixie Dean and Tommy Lawton are still around the place.

NR: That's how I feel about Goodison Park. The sense of history. You can imagine it. You can smell it.

Alex: Goodison is such a fabulous ground. A lot of old players love the club and I'm no different. I see the lads from those days every now and again. But you do lose touch unfortunately. But I can never forget the club, the town and how welcome I was made. And I'm not shooting any muck when I say that.

Gary Lineker

It's said that Everton has that effect on players. It touches them. Something about the club stays with them. Whoever they go on to play for, they feel a special bond with Everton. An affinity. Often to the exclusion of other clubs, even if they played more for other clubs or won things with other clubs. Take Duncan McKenzie. Forget Forest. Forget Leeds. Forget Chelsea. He's an Evertonian. At Everton, he was appreciated. He was loved. His skills were adored. There was a natural home for his talents at Goodison Park. Even if the manager Gordon Lee did try to stifle them.

Goodison Park also provided a home for the talents of Gary Lineker, albeit for one season only. We signed him from his home town team, Leicester City, to replace Andy Gray. He cost £800,000. One summer later he was starring for England in Mexico in the 1986 World Cup. Our player of the tournament who kept us alive until the curse of the 'Hand Of God'goal by

Maradona. But then he was gone, to Barcelona, for the princely sum of £2.2m.

Gary Lineker was a short-term servant to Everton. No long-term devotion to the cause for him, like Howard Kendall. Not even a darling of the terraces for his head-turning genius, like Alan Ball or Alex Young. Not even the talisman figure like Duncan Ferguson – or even his predecessor Andy Gray who, like Lineker, ultimately graduated from football to a career in front of the TV cameras. No. Lineker's gifts were purely and simply in his goalscoring boots.

This was no Golden Vision. This was Golden Boots. Everton haven't seen his goalscoring talents since. They hadn't really seen them before, since Bob Latchford at least. Gary Lineker plundered 40 goals in 57 Everton matches. And he won absolutely nothing. He starred in the team that finished double runners-up ... to double winners Liverpool.

I went down to Television Centre in London to interview Gary Lineker after he'd appeared on *Football Focus*. I wasn't kidding myself. I knew that 'Everton effect' would hardly have rubbed off on him in just one season. He freely admitted that Leicester City were his team. But where would Everton sit alongside his later clubs, Barcelona and Tottenham? I was intrigued to find out. And again, I found a huge name perfectly willing to speak to *The Evertonian*.

NR: Gary, I want to know how you look back at Everton. Tell me one thing that stands out.

Links: The thing about Goodison is that there's such a fantastic atmosphere when things are going well and it's one of the most incredible grounds in terms of noise. It doesn't compare with the Nou Camp in terms of size. But the fans who go to Barcelona are slightly different to Evertonians in many ways. The people there are very much the well-to-dos and they are the same people who go to the opera. In England and at Everton, football is the people's sport. The working classes go and they are more vociferous and more enthusiastic.

NR: So it's official? Goodison Park is noisier than the Nou Camp?

Links: The only time there was anything like that in Barcelona was when they played Real Madrid. There were 120,000 in the Nou Camp and they were all supporting the home team.

NR: So why is it that you're remembered for your time at Tottenham, at Barcelona and even at Leicester, but Everton hardly gets a mention?

Links: It's probably because I only had one year at Everton. It was an enjoyable year but it's nearly ten years ago now. Everton is a club that often gets forgotten when people list my clubs but it's not forgotten by me. It's a part of my football life because in many ways it launched me on to the international scene.

NR: So Everton is a major part of your life because they helped your England career?

Links: Handling the move to a big club like Everton helped confirm my status as an international footballer. Also, it was certainly the best club side I have ever played for. It was the only time I played for a team that had a genuine chance of winning the title.

It took me back to the decade before. Back to when I believed we would win the double. As my father told me, LIVERPOOL had never done the double. Yet we were going to do it. We were going to do something they had never done. We were going to humiliate them.

Except the plan went all wrong. And we were the ones feeling humiliated. Liverpool won the double. We won nothing. Gary Lineker was an unstoppable goalscorer. He'd had to fight to win over the fans when he replaced a Ferguson-like talisman for the Gwladys Street faithful in Andy Gray. Gary Lineker DID score a hatful of goals and he DID win over those fans. But with Gary in the team, we won nothing.

NR: We didn't win the title when you were there, of course. We were champions when you arrived ...

Links: Everton had got in touch with Leicester City and I remember meeting Howard Kendall in a hotel in Stoke. We went out for a meal and he didn't have to sell the club at the time because they were champions and they had won the European Cup Winners' Cup. He impressed me straight away and it just seemed like the perfect move for me.

NR: Even so, the man you replaced was an Everton hero and that can't have been easy.

Links: It was a bit difficult at the start because I had to replace Andy Gray who, quite rightly, was a legend with the fans. We were different in our styles and our characters and that didn't make it easy. There was a lot of pressure on me and the letters in the *Football Echo* weren't very kind in the first few months.

NR: So what was your relationship like with the fans? Not that easy?

Links: I got a bit of stick at first and it wasn't until a couple of games around Christmas when I scored a few goals and we had a couple of good wins that the fans took to me. From then onwards, the reception I received was fantastic. Evertonians are demanding like all fans, but they are knowledgeable and if you are getting stick there's generally a reason for it, even though players never like to admit those things. But if you are giving your all they will know. They are used to very good players and they have had a lot of great players, especially centre-forwards ... people like Dixie

Dean before my time, the Golden Vision Alex Young, Joe Royle and Graeme Sharp.

NR: And they were all a very hard act to follow.

Links: The standards that have been set at Goodison before are very difficult to live up to. Even so, the year I was there we should have won the double. But Liverpool won almost all of their last 12 games or something silly. I think we lost it at Oxford.

Ah yes, we lost it at Oxford. The scene of the remarkable Everton turnaround under Howard Kendall. The scene of the Kevin Brock back pass. The scene, in 1986, of a Gary Lineker without his shooting boots.

NR: I remember that game. It was towards the end of the season and I listened on the radio. We needed to win but you just didn't have your shooting boots on. Literally ...

Links: I had this pair of Adidas boots and I changed them just before Christmas. I had scored about a goal a game in the old ones so I changed back to them when the goals dried up. But for some reason they weren't in the skip to Oxford and I had to borrow a pair. Anyway they weren't the ones for me and I had a couple of half chances in that game but didn't put them away. We lost it and that cost us the league.

NR: And let's face it, we were better than Liverpool.

Links: We had great pace at the back and a great goalkeeper. The midfield was sensational and we didn't have that many injuries. There was great supply from wide and that tremendous engine room in the middle, Peter Reid. Plus if Paul Bracewell hadn't got that terrible injury, he would have been an absolute regular in the England team for years to come. He was a marvellous player.

NR: We got to Wembley and you scored the first goal. But we lost the FA Cup Final too.

Links: The goal I scored in the 1986 cup final against Liverpool was the most memorable goal I had scored at that time. We had made a couple of slips towards the end of the season but that team had quality and we were trying to make sure we didn't slip up in that final. It's very rare that I have had a buzz like the one I got from that goal. But then we had to go through a dreadful couple of days after the match. We thought we would win the double and ended up with nothing. It was a bit of a choker.

It was a choker all right. Watching that 1986 final at Wembley was painful at the time and became even more painful with subsequent viewings. So much so that I had to stop watching it. But Gary Lineker is more than just a footnote in the Everton story. More than just part of a painful season. In any list of our great number 9s, Gary Lineker will be a standout figure. Even if it was just for one solitary season of true greatness.

NR: You forged a great partnership with Graeme Sharp for Everton and with Peter Beardsley for England. Both Evertonians, of course. How do you compare them?

Links: Sharpie was a different kind of player to Peter but he was a fantastic target man, especially the way Everton played then with getting balls from wide positions into the area. He was as good a target man as I have played with and put himself about and we combined really well. Graeme would go short and I would get behind him and to forge such a partnership in such a short time was good going. It's just a shame Peter went to Everton a few years too late. He was fabulous.

NR: And so has Everton touched you in the way other players say it has touched them?

Links: I will tell you the absolute truth. Leicester City is my team and I don't think you change allegiances. But you certainly get an affection for your old clubs, especially if you have been successful and leave on happy terms. Thankfully, that's been my experience with all my former clubs. I have always left on good terms and in good faith and after Leicester City the results I look for are Spurs and Everton.

NR: In that order though, right?

Links: I honestly don't favour one over the other. I was hoping they would meet in the FA Cup Final. In an ideal world, which is something you can never totally predict, it would have been nice to have had a little bit longer at Everton, for sure.

Perhaps that's because Everton won the league the season BEFORE Gary left and the season AFTER Gary left. In truth, he's not a legendary Evertonian. Not for me. But he had that legendary season. And the way he joined and left in a whirl, with 40 goals swirling round inside that hurricane, was always something of a mystery to me. He had his own Magical Mystery Tour to Merseyside, if you like.

Gary didn't get his wish of an Everton–Tottenham FA Cup Final in 1995. That's because we walloped Tottenham 4-1 in the semi-final at Elland Road. I remember getting the feeling that we'd win that game. My dad and my sister came with me to Leeds. Evertonians had three sides of the ground. And Matt Jackson and Graham Stuart put us on the way, before two late goals from the substitute Daniel Amokachi turned it into a rout. Apparently, he wasn't even supposed to be on the pitch. Joe Royle was hoping to make a change and Amo just wandered on, by which time it was too late. Somehow I can believe that. This was a man who watched his dog mauling my suit, then had the temerity to tell me off for playing with his dog too much. Good old Amo. Not an Everton legend either, but one with his own place in the Everton history books.

I interviewed everyone from the Everton chairman to the Everton groundsman. I walked across that pitch and saw the camber. How it's about ten feet higher in the centre circle than it is on any of the sides. How you can't actually see the bottom of either goal from the halfway line. I walked out there and gazed at the empty stands. As the rollers got rolling and the sprinklers got sprinkling, I was daydreaming again, looking up at those painted numbers on the brick walls at the backs of the stands. At the wooden seats in Upper Bullens and Upper Gwladys. Daydreaming about Dixie. About Tommy. About Dave Hickson even. About the Golden Vision. It was a time in my life when I had to pinch myself. I was living a dream. Living with legends. I interviewed them all. I met them all. And not one of them let me down. Not even Gary Lineker.

Wembley

Mike Dunford was Everton's managing director, club secretary and top admin guy. Something like that. I walked into his office. On his broad oak desk, a huge pile of tickets. Hundreds and hundreds of them. FA Cup Final tickets. Stacked into a perfect pile. Worth their wait in gold.

'I want one, I want one, I want one!'

That was what I thought, not what I said. But looking back, my tongue could barely have been hanging out any lower had a scantily- clad Anna Friel been sprawled backwards over that desk in front of me. Those FA Cup Final tickets were like gold dust. And I wanted one.

Now you might have thought that my position as the launch writer of *The Evertonian* would have guaranteed me a Wembley ticket. But not so. I had my season ticket to fall back on. I had the possibility of a press box pass. And here I was in Dunford's office, staring at a foot- high pile of gold-plated, bona fide FA Cup Final tickets.

'Mr Dunford, sorry to ask. Is there any chance at all of a ticket for the final?'

That's what I did ask. And thankfully, that's what I got.

'There you go young man,' he said. All quiff and Derby accent. A solitary ticket.

I walked out of Goodison Park as if I'd just been offered the best job in the world. Mind you, I already had that. So I had the next best thing in my back pocket. A cup final ticket. Everton versus Manchester United on 20 May 1995. Now to get tickets for my father and my sister, both of whom had come to the semi-final with me at Elland Road.

A few weeks before Wembley, the tickets went on sale to season ticket holders. I was still a season ticket holder. I hadn't used it for every game, because sometimes I'd had to go in the press box. My duties for *The Evertonian* sometimes required it. But wearing a suit and cramming into the Goodison press benches was never as good as being in the Gwladys Street End. Even if the sandwiches were quite good. And you got to see both managers up close and personal when they got the Goodison Park lift up to the Goodison Park press room, to meet the assembled ranks of the print media. No, that was interesting enough. But nothing beat being a fan. You could meet all your heroes and mix with all the players. But nothing really compensated for what you loved most in the world. Your passion. Going to the game. Supporting Everton.

The tickets were going on sale at 11am on a Saturday morning. I got to Goodison Park at 11pm on the Friday night. I say got to Goodison Park. I got to about half a mile away. Because the queue for tickets, already four wide in places, was snaking its way in and out of the side streets behind Gwladys Street. I followed it. And followed it. And followed it. From my arrival at Bullens Road, I walked alongside the queue. Down Gwladys Street. Along Walton Lane. Up Bardsay Road. Along Hans Road. Down Milman Road. Along Walton Lane again. Up Bodmin Road. Along Hans Road again. Down Cowley Road. Stop. The end of the line. This is where I'd make my bed for the night. I already knew the ins and outs of L4 like the back of my hand.

How many people were in front of me? It was impossible to tell. Perhaps Everton had 30,000 tickets to sell. Perhaps there were only 5,000 people in front of me. Mind you, perhaps Everton had 20,000 tickets to sell. And perhaps there were 10,000 people in front of me. The club – in its infinite wisdom – had decided to offer four tickets to every season ticket holder. Four tickets to every season ticket holder. Shit.

I stayed out all night. Suffered the cold. Even worse, suffered the boredom. As much as I love Evertonians, there's only so much mindless chit-chat you can take overnight on the pavement in suburban Liverpool. I'd stocked up on Coke. Stocked up on pork pies and crisps. I was set for the night. But it dragged on and on. It seemed to stretch further than the queue itself. Until the morning came, and the feet in front of me slowly began shuffling forwards. Slowly we shuffled. Inch by inch. Up Cowley Road. Along Hans Road. Down Bodmin Road. Along Walton Lane. Up Milman Road. Along Hans Road again. Down Bardsay Road. Along Walton Lane again. We turned the corner. The towering Bullens Road stand inched into view. Up Gwladys Street. Along Goodison Road. Stop. The end of the line. Still a hundred yards from the Park End ticket office. And the shutters had come down.

It was heartbreaking. And even more so for those around me. Those insufferables who I now felt total solidarity with. We'd missed out on a ticket. All of us. I kept quiet. I wasn't that badly off. Yes, I'd stayed out all night. Yes, I'd endured 12 hours of Liverpool cold and boredom. But actually, secretly, I had a ticket. I had that one from Dunford's office. And I could get a press box ticket. So I would at least get to Wembley. So would my dad. But sadly for my sister Caroline, there was no FA Cup Final ticket. I'd interviewed all the greats. I knew the manager and the captain. I spent every day at Bellefield. But I couldn't get her a ticket.

When the day came, Wembley was a whirlwind. It happened so quickly that it was hard to take it all in. Like a wedding. And it truly was a happy occasion. I took my press box pass so that meant I had to wear a tie. I took an Everton tie. And I ignored the stipulation that you must remain non-partisan in the Wembley press box. Sod that. My dad had the ticket from Dunford's office. Behind the goal. The only downside to this? Not the goal that Everton scored in.

The one piece of football that stood out from that day stands out in my memory now. Anders Limpar was given the freedom of Wembley. He charged down the middle of the pitch without a Red Devil soul in sight. He ran almost the full length of the pitch. At speed. Tore towards the United goal. Matt Jackson was outside him. He took a pass from Limpar and crossed into the penalty area. Graham Stuart collected the ball and rattled the United crossbar. The ball came back. Paul Rideout outjumped Gary Neville. The ball went past Steve Bruce on the United goal line. The ball went into the net. Steve Bruce and Peter Schmeichel started fighting. We started cheering. Me included. Everton 1 Manchester United 0. And that's how it finished. We won the cup. Now nine league titles, five FA Cups and one European trophy. And we haven't won a trophy since.

After the match, there were some minor scuffles between the rival supporters. Some sporadic fighting broke out. But I was oblivious to it as I picked my way around the outside of Wembley Stadium to the rendezvous point where I was to meet my dad. There he was, in front of me.

'Have we just won the cup?' I asked him. 'I think we have,' he said.

Nothing more needed to be said. *Nil Satis Nisi Optimum.*

Back To The Egg

Rovers Return

There was no time for a major celebration. At least, not of the ordinary kind. I was still working on *The Evertonian*. And Everton's triumph meant I was needed in Liverpool the next day to cover their victory parade.

I drove back up north, straight to the point from which the team bus would leave. The team bus and the press bus. But I was cutting it fine. And when I got there, the *Echo* had also despatched my friend and colleague Martin Dillon to cover the parade for the next day's paper. Now Martin is an ardent Red, so this seemed to me to be the cruellest and most delicious of ironies. Especially as he has relished every opportunity to lord it over me since. But on this sunny, late Sunday morning, the gloating opportunities were all mine.

It got better, too. Because we accidentally got on the wrong bus. Without even knowing, we were on the team bus, not the press bus. We just simply waltzed on to the wrong bus. The players were on the upper deck with the cup. And before I knew it, Joe Royle had climbed on board too. 'Well,' he told the driver, 'are we going to get this bus moving or what?' Martin and I looked at each other. Should we stay? Errrr. Yes. So we did. And we went up on to the deck to mix with the players and their families. And wave to the crowds. And touch the cup. And feel the euphoria. And join the celebrations. Well, I was celebrating. Martin wasn't.

The bus pulled on to Queens Drive and began its tour of the city. Everywhere below us, en route, a sea of blue and white. There must have been more than 100,000 people with scarves, flags, banners and rosettes. Perhaps 200,000 Everton supporters.

Young and old, babies and grannies, grown men and women. Teenagers and families. Imagine how Everton would transform the city if we won the league again. Or another European trophy. Or even the European Cup, as Peter Johnson had promised. I interviewed a couple of the players. I joined in the banter. I managed to pick up the Everton scarf that Dave Watson was wearing. The same scarf he'd been wearing when he accepted the FA Cup from the Prince of Wales the day before. Perhaps he'd never taken it off. Perhaps he'd slept with it. Perhaps I should find its rightful owner? Nah. Perhaps I should keep it, more like. Years later, I lost it.

Back in the office at Old Hall Street, I was immediately presented with a dilemma. Perhaps the same dilemma Howard Kendall was presented with after winning the league title with Everton in 1987. Or perhaps not. But the question was the same. Should I stay or should I go? John Griffith, the *Echo* editor, offered me the chance to stay on *The Evertonian* for the following season – to make it a permanent position. I declined. To this day, it's a career decision I look back on with regret. But back then, I was still a fledgling journalist. I wanted more news under my belt. I knew I could come back to sport. And there was a sense of having been there and done it. Don't get me wrong, I loved every second of 'working' on *The Evertonian*. Of 'working' at Bellefield and Goodison Park. It was a dream but a real one. A real dream that actually happened. But it was time to snap out of the dream and begin building my journalism career. So I went back into news.

Now, news in Liverpool is not exactly a bad option. In fact it's a great job. And sport – or namely football – plays a very large part in it. In my early days on the *Echo*, even before the launch of *The Evertonian*, I was thrust in at the football deep end and thrust on to the front page. Not just my byline but my ugly mug.

Brian Clough, the Nottingham Forest manager, had made some insensitive and ill-considered comments about the Hillsborough disaster. He said that Liverpool fans were to blame for the tragedy. And of course, his Nottingham Forest team had been Liverpool's opponents on that awful day five years before. Clough's comments were hurtful. Not just to Liverpool fans but to the whole of Merseyside. They would have been hurtful anyway. But the fact that his son Nigel was a Liverpool player at the time made them really sting.

Being the new boy, I was despatched to Melwood to get a reaction from Nigel Clough. None of the seasoned hacks would walk into the bear pit like that. So send a junior reporter. Send a junior photographer. It was the end of a training session and I waited and waited and waited for Clough Junior to emerge from the changing rooms. John Barnes came out and joked with the assembled media. He wondered why no one wanted to interview him any more. 'Probably because you're fat and past it.' I thought it. Didn't say it. Robbie Fowler appeared. Steve McManaman. Boyhood Blues. 'Traitors.' Again. Thought it, didn't say it. Ian Rush. David James. Neil Ruddock. Jamie Redknapp. Phil Babb. Okay, we'd gone from the sublime to the ridiculous now. But where was Nigel Clough?

Suddenly he appeared and he knew what was coming. He knew because I'd tried to grab him on his way in. Now, he was single- minded. He headed for his car, head down. My photographer, Andy Teebay – another raw *Echo* recruit thrust into the lions' den – was positioned nearby. So I grabbed my chance with Clough Junior. I reintroduced myself. I explained again that we wanted a reaction to his father's comments. I asked for his response.

'It's not a good time to say anything,' Nigel said. 'It just tends to make things worse.'

Perfect. Not just a 'no comment'. A quite elaborate 'no comment'. More than enough for me to make something of. And unbeknown to me, Andy had snapped not just Nigel – but ME with Nigel. A look of pleading agony on my face. As if to say, 'Please, Nigel. Please say something.'

The story appeared on the front page of that night's *Echo*. The headline:

LEAVE ME OUT OF IT
Soccer star Nigel Clough today refused to be drawn
into the outrage over his father's Hillsborough
outburst.

And so it went on. I'd asked Nigel for his response on his way into training and got a fairly brisk 'no comment'. I waited for him and asked him again when he came out. This time I got a bit more. And I got my story.

There's no doubting that news journalism is like a drug. Whereas sport allows you to indulge your passions, news allows you that surge of adrenaline. I went to work in the *Echo*'s Wirral district office, with Martin.

Both of us operating from our respective bedrooms. His in Bebington, mine in Prenton, just around the corner from Tranmere Rovers' ground. We'd cover inquests. The council. Fatal fires. Car crashes. Gas explosions. Ian Rush's decision to quit Liverpool.

Exactly. It was things like that which occasionally jumped out. Occasionally lifted the job out of the humdrum and on to the front pages. Into the spotlight.

I was woken one morning by a phone call from my news editor, Red nose John Thompson. Ridiculous tache. Ridiculous team. Good guy. He told me there was a rumour that Ian Rush would be leaving Liverpool. There'd been talk about it in some of the nationals. Please could I go and get the story?

Errrrr ... okay.

So I did. I drove to Caldy, where Rushie owned a giant gated house on top of a big hill, overlooking the Dee estuary and into north Wales. I got there at just before 8 o'clock. Just before the school run. And I buzzed the intercom.

'Errr, hello?' (That was Rushie, not me.)

'Hi Ian. Neil Roberts from the *Echo*. Wondered if I could get a quick interview about whether you'll be leaving Liverpool.'

'Not right now you can't, no.'

My heart sank. But then Rushie continued:

'Gotta take the kids to school. Do it when I come back.'

And fair play to him, he was good as his word. Yes this might have been the guy who once scored four times at Goodison Park in a 5-0 win for Liverpool, the biggest derby defeat of my lifetime. This might have been the guy who scored more goals against Everton than against any other team. This might have been the best striker in the league who once supported Everton but instead turned into a true legend for our most bitter rivals. But fair play to him. I respected him. Not sure who I had to blame for the headline in the *Echo* though.

THE GREATEST
Liverpool soccer legend Ian Rush today spoke
emotionally of his decision to head out of Anfield and
said: 'I'll be leaving the greatest club in the world'.

Never let it said that I could not be dispassionate. Despite my passions. But that headline was pretty subjective. And it certainly wasn't my doing. Even so, Rushie gave me one of the most memorable interviews of my life in those few minutes. He gave me a genuine news exclusive.

> Liverpool want me to stay but I want to play and thankfully I have come to an amicable arrangement with Roy Evans. I don't even think the other players know about it yet.

Well they did now. The whole world did now. And I was the Johnny on the spot, just like Rushie himself had been so many times in opposing penalty areas – Everton's chief among them. Colin Lane, my photographer, got a picture of me with Rushie as my shorthand worked overtime to take down everything he said. Ian Rush had announced he was leaving Liverpool. And I got the story. Me. An Everton supporter.

Of course such stories were rare when you were working the Wirral patch. But there was genuine news too. I went to Dunblane, the scene of a terrible gun massacre in a school, because a five-year- old from Wirral moved up there and survived the shootings – two bullets passing clean through his body.

I covered murders. Court cases. Human interest stories. Tragedies. But I had to fight a constant tug of war inside myself. News or sport? News or sport? And it was a dilemma which would continue.

Ken Rogers was the *Liverpool Echo* sports editor. Like me, he was a True Blue. And he could clearly see that I was battling some inner career demons over which direction I should go in. He'd been my boss when I worked on *The Evertonian*. He was going to be my boss again. Because he met me in a pub in Oxton in Birkenhead and he asked me to be the Tranmere Rovers reporter. More than that, I'd have to double up as a general sports reporter when required.

So I went back to the sports desk. I interviewed the England manager Terry Venables on the phone. I even managed to get a few words with Tommy Lawton, now 76 and not in the rudest of health, from his care home in Nottingham. Sadly, I no longer have a record of what he said to me and I'm not even sure how I used it in the paper. But even a minute or two on the phone with Tommy Lawton was worth recording in this book. This was the man who was told he would 'never be as good as Dixie'when he got on the bus to Goodison, having arrived in Liverpool from Burnley. The man who scored 65 goals in 87 games for Everton and was just as good for Chelsea and Arsenal. The man who scored a goal a game for England. The man who almost WAS as good as Dixie. And that was saying something.

Within days of that brief phone call,I was sitting next to Liverpool's old striker John Aldridge on the Tranmere team bus during a pre- season tour of Ireland. I was ghostwriting Aldo's *Football Echo* column every week. I was interviewing former Evertonians like Pat Nevin and Gary Stevens, now Tranmere players. And now Tranmere weren't the Fourth Division rubbish I remembered from my earliest first- hand football experiences in 1980. They were First Division now. First Division rubbish.

A lot happened in a short space of time. One player literally ripped the shirt off my back during that pre-season tour. He thought I was taping the players' private conversations. As if they were that important. "I don't trust that c***," he said, as my buttons went flying. There was I, shirt ripped, bare-chested and not a wire-tap in sight. What a surprise. Who said footballers weren't the brightest.

But there were more enlightened moments. Pat Nevin would speak to me about Everton. And music. And poetry. And then there was Kevin Sheedy. Ah yes, Kevin Sheedy. My boyhood hero. The cultured left foot on Everton's left flank. The man who performed so much magic when Everton ruled the football world. Now he was John Aldridge's assistant manager at Tranmere. He had so much to give football. Sadly, he didn't have so much to say in interview.

Either way, my Rovers return was all over in ten matches. But for several weeks, I ploughed a lonely furrow up and down the country. It was a life on the motorway. A life of pokey press rooms in pokey, run-down grounds. A life of waiting outside Victorian football terraces, and among Victorian terraces, for journeymen players to board team buses. A life in bed and breakfast hotels. I went to Southend and Shrewsbury. Bradford and Huddersfield. And Swindon and Oldham, where the respective managers were Steve McMahon and Graeme Sharp. Where I got my only chances to interview Steve McMahon and Graeme Sharp. Funny how football throws up such ironies. Coincidence? Fate? Luck? Who knows. But I was something of a lucky charm for Tranmere. In those ten matches they notched up five wins and three draws with only two defeats. And I met everybody. Everybody who was ever anyone to Everton. Except Peter Reid.

The Song We Were Singing

All around Prenton Park there were giant posters sporting my spotty ugly mug. I was the Tranmere correspondent. Read all about it in the *Echo*. Or something like that. One night, a vandal scaled a lamp post on Borough Road in Birkenhead and stole one of those posters. It was a Bebington taxi driver called Leo Roberts. 'Dirty Leo'. Dad's cousin. The poster turned into a present for my nanna. She was probably the only person in the world who'd be so delighted with such a gift.

And it soon became a keepsake. Because I abandoned Tranmere for a life of crime. No, I didn't turn scally. Didn't go on the rob or start dealing drugs. I became the *Liverpool Echo* crime reporter. John 'Thommo' Thompson poached me back to news from Tranmere Rovers. The crime brief was incredible. I was told it was the best job on the paper. And journalism-wise, it was. I was mixing with police officers and criminals. Sometimes the police officers WERE the criminals. That's what made the job fun. One of my best contacts, Detective Chief Inspector Elly

Davies, trod that line himself. A great copper. Also a convicted criminal. He went to jail for taking a ten grand bung to fudge an attempted murder charge ... he somehow got caught up in the tangled web woven by Interpol's 'Target One', the Liverpool crime lord Curtis Warren. Curtis Warren, listed by *The Sunday Times* as one of Britain's richest men. Curtis Warren, 'property developer'. He had actually built his empire on drugs and firearms.

I covered the Curtis Warren story from start to finish. I went to Holland for his trial. I should have written a book about him. My opposite number from the *Daily Post* got in before me. But I got scoop after scoop. A string of exclusives. And even on the day I eventually left Liverpool, I'd brought in the story of how £1 million was found buried in a garden in West Derby. Not Bellefield, thankfully. But the garden of one of Curtis Warren's henchmen. It had been found as part of the investigation into Elly Davies.

The city of Liverpool was no longer just my spiritual home, it was my actual home. Okay, I was still living 'across the water' but my day-to-day work was on Old Hall Street. And Liverpool offered me everything I wanted. Football, booze, girls and music. All right, this was hardly the time of Beatlemania, but it was during this period that I reconnected with Paul McCartney.

My Beatles senses had been stirred by the recent *Anthology* programmes featuring Paul, George and Ringo with clips of John interspersed. It was the story of all four Beatles, told by all four Beatles. Soon afterwards, Paul released an album called *Flaming Pie*. Because a man on a flaming pie came to John Lennon in a dream and said: 'You are Beatles with an A.' Here was Paul reconnecting with John. Here was my opportunity to reconnect with Paul.

On one track, he wrote about his old musical brother. Someone he'd sit, talk and write music with through the night. It's called 'The Song We Were Singing' and it's the opening track on the *Flaming Pie* album. I didn't buy the record straight away, even though it went straight to the top of the album charts. I bought it from a little independent music shop in Keswick, on a trip to the Lake District with a girlfriend. And so began my reacquaintance with 'the song I was singing'. And while I'd given up on sports journalism, I knew that one day I'd go back to the song I was singing – just as Paul McCartney seemed to be going back to his.

'The Song We Were Singing' signified two more reconnections for me. First, Joe Royle left Everton because Peter Johnson wouldn't let him sign Tore Andre Flo on transfer deadline day in 1997. In truth, Everton had faltered since the cup win. The next season they finished sixth in the league and new record signing Andrei Kanchelskis put in some breathtaking performances on one wing, with Anders Limpar on the other. I was a fully paid-up, signed-up season ticket holder once more. But the sparkle of the previous season wasn't quite there. And by 1997 we were on the downward spiral once more, despite the addition of yet another record signing in Nick Barmby, who we re- established as an England regular but who would one day betray the Blue cause, confess a lifelong love for Liverpool, and scuttle off into the Red corner where he lasted about five minutes.

So Joe Royle left the club in a dispute over transfer policy. His predecessor Howard Kendall had left for the same reason. So who would take the helm at Goodison Park? None other than Howard Kendall for his third and final time. That was reconnection number one.

Reconnection number two came in the form of a fax. This was before email. Before the web. Before Facebook and Twitter. We'd only just given up telegrams and the Telex. But one day, the news desk fax machine ticked into gear with its printer clicking out Times New Roman type on to shiny white fax paper. From out of the blue. From six years ago. A message from Dawn. Wondering how I was, wanting to be friends again. Reconnecting with me. Funnily enough, it was the song I'd been singing too – though I hadn't dared admit it to myself.

Everything in that *Flaming Pie* album seemed to speak to me. From: 'He's just a young boy, looking for a way to find love', to 'It was written that I would love you, from the moment I opened my eyes.'

Yes it's that saccharine style of McCartney's that alienated so many and found him 'treading the line between hip and naff ', as an unnamed rock legend is quoted as saying. But McCartney has that ability. Maybe not Lennon's lyrical ability but an ability to connect. To speak with simplicity. With simple words and simple melodies. At his worst, maybe he is naff. But at his best, there's nobody to touch him. Nobody.

And I found meaning even if there wasn't any. I read things into lyrics that I felt must have applied to me. I was soul-searching. Thinking about what to do with my life and where to go with it. I'd lost two loves in my life, and in truth, I'd given them both up. Dawn and Everton. Of course, I'd never actually give up Everton. But I gave up the job. And already it was starting to hurt. I gave up the girl, too. And likewise, that was hurting. It had been hurting for a long time.

So I'd gone back to the egg with my switch from sport back into news. I'd gone back to the song I was singing. Now I needed a rebirth. So I went back to Bermuda.

Here Comes The Sun

Gone Troppo

My job interview for the *Royal Gazette* in Bermuda consisted of two questions. I was talking to David L. White, OBE. On the phone. The editor. The same editor who'd been in place when I was a child in that newsroom, tapping away at a typewriter beside my father's desk. Only I wasn't getting paid for that.

'How much notice do you have to give?' he asked. Followed by: 'And can you ride a moped? We've had terrible trouble with British journalists who can't ride mopeds.'

The job was mine and I was returning to Bermuda for the first time in 14 years. It was more than half my life ago that I was last there. During that period, George Harrison's album *Gone Troppo* inspired images of life in the sun. I heard it in Bermuda first time round. Well this was my voyage of rediscovery. This was me 'going troppo'.

I didn't really know what to expect of Bermuda. I knew it was a tiny island. I knew it had just 60,000 people. And I knew there was a speed limit of just 20 miles an hour. Even so, I knew I'd have to be careful on that moped. But it had some dark memories for me as well as some sunny ones. This is where my parents separated. This is where my family divided. This is where I lost two of my young school friends – one to a brain haemorrhage in Wales, the other to a speedboat accident in local waters. This is where I broke my arm as a seven-year-old and had six operations to fix it. This is where my sister Caroline fractured her skull after being knocked down by a van when she was only four. This is where I lived when my grandad died. This is where we said goodbye to our father, not knowing when we'd see him again. This is where my sister and I left him. 'All those years ago.' It was like listening to George's musical tribute to John.

So why go back to this 'Devil's Isle', as it's known? Why reopen that closet, for the bare bones of that skeleton to come tumbling out? Because it gave me the happiest times of my childhood. My happiest times away from Bromborough. This is where I began collecting football programmes. This is where I dreamt of being Paolo Rossi after the 1982 World Cup Final. This is where I pulled on my first Everton top. This is where I met Duncan McKenzie when he toured with a visiting team from America. It's also where I discovered the entire catalogue of Beatles records. It's where I learnt to play the guitar. And it's where I sat on the porch with my father, playing Beatles and John Lennon songs together, somehow hoping the world's greatest musician, songwriter and person would come waltzing up to us and ask for a cup of tea. Or a lemonade. These were the memories which drew me back. This is what I was looking to rediscover.

One of my colleagues at the *Gazette* was a young Bermudian called Patrick Burgess. Like me, Patrick loved his sport. He loved cricket, particularly. But probably not quite as much as he loved the Beatles. I shared the grief with him when Linda McCartney died of breast cancer six months after I arrived on the island. I mused with him over how 'Blackbird' became 'Bluebird', and tried to work out if magical Paul had just become whimsical Paul. We discussed the various merits and demerits of all four Beatles. Paul may not quite have been John. But Ringo wasn't even the best drummer in the band. Et cetera. We talked about the mystical Beatle. About George Harrison. About the Indian music. About 'Something'. About 'Here Comes The Sun'. About 'My Sweet Lord'. And of course, we talked about John Lennon. And about his visit to Bermuda back in 1980, in those months before he was murdered.

That 1980 summer, my dad and I had tried so hard to meet John. We went wandering around the estate where we thought he might have been staying. We took a trip out to St George's to look for his yacht, only to find *Strawberry Fields* – which turned out not to be his. We sat there on our porch playing into the Bermuda breeze, hoping John Lennon's vocals might somehow come floating back to us. The near miss was perhaps not so painful for me at the age of eight. I had no concept of how rare an opportunity it might be. 'To meet a Beatle? Oh that'd be cool. But hey, there'll be other opportunities. If not now, some day.' Of course. Easy. Yeah, right. But for my father ... to be so close to a man he'd admired all his life; to know there was every chance of bumping into him in Bermuda where everybody knew everybody; to know that one of his best pals had actually been drinking with him in a nightclub in Hamilton ... now that was cruel.

I relayed the story to Patrick in the office one day.

'That sounds pretty tough,' he said. He looked at me. He paused.

He said 'Errrm'.

He continued: 'Of course, I met him.'

What!? Pause. Shake head vigorously. Are ears deceiving me? Did he say what I think he said? Come back to senses.

'What?'

'I met John Lennon.' 'You met John Lennon?' 'Yeah, it was cool.'

I'll bloody bet it was cool. Lucky, lucky sod. Lucky bastard. 'How?'

Patrick relayed the story. His brother was a waiter at Elbow Beach Hotel and John would frequently enjoy the paradise which Elbow Beach itself had to offer. He'd sit there on a sunlounger, under a parasol, reading a book. Acoustic guitar by his side, just in case he got the urge. Just in case the creative juices started flowing.

One day Patrick's brother came home and casually mentioned that John from the Beatles was hanging out on the beach. That he was being served by him. That he tipped quite well and that he was a nice guy. Patrick couldn't believe it. It was probably a case of: what!?; shake head vigorously; check if ears being deceitful; come back to senses.

Patrick went to the beach the next day, nervously clutching a copy of *Sergeant Pepper*. By Patrick's account, John saw him coming and looked up to peer over his Windsor-style spectacles. He put the young boy at ease.

'Hello there,' he said.'

'Hello Mr Lennon,' said a young Patrick.

'I see you have a copy of *Sergeant Pepper*. Do you like that album?' 'Yes, very much.'

'What's your favourite song from it?' '"Fixing A Hole".'

Gulp. Looking back, that's probably not what John expected to hear. He probably thought Patrick would say 'A Day In The Life' or 'Being For The Benefit Of Mr Kite' or 'Lucy In The Sky With Diamonds'. Not some Paul song. Not some song from his musical partner. His musical brother. His friend, but his arch-rival. His some- time musical enemy. His nemesis. The brother he'd fallen out with.

'Oh,' said John, according to Patrick's story. 'Why do you like that one?'

'Because it reminds me of how my family has had to pull together through some difficult times.'

John smiled. John understood. John told Patrick that music was a good thing. He told him it was good to like music. He told him that music meant something. Then John signed something for Patrick. Not the album, which young Patrick didn't think to offer up. But some scrap of paper. And then Patrick turned and left. He'd met John Lennon when I was probably just a couple of miles away, looking for John Lennon. Lucky, lucky sod. Oh to be able to meet an actual Beatle. A John Lennon or a Paul McCartney.

Some weeks later, I relayed this story to a new love in my life as we relaxed on a boat owned by her family in the Fairylands area of the Bermuda parish of Pembroke. We swam, we drank, we fished. We talked about John.

'Yeah, he stayed over there,' said Kim. 'My mum saw him too.'

Mersey Blues

Of course, when you're living 3,000 miles from Goodison Park it's even harder to get there than when you're living 200 miles away. So apart from some early games in the first part of the season – including my one and only pilgrimage to Hillsborough – I didn't see Everton in the 1997–98 season, except for on the telly at the Robin Hood pub in Bermuda. In that pub, every Saturday morning meant a cooked breakfast and a live Premier League match. And uncomfortably often, that involved Everton.

I say 'uncomfortably' because we were only shown so much by virtue of the fact that every one of our games was a relegation scrap.

I'd settled on the Robin Hood because they liked showing Premier League football. Not Scottish Premier League football. Once in Flanagan's on Front Street, largely frequented by Scotsmen, someone had the audacity to turn the Rangers game off in favour of the Merseyside derby. It didn't go down well. Rangers against St Mirren or someone was far more important than Everton against Liverpool. I wouldn't have minded so much except that this was a game Everton won. Danny Cadamarteri's scene-bursting goal which saw him catapulted into the Goodison spotlight as the next great thing. The next great thing that never was. But on that day, the next great thing. And on that day, he was relegated by the Rangers match. So I retreated to the English pub ... and I saw a lot of Everton's season.

If Howard Kendall had been magical in his first incarnation, he was simply effective in his second. But his third spell in charge of the club he loved, and the club to which he'd brought so much glory, was just a case of his heart ruling his head. He'd once talked of a love affair with Manchester City and a marriage to Everton. Well he'd been married to Everton twice before, and like Elizabeth Taylor and Richard Burton, he really should have learnt his lesson. Once a love is lost, don't go back. Don't go back.

As well as promising Evertonians hope of winning the European Cup, Peter Johnson promised Evertonians that we'd never again endure the last-day drama of 1994. That never-to-be-forgotten comeback against Wimbledon would be a one-off. We wouldn't put our supporters through it again. The agony of final-day survival would not be something Everton would inflict on their supporters again.

Except they did. In May 1998 we were back in trouble again, and this time, instead of being at Goodison Park to lend my support, I was watching on from the helpless confines of the Robin Hood bar. We were playing Coventry at home. Bolton were playing Chelsea away. Bizarrely, Chelsea had a role to play once more, just as they did four years previously when they played Sheffield United. But this time the permutation was simple. We needed a better result than Bolton to stay up and send Bolton down. Getting the same result as Bolton was no good. If both teams won, drew or lost, it would be the Toffees in the second tier. Not the Trotters.

Howard Kendall had done it all with Everton. Won league titles, won FA Cups, won a European trophy. Turned us into the best team in Europe. Now here he was, the great man who'd bought me a drink and spoken so passionately about Everton and his fortunes with the club when I interviewed him three years before, standing on the brink of getting us relegated. Of sending us down. It was more than the football gods would allow, surely. It was agony. There were twists and there were turns. We took the lead when Gareth Farrelly wrote his own footnote in Everton's history. An unremarkable player in Everton folklore except for this one sublime moment – a 25-yard strike which gave us the lead and all but secured our survival. But still we were on tenterhooks. The thousands at Goodison. Me and a handful of others in the Robin Hood. And, I guess, millions more watching around the world. With the clock ticking down, Everton were winning 1-0. And at Stamford Bridge, it was still 0-0 between Chelsea and Bolton. This meant that Everton would be relegated if Coventry scored a late equaliser. But for now, we were safe.

The clock continued ticking down. Then that Coventry equaliser came. And who should score it? Who would be the man who might destroy Howard Kendall's career? Who would dare leave that man's football pedigree in tatters, a fate he would never deserve? Who would dare break the hearts of Evertonians everywhere – and bring to his knees the man who'd possibly done more than anyone for Everton

Football Club? Dion Dublin. The man who prompted Howard Kendall's resignation after his second spell as manager. The man who Kendall wanted to sign for Everton, only for the board to turn him down. Was Dion Dublin on the brink of relegating Everton? It was pure tension.

Bolton had gone behind to two late goals at Chelsea. But Everton would be relegated if Coventry struck a goal in injury time. They didn't. It finished 1-1. Everton survived by the skin of their teeth and the width of a goal line. Because earlier in the season, in a goalless draw at the new Reebok Stadium, Bolton were denied the points that would have kept them up at Everton's expense. They had a goal disallowed against Everton, even though the ball crossed the line. Bolton, my former girlfriend's team, suffered relegation. They went down with Barnsley and Crystal Palace. We were safe again. But we suffered too. And Howard Kendall suffered by losing his job. He resigned and returned for a brief spell managing in Greece, knowing he had taken Everton right to the edge of oblivion, only avoiding relegation on goal difference. Those pitch invasions at Goodison. Pitch invasions prompted by the delight of having saved our Premier League skins. First in 1994 and again in 1998. Just like that pitch invasion back in 1984 at Highbury, when we made it to our first cup final in 14 years. Only this time, the reasons for such delirium were just not good enough. They were not in the Everton motto. They were not *Nil Satis Nisi Optimum*.

By the start of the following season, Walter Smith was the new manager of Everton. He came with a rich pedigree, having won everything there was to win for Rangers in a league where only two teams ever COULD win anything. And there was the stumbling block. Everton, themselves, continued to stumble. I saw them twice that season. The first time was at Charlton, where Everton were playing at the Valley for the first time in goodness knows how long. The Valley had been closed for years, overgrown and run down. A famous, derelict old football ground. Home, once, to the biggest attendance in domestic league football. It had been left to rack and ruin. But Charlton summoned all the spirit that only genuine football supporters seem able to summon. And they rescued their club. And they rescued their ground. And now Everton were back there at the Valley. I was back in England on holiday and dad and I had only managed to get tickets with the Charlton supporters. We decided against taking our scarves. We decided against engaging in too much banter with the locals.

Then the tannoy announcer piped up: 'Ladies and gentlemen, for today's game we welcome Everton to the Valley. And we offer a very warm welcome to their players, staff and supporters.' No boos. No jeers. Not even the occasional hand gesture. Not much more than a ripple, but nevertheless applause around the ground. I thought we would be okay. And so it proved. Everton won the match with two goals from Danny Cadamarteri, and I was left with warm feelings for Charlton and their supporters.

A few days later, dad and I went to Goodison to see a 0-0 home draw with Chelsea. It was unremarkable apart from it being the only time I ever saw Marco Materazzi in an Everton jersey and still the only time I've been to Goodison with the chairman too afraid to show his face. Both Materazzi and 'Agent' Peter Johnson achieved a fair amount of football notoriety. Materazzi for his foul abuse of Zinedine Zidane, which provoked a headbutt and a red card for one of the world's greatest ever footballers in the 2006 World Cup Final. And Johnson for selling Duncan Ferguson behind the manager's back.

In the previous home game, and the game before that Charlton match, Everton had beaten Newcastle 1-0 thanks to a penalty from Michael Ball. For me, it was a working holiday as much as anything else and I was working a few casual shifts on the *Sun*. One night, I caught the result. The next morning, I read the fallout. Duncan Ferguson hadn't been playing. Instead, he was being sold by Peter Johnson ... to that night's opponents ... in the boardroom. Behind closed doors. Out of earshot and eyeshot of the manager. Walter Smith was conducting team affairs from the touchline when the deed was done. He didn't have the faintest idea of the back-room dealings which saw Johnson sell our talisman for a club record £8 million. Apparently he needed to balance the books. Apparently he'd spent what Everton didn't have. Apparently Ferguson was dispensable. According to Agent Johnson.

Immediately, Peter Johnson became *persona non grata* at Goodison Park. And Walter Smith secured his greatest victory in an otherwise fairly uneventful four seasons at Everton Football Club. He got rid of the chairman. He beat Peter Johnson and Bill Kenwright rode to the rescue. And the club has been on a much more stable footing ever since.

Before returning to Bermuda, I had a couple of very important diary dates. Apart from those two Everton matches, that is. One was to meet up with Dawn for the first time in seven years. The other was to be interviewed for a television series called *Mersey Blues*. This was a fly-on-the-wall documentary series, screened on BBC2, about life on the streets with Merseyside Police. One of the crew's hosts for these programmes was a certain DCI Elmore Davies. My old mate Elly. The top copper who'd gone bent and took a bribe to damage an attempted murder charge. Elly was trapped by Merseyside Police's internal investigations unit while the series was being filmed. In fact, unwittingly, I'd called Elly at home around Christmas 1996 when he was actually under arrest. I simply wanted to see if there was anything going on but mostly I wanted just to have a chat and to wish him all the best for Christmas. 'I know why you're ringing me,' he said. The fact is, I didn't.

But I did know the man, the copper, the personality. In the year in which I got to know him, I got to know him pretty well. I went to his office. I went on raids co-ordinated by his team. I went to his office. We went for lunch. We went for drinks. I liked him. He was a laugh. He was a tough, old-school copper. He was a true, archetypal, old-fashioned detective. A proper dick. He took it too literally, unfortunately. Because Elly got caught red-handed. And the *Mersey Blues* team were there to film it.

I gave them an interview. I told them about my own dealings with Elly. About how his arrest had shocked me as much as anyone. I told them all the anecdotes. About how at his committal hearing at St Helens Magistrates, Elly could barely look at me. About how the senior investigating officer told me he already knew me, even though I didn't know him. About how they'd got my voice on tape because of the wire taps they had running on Elly's phone.

Of all the people to get caught up somewhere deep inside the Curtis Warren crime empire, Elly Davies seemed one of the least likely candidates. On the face of it, anyway. So I spoke to the BBC crew. I gave them my insight. I appeared on the show. And that was my first introduction to television.

A few days later, and I had my second introduction to Dawn. We met at my mother's house. We went for dinner. We had a drink. We kissed on the cheek. It was all very friendly. All very platonic. All very platonic 'plus'. But I had a girlfriend. She had a boyfriend. And I was going back to Bermuda. But the seeds for a future relationship were sown.

Back in Bermuda, the Gone Troppo life continued. The sea, the sun, the sand. The Dark 'n' Stormies, the mopeds, the cricket matches, the rugby matches, the beaches and the golf courses. Playing football with the Italian waiters and watching Everton at the Robin Hood. But after 18 months, enough was enough. I'd lived one dream at *The Evertonian*. I'd lived another in Bermuda. Before long, I heard that my nanna was getting very ill and may not last that much longer. Then the *Liverpool Echo* wanted me to come back. The *News Of The World* wanted to hire me. And once again, Bermuda represented familiar shores to me. That was why I went there. That was why I felt able to leave. I'd gone back to that song. That 'song I was singing'. Now I needed to go back to the familiar shores of England. Back so I could properly reinvent my career. Back so I could watch Everton properly again. Back so I could see Dawn.

The Long And
Winding Road

Heart of the country

The B842 winds for 31 miles through the Mull of Kintyre, a
windswept western Scottish peninsula famous for its rugged
coastline, its remoteness, its beauty, its sheep. And its Paul
McCartney. McCartney made his home away from it all in a
farmhouse near Campbeltown. Oddly but perhaps suitably
enough, it's called Home Farm. The road which leads to its door
carves a path all the way down the east side of the peninsula,
from Lochgilphead in the north, through Ardrishaig and Tarbert
and all the way down to Campbeltown. It always leads you here.
It's the long and winding road.

Around my 28th birthday, my girlfriend Jacqui and I drove
down the long and winding road in search of that remote
farmhouse and that remote Scottish land which also inspired
another of McCartney's better-known ballads. Perhaps not quite
such a good one, but a smash hit nonetheless. The Mull Of
Kintyre is the perfect backdrop to playing 'Let It Be' on a car
stereo. When the wind is lashing down on the windscreen, when
you're stuck behind another tractor, when you're consumed and
confused by the mix of bleakness and beauty. Then just Let It
Be. And roll back the years to 1969.

We stopped at a bed and breakfast beside a golf course. We
chatted to the locals. So where is Paul McCartney's farm? Few
would answer that question. Not out of unfriendliness, but out
of respect for their famous neighbour and his privacy. Finally, I
got one of them to talk.

'Oh it's up that road there, about a mile up,' she pointed. 'Get to the brow of the hill and look down to your left. It's quite a modest little place but that's it. It's called Home Farm. If you get stuck, the postman will probably show you.'

It was generous. She could tell I was interested for genuine reasons. For curiosity rather than to stalk the man, who wouldn't be there anyway. 'He comes up most Easters,' she said. 'You see him driving around in his battered old Range Rover. Very scruffy, he is. All unshaven and wax jacket. You wouldn't recognise him at first. You'd have to look twice. Everybody likes him. He goes down to the beach on the Easter weekend. He gives donkey rides to the kids. He's one of us.'

This was what I wanted to hear. This was the sort of thing that always inspired me about McCartney. How he shunned the limelight despite being one of the most famous men on the planet. How he brought his kids up as normally as possible. How he was unassuming. A down-to-earth sort of guy.

We trundled up towards the farm and sure enough we found it. Indeed, it was a modest place. Well, not exactly humble. Maybe a six-bedroom farmhouse or similar. But in a little valley of fields. Acres and acres of open countryside. Mist rolling in from the sea. Macca's desire was always to be here. And you could see why. This was where he wrote *McCartney*, his first solo album since the Beatles. His eponymous debut album, written on basic home recording equipment here at Home Farm. This is where he also wrote the *Ram* album, with 'Heart Of The Country' as one of a number of standout tracks.

Paul had looked high and low for a home in the country. And the thing is, McCartney's words from 'Heart Of The Country' absolutely typified the Mull of Kintyre. They may be simple. They may not tug at the heartstrings. But his simple words, with a simple ode to country life, reassured me that coming home was the right thing to do. This was the sort of adventure that was impossible in Bermuda. I didn't just come back to the UK to camp out in the bushes by McCartney's house. Okay, I've driven around the village near his Sussex home too. And I've walked by his place in St John's Wood. But stalkerish behaviour? Erm hmm. Clears throat. Errr. No. Well, maybe just a bit. But only in a good way, you understand. I came back to the heart of my own country.

I didn't come back from Bermuda for Beatle-missions. Nor did I just come back from Bermuda for football. Okay, I could hardly watch Everton from that tiny island, except on the big screen in the Robin Hood. But where else was I likely to bump into the England goalkeeper David Seaman while he was out shopping? Where else would my hairdresser – a Scouser whose brother had been Rod Corkhill in *Brookside* – tell me to get down to the Sonesta Hotel because Jamie Redknapp and his pop star girlfriend Louise were there, waiting to get married. (I covered both stories, incidentally. And sold them both to the *Sun*. It was about time they paid up after lifting my quotes from Duncan Ferguson.)

No, I came back from Bermuda to lay down proper roots in the heart of my own country. To build my career again. To build my life. And just like anyone's life, mine has always seemed to be a journey down a long and winding road. I stayed at my mother's house in Dorset. With her, her husband and their eight-year-old son: my brother Matthew. I stayed with my best friend Adam, an Oxford United supporter who took me to the Manor Ground – that scene of Everton's great turnaround (whatever Howard Kendall told me) to see them play Everton in a midweek League Cup tie. And I eventually got myself a little flat in London so I could take my job at the *News Of The World*.

The problem with working on the *News Of The Screws*, for me, was the lengths you'd have to go to to nail their kind of story. Trust me, I have never had any desire to live in Swansea, lovely though I'm sure it is. But after I did a big exposé one week on a sex cult, they asked me to infiltrate. It wasn't the six months of sex that bothered me too much. It was the thought of living in Swansea. No thanks.

So it quickly became apparent that the *Screws* wasn't for me and I abandoned Fort Wapping and went into a television career instead, all guns blazing. I worked on regional television news programmes in the south-east, firstly at Meridian and then at the BBC. Both jobs were based in Kent. In the heart of the country. Transmitting to Paul McCartney's Sussex home. 'Get me an interview with Paul McCartney and I'll give you the whole show,' said Alan Rook, my programme editor at Meridian.

So I tried. I rang up McCartney's press man, Geoff Baker. I began calling him about various story ideas. I struck up a telephone relationship with him. I didn't harangue, but gently inquired. But every time the answer was no. Every time, Paul didn't have enough time to do it. Or so Geoff said.

I tried again at the BBC. McCartney had done some songwriting workshops for BBC Television and he was featuring in an advert for them, which showed him cleverly playing around with the pace and instrumentation on 'Band On The Run'so it sounded like a completely different song. Could this be the basis for an interview? An interview for the BBC staff magazine? 'Sorry, no,' said Geoff Baker. I just couldn't get past him. Every avenue was being shut off. He said it was not the sort of thing Paul would be interested in.

Everything I tried, failed. Every time I knocked on the door, it was closed in my face. There was no chance of getting an interview with Paul McCartney. I wasn't a music journalist. I was a news journalist. At best, I was a sports journalist. And Paul McCartney wasn't someone I could just ring up and sit down with over a cup of tea in the kitchen or a pint of lager in the corner of some bar. He wasn't Graham Stuart. He wasn't Howard Kendall, even. This was Paul McCartney we were talking about. One of the most famous men on the planet.

Then I heard that Macca had a book coming out. A collection of paintings he'd done. And he was to do a signing session at Waterstone's on Piccadilly. It started at 10 o'clock or something, one weekday morning. So I took the day off. I thought I'd get there very early. I rolled up at 5 o'clock. And the memories came flooding back. The memories of queuing up in those streets in the shadow of Goodison Park, waiting overnight in the cold and getting so close to the ticket office only for the shutters to come slamming down before I could get an FA Cup Final ticket. Surely this couldn't happen again. But it did. There was I, clutching my Tesco carrier bag with my copy of *Ram* hoping to get it signed. There was I waiting with the other mugs. Only to get nowhere near him before he 'left the building', like Elvis. Actually, I did get reasonably close. Because when Paul did leave to get into his chauffeur-driven car, he was literally mobbed. And the picture of the hordes surrounding him appeared in the *Sun* the next day. You could barely make me out. But I was there.

Irony of ironies. Meridian had a reporter there. All I needed to do was phone up and I'd have known. I'd have jumped right to the front. I'd have met Paul McCartney. But I didn't. I didn't shake his hand. Didn't get to say hi. Didn't get anything signed. I rang Geoff Baker and told him what had happened. He expressed sympathy. Told me to send him a couple of my CDs. Told me he'd get them signed for me. I never got my CDs back. I never phoned Geoff back. I'd given up on any chance of meeting Paul McCartney.

It was just like when dad and I were looking out for John back in Bermuda, first time around. Back in 1980. It was a case of nearly, but not quite. Perhaps the harder you looked, the less you had to find. My friend Patrick just waltzed up to John Lennon on a deserted Bermuda beach. A girlfriend's mother had some chit-chat with him. And dad's colleague at the *Gazette* spent a night drinking with him and ended up with a world exclusive. And my friend at the BBC, James Clarke, just so happened to have a similar story. It wasn't his personal story, but that of a friend of his.

'She was driving in Sussex one day and she broke down,' he said. 'The car behind stopped and two guys got out to see if they could help. It was George Harrison and Ringo Starr. They'd been to Paul's place and they were just heading home.'

So some girl just so happened to get a puncture or blow a couple of spark plugs on some country road in Sussex. And as she flipped her bonnet lid, she looked up to see George Harrison and Ringo Starr cheerily peering round the side of the car to see if they could help her out. It was probably all thumbs-up and 'all right lass'. She literally just bumped into two Beatles in the countryside. As you do.

The nearest I came was to see Paul McCartney in concert for the first time. Twice, within the space of a few days. First at the National Exhibition Centre in Birmingham and then at Earls Court. I went with my dad and my sister. I went with Dawn, who I'd now rekindled a relationship with. It was an incredible experience finally to be under the same roof as Paul McCartney. Even though I was probably 150 yards away with 20,000 people between me and him.

Another Rovers Return

The way was clear for me to try again with Dawn after she broke up with her boyfriend. And after I broke up with Jacqui. Or rather, after she broke up with me. It was a painful period in my life. A period in my life when everything I touched seemed to just crumble away. Disintegrate. Turn to dust.

I resorted to poetry. It was cathartic. Something I could do to lose myself on a sheet of A4. To lose myself in some meaningless words. Meaningless to most people but full of meaning to me. I became a wistful, mournful amateur poet. Writing miserable lines about a miserable life. Whenever I was down, I got the pen and paper out. Every poet needs something to inspire them. And for most, I think it's pain. The pain of a death or of a lost love. The pain you can only feel during life's lowest points.

For me, one such low point came at Goodison Park on 27 January 2001. Everton were playing Tranmere Rovers in the FA Cup at Goodison. The last time this had happened, my dad's old pal Kenny Beamish was playing for Tranmere. Back in the late 1960s, it provoked in my father a sort of agony. An agony that one of his best mates was playing at Goodison Park. An agony that it could have been him. It should have been him. An agony not even deadened by a comfortable victory for Everton.

This game provoked agony of a different sort. Paul Rideout, Everton's FA Cup winner in 1995, was in the Tranmere team in 2001. And he was the architect of their extraordinary triumph that day. And our dismal demise. My sister, my father and I ... along with a couple of dad's cousins ...were in the Goodison crowd. And we lost the game 3-0. I hate to patronise Tranmere because I hold genuine affection for them, but Rovers were our little cousins from across the water. This was not supposed to happen. In fact, re-reading that sentence I want to delete it. Because doubtless it IS patronising. The way Liverpool supporters patronise Everton was perhaps the way Everton were now patronising Tranmere.

This was how far we had sunk on that day in the fourth round of the cup. And the result was that we got spanked out of the FA Cup. Tranmere Rovers were patronised. So Everton were humiliated.

It was agony. Real agony. It hurt. It caused pain. I tried to escape the sense of it at the full-time whistle, when I aimed a badly-timed wisecrack at my father. 'This is all your fault,' I told him. 'Why did you bring me up to be an Everton supporter?'

It was a joke. Black humour, yes, but a joke nevertheless, not that my father took it that way. He was hurting too – I could see it in his eyes. So it went over his head. It went right through him. And he looked right through me. Tranmere, a club he had even more affection for than me, whose ground he had starred at by scoring a late penalty winner for Port Sunlight in an amateur match, had just totally turned the tables on an Everton side. Tranmere, who I'd covered as their correspondent for the *Echo*, and where giant posters of me lined the streets, had humiliated us. Had wrecked our season. Had heaped agony on Evertonians everywhere. It inspired me to write a poem.

Everton Forever
by Neil Roberts

Tales of greatness map the legend of this place.
It's a story about style
Based on passion, but with grace.
It's still in the air
And it's still on the walls.
But the sounds have now gone,
Drowned out by catcalls
While the pains of today paint the looks on every face.
The blue shirts disappear down the tunnel of despair.
Another 90 minutes Without an ounce of flair.
It's a weary trudge down To a lonely dressing room
As the thousands who left early
Darken the shadows and the gloom
And repeat to themselves: 'They don't care. They don't care.'

BLUES & BEATLES

The arena stands empty as the floodlights start to fade.
Another side has come
And left the home team in the shade.
The players have now gone
While the fans try to solve the riddle.
But one man still remains,
He's the man out in the middle ...
A man who's seen it all in this place where dreams were made.

He cuts a lonely figure as he patches up the grass,
The turf no more surrounded
By the howling, baying mass.
There was Dean, there was Lawton,
There was Young, there was Ball.
Even years later,
There were men who'd walk tall
But today there were jeers for a team without their class.

The gates are all locked and the place has now gone dark.
The man starts walking home
But the facts, for him, are stark.
Through these streets around the ground
There was once a sense of pride.
Now there's not a soul in sight
Just a place for fans to hide
From the outlook just as bleak back inside Goodison Park.

But tomorrow's just another working day, that's his thought
And there's still that time
We beat United five-nought.
We may not get back to Reid
Or Sharp or Trevor Steven
But let's think for a minute
And let's keep all things even.
There's more to this place than any name we might have bought.

He thinks towards the future and he wonders what it will bring.
Maybe soon we'll find a team

That can make the thousands sing.
Once again there could be magic
And even if we move
We'll always have a home
Where our greatness was once proved
With spirit and with dashing and with dazzling on the wing.

So to the groundsman, to the keeper, to the man without a name
There's more to this club
Than a team that is so tame.
Everton forever.
It's something to draw the breath.
And he remembers well that rival
Who said: 'Football, life or death.'
One misguided phrase because, in fact, it's just a game.

It summed up exactly how I felt. And even in the anguish of being dumped out of the cup by Tranmere, I couldn't resist a little dig at Bill Shankly's most famous saying. That football wasn't a matter of life and death. It was more important than that. Even I wouldn't dare to besmirch that man's memory – I know exactly what he meant by that. And it's a beautiful, ironic phrase. But he is the person who also said there were two teams in Liverpool – Liverpool and Liverpool reserves. He is the man who also said that if Everton were playing at the bottom of his garden, he would draw the curtains. I could hardly blame him that day at Goodison. I'd have drawn the curtains myself, if I could. But this was my opportunity to vent my football spleen. And to remind myself that too often, we take football as a matter of life and death. It isn't a matter of life and death. It feels like it's more important than that. But it isn't. It's just a game.

Little more than a year later, Walter Smith lost his job as Everton manager. He was a decent enough man and he did a decent enough job. Yes, we fought relegation battles. But we always escaped comfortably enough. Well, by that I mean not on the last day of the season. Maybe a few games before the end of the season. But Walter Smith OBE (like David L. White OBE) assembled teams that were unimaginative, uninventive.

Sometimes we would seem to play with defenders all over the park. It was utilitarian. Dull football, only occasionally lifted by a bullet Duncan Ferguson header or a thumping of West Ham (usually). Bizarrely enough, there was the odd headline-grabbing signing, but normally of someone who was past their best; someone like Paul Gascoigne or David Ginola. Past their best like Everton. Walter Smith had represented another false dawn.

Bill Kenwright, a loyal man, finally decided it was time for a spring clean at Goodison in March 2002. Walter Smith was his friend. But he called him into his office and he explained that it just wasn't working. It was a mark of Walter Smith – in fact of both men – that they immediately sat down to discuss who would be the best option for Everton going forward. Walter recommended his young compatriot at Preston North End, David Moyes.

The next few seasons would indicate that this appointment wasn't one of those false dawns. After eight years, David Moyes became one of our longest-serving managers in a continuous spell, second only to Harry Catterick. Howard Kendall served the club as manager for more than ten years, but he had three bites of the cherry. I've already mentioned his 'marriage' to Everton, but it's worth repeating. It was a great romance. Like Elizabeth Taylor and Richard Burton. Like me and Dawn.

Dawn and I steadily became friends again. And then we fell in love again. She came with me to those Paul McCartney concerts. She traipsed around Peasmarsh with me. Around the Sussex countryside that envelops McCartney's home. She put up with my endless psychobabble about the Beatles. About Everton. She even came to matches with me. This was something that was meant to be. It had been a long and winding road, but eventually we merged together again after ten years apart. Within two years we were married. Within three we had a little boy. The world's newest Evertonian.

George

George Jack Roberts was born at Maidstone Hospital in Kent. He was born weighing eight pounds and one ounce. He was born at 8.49pm. He was born on Friday 18 June. It was Paul McCartney's birthday. And it was as if I'd planned it for that day. Except of course I hadn't. It's not that George was unplanned. He certainly was planned – and long hoped-for. But his arrival came quicker than Dawn and I expected. She fell pregnant shortly after our honeymoon in America. And no sooner had we got married, we became parents to a beautiful boy.

There's nothing like fatherhood to put your whole life into perspective. All of a sudden, your life is transformed. You worry about your child choking. You worry about him not eating properly. You worry about his constant cries. You worry about what used to be a simple plane journey. Now you're responsible for a child. You're worried about leaving the door open. You're worried about crossing the road. You're worried what will happen if your little boy grows up to be a Liverpool fan.

'One day Mr Roberts, you'll have a grandson,' Martin told my father on my wedding day. 'And make sure Neil doesn't repeat the child abuse you inflicted on him. Make sure he doesn't bring that boy up as an Evertonian.' Oh, very funny, Mr Dillon. Another one of Martin's little jokes.

'I'd rather he was gay than a Liverpool supporter,' said dad. 'You never know,' quipped Dillon. 'He could be both.'

Quite. Whatever's mapped out for them is mapped out for them. You can't control it. It's their life, not yours. All you can do is try to show the way. Which is why I put George in a little Everton top as soon as practically possible. And got the camera out for evidence.

He was a beautiful boy. And planned though he was, I simply couldn't have been prepared for the effect he had on me from the minute he was born. I could hardly wait to see him grow up from a baby to a little boy, from a little boy to a little man. Yet, as John wrote, you can't map out everything in life. I might have been 'busy making other plans'but life happens to you anyway. And that sentiment could never have applied to me more. Beautiful Boy. That's exactly what George was. As soon as he was born, I rang my father.

'He's called George Jack Roberts,' I told him.

'George Jack! George Jack Roberts,' he repeated. And his reply was enough for me. Jack was my grandfather's name – my

Evertonian grandad. George was one of the Beatles. George Jack Roberts was an Evertonian, Beatle name. He'd be an Evertonian Beatle. Poor lad. Whatever I wrote a few lines ago, perhaps the little fella never really stood a chance. Especially considering he was born on Paul McCartney's birthday.

One thing was certain. They may have been addictions and afflictions for me all my life. Especially given the turmoil Everton like to put their supporters through. But if I could, I'd share every ounce of enjoyment I've ever had from football and music with my son. Just as my father shared those passions with me, I'd share them with him. They'd be a bond between us, I'd hope. And if not, 'I'd just have to be patient,' as John would say. And whatever the outcome, life would be whatever happened while I was busy making other plans. So I certainly took nothing for granted. It all went round in my head. If George did follow another team, I guess I'd just have to take him to watch them. Whatever passions he followed in life, I'd support him. But if he supported Liverpool? Errr. Scratch that. No chance.

The start I've made has been a good one. Now, six years later, George refers to red as 'the colour of evil'. He draws me pictures with the Everton badge on. He loves Marouane Fellaini for his Marge Simpson-style hairdo. George likes Everton and England, even though England play in red. That was the one exception, I told him, that made red tolerable. I conveniently forgot that George's school uniform is red.

But there is a serious point underneath all this irony. And that is that I wanted to share my passions with George. I wanted to share them with him because I loved him. Would always love him. Will always love him. And what I loved most, I hoped he would love too. So we could share those passions. Spend those times together. Pick each other up when Everton were failing us. Celebrate together whenever there was a triumph. It was the way I had lived my life with my own father. It was the way I wanted to live my life with my son. But where my relationship with my dad NEEDED our mutual love for things like Everton and the Beatles, I didn't want any prerequisites for my relationship with George. He wouldn't NEED to be an Everton fan. Or a Beatles fan. Or even, really, to have any passions in common with me.

I just wanted him to share them with me if he could. For me to share them with him and for him to share them with me. Despite that, music isn't everything. And football isn't everything. It IS just a game, however we supporters feel. Whatever Bill Shankly said. And I resolved to keep remembering that.

One thing which helped me to keep that in focus was the last match I ever went to with Dawn. In February 2004, my journalism career had taken me back into sport from news. I was working on *Grandstand* and *Sunday Grandstand* for BBC Sport. And one night, Dawn came to meet me from work at Television Centre. She was five months pregnant. And I took her to Loftus Road, the home of Queens Park Rangers and at that time a temporary home to Fulham. It was just around the corner from the office and we went to see Fulham play Everton in an FA Cup fourth-round replay. It was a decision I came to regret.

Junichi Inamoto put Fulham ahead just before the hour mark. And then the abuse started. We were sitting behind the goal in awful seats. Awful for the view. But even more awful for the company we were keeping. Loathsome, loathsome company. Anyone who has ever heard my language at a football match might now be crying: 'Hypocrite!' But it wasn't just the foul language which was beyond the pale. It was the nature of it. Racist. Sexist. Utterly abusive. Fuelled by gallons of alcohol. Looking like it. Smelling like it. Sounding like it. And from so-called Everton supporters.

I was trying to protect my wife. Trying to protect our unborn child. I hated being there. Going to the match was regret number one. Regret number two was that we should have left. In injury time, Francis Jeffers equalised for Everton. I didn't even cheer. It was the first time I had ever not cheered an Everton goal. This was the first match, in truth, where I genuinely didn't care what the result was. I just wanted out of there. We should have left earlier. We certainly should have left after 90 minutes. But something made me stay. Perhaps I didn't want to be beaten by these morons. I didn't want to have to suffer for their behaviour. So we did stay. And we endured another 30 minutes of it. Steed Malbranque scored the winner for Fulham and Everton were knocked out of the cup. On any other night, great disappointment.

On this night, great relief just to be out of the ground. On this night, so what.

I wrote to Everton the next day. I sent an email to express my anger. To express how appalled I was. How ashamed I was of these Everton 'supporters'. How I never again wanted to feel that way. The club wrote back. It was a responsible reply, one of genuine concern. It was treated the right way. They wanted seat numbers. They wanted details. And I provided them. I doubt if anything happened as a result of my email. After all, at the match itself, there were stewards everywhere seemingly too weak or too frightened to stop the abuse.

On reflection, I know it has nothing to do with football. And it certainly has nothing to do with Everton. It's not an ugly side to Everton. It's an ugly side to human nature. Unfortunately, away from home, you can't really control where you sit. We got unlucky. We ended up with half a dozen imbeciles. And they spoiled the entire experience. And they made me ashamed to be associated with them. This wasn't my Everton. I shout and swear with the best of them, but even I have a limit.

Dawn never came to a match with me again. Before long, she was at home with George on a matchday if I was going off either alone, with friends or with my father. And before much longer, Dawn and I were no longer married. A little more than three years into our marriage, and almost seven years into our relationship, I called it off. It was the lowest point in my life. But I was no longer 'in love' in the way I wanted to be. Our relationship was once so passionate. It had become so platonic. And only just into my thirties, I couldn't deal with it. Perhaps it was wrong. Perhaps it was my failing. But Dawn and I divorced. I'll repeat. It was the lowest point in my life. I ached at the prospect of splitting up George's parents. I ached at the prospect of not seeing him nearly as often as I should. I was in turmoil. I lost about a stone and a half. I got dreadfully down. I wasn't eating. I was only drinking.

But it was the right decision. The test of time has proven that. And George is not subjected to constantly squabbling parents. He has two parents who love him very much and always will. And he's got one, at least, who's trying to instil in him the true virtues of being an Evertonian. Swagger but sportsmanship. Style but substance. Genuine passion and genuine pride: for me, being an Evertonian is a badge of honour. You are a member of an elite club with an identity to be proud of. *Nil Satis Nisi Optimum*. But cover your ears sometimes if you sit next to me at a match. *Nil Satis Nisi Hypocrite*.

Like me, George Jack Roberts is a Home Counties boy. I always felt like a Scouser in all but the accident of my birth. But of course, I had that constant association with Merseyside to fall back on. Those extremely close family ties. Those regular trips to Bromborough. Every school holiday with my nanna and grandad. George won't have that, because there's no family left for us on Merseyside. Not in the direct line, anyway. Cousins, yes. Dirty Leo, yes. But it's not enough to give George that same emotional pull.

When I was a boy at school in Chelmsford, nobody would say: 'Everton who?' When I scored a tennis-ball hat-trick in the playground and celebrated like Trevor Steven, everybody knew who he was. Yes, they may have followed Tottenham and Arsenal, West Ham or Chelsea, Manchester United or Liverpool. But Everton had one or two followers as well. We were the best team in the country.

It doesn't look likely that George will have that luxury. Only a radical turnaround in fortunes will turn Everton into league champions any time soon. And this time, they'll need more than a Kevin Brock back pass at Oxford. So Everton may be a harder sell with George than it was for me. I just hope that there'll be enough pride for him in following the passions of his father, his father's father and his father's father's father – even his father's father's father's father, if we go back to the Roberts family myth of Charles Roberts and Edgar Chadwick. 'If you know your history,' as we Evertonians like to sing.

In the end, becoming a fully-fledged Everton supporter will be a choice for George and George alone, no matter how much I try to encourage and influence him. I've even been accused of brainwashing him. I hope he'll get bitten by the bug. But either way, the Beatles may prove to be an easier sell. At his christening, my friends John and Paul became George's godfathers. The odd one out was George's godmother, Dawn's friend Clare. She had to become Ringo for the day. A christening? Welcoming George into the Christian family? Setting him on the right path? Exactly. Never let it be said that I don't get my priorities right in life.

George has already watched the *Anthology* with me on DVD. He's already got all my old Beatles CDs, now that I've replaced them with the remastered versions. He already wants to know how John Lennon died, which is a tricky conversation to have with a five-year-old. He already loves 'I Want To Hold Your Hand' so much that one day they played it for him in reception class. In fact, George has moved on from 'A Hard Day's Night'. His new favourites are 'Eleanor Rigby' and 'Drive My Car', usually singing along to Paul McCartney's concert DVD, even doubling up a cushion as both a guitar and a microphone. Good boy. Beautiful Boy.

The People's Manager

'I am from a city that is not unlike Liverpool.
I am joining the people's football club.
The majority of people you meet on the street
are Everton fans.'

David Moyes, 2002

David Moyes

David Moyes began with a bang. The roar which greeted the announcement of his arrival, and his first walk out on to the Goodison Park pitch, was like a two-minute long thunderclap. The thunder had barely subsided before his first game kicked off. It was pierced by the blast of the referee's whistle. And within 30 seconds, David Moyes' Everton team had scored ... David Unsworth drilling the ball low into the Fulham goal, as the new boss kicked off his Everton reign with a 2-1 win.

I've been privileged to be at some of Goodison Park's greatest occasions. And this was one of them. Never before had I heard such a welcome. Such adulation. Such a roar, just for the announcement of a new manager. These were fans who were willing David Moyes to succeed. As Alex Young once told me, you 'could feel the goodwill emanating from the terraces'. This was the People's Club.

We'd always been the Toffees, or the Toffeemen. The Blues or the School Of Science. Now you could add the People's Club to that list of Everton monikers. It was David Moyes' phrase. And it instantly lifted the new manager into the highest of heights as far as the faithful were concerned. Those lofty areas normally reserved only for Goodison legends. In the eyes of the fans, he had god-like qualities as soon as he uttered those words. And his team hadn't even kicked a ball in anger yet.

The phrase came from David Moyes at the press conference to announce his appointment. Whether by accident or by design, this was a man who was clearly a master at public relations. He knew how to master language. And he would know how to master his team.

Remembering their first meeting, Bill Kenwright is quoted as saying: 'It was midnight when he arrived at my home and we talked for two hours. He looked at me with those eyes – and when you've not met him before, they're very frightening – and he mentioned the word "win" ten times in the first minute.'

Then came Moyes' statement of intent at the press conference to announce his appointment. His statement was a statement of pride. It was like a rallying cry. From a Glaswegian to an Evertonian.

> The Everton supporters deserve a good side. I am from a city that is not unlike Liverpool. I am joining the people's football club. The majority of people you meet on the street are Everton fans. It is a fantastic opportunity, something you dream about. I said yes right away as it is such a big club. I would be lying if I said it wasn't a big job. It's been a big job for all the previous managers here. I have great faith in what can be achieved here.

David Moyes came to Everton with a steely determination and a winning mentality. And with piercing blue eyes. And those qualities paid dividends at the People's Club. Gascoigne and Ginola departed. So did Jesper Blomqvist. And the old guard began making way for the new. Soon, he was building a team around a new generation of Everton stars. A new generation which became the best clutch of players the club had had in a generation. In came Tim Cahill and Mikel Arteta. In came Steven Pienaar and Leighton Baines, Louis Saha and Phil Jagielka. All captained by Phil Neville, whose own career was resurrected having won everything with Manchester United only to stare at the Old Trafford substitutes' bench. In came some club record signings. James Beattie, then Andy Johnson, then Yakubu, then Marouane Fellaini. And in came some new home-grown talent. Leon Osman. James Vaughan. Jack Rodwell. Wayne Rooney.

Rooney was the first. He burst on to the scene like David Moyes did. I saw Rooney as a 16-year-old, making his debut at home against Tottenham in August 2002. He may have been only 16, but he looked about 28. He was big, strong, fast and beautifully balanced. He had awesome control. But I already knew all about him. My dad had been to a Youth Cup semi-final a few months before – also against Tottenham – and watched Rooney crash the ball into the net from 35 yards at White Hart Lane. He texted me straight away to tell me that he had 'just seen the best player we've produced since Colin Harvey'. And he was right. A couple of months later, Wayne Rooney became Everton's youngest ever goalscorer, eclipsing Joe Royle's record. He slotted a 25-yard curler past David Seaman to secure a last-minute win for Everton against Arsenal at Goodison Park. There was one of those thunderclap roars. The crowd went into raptures. So did the ITV commentator Clive Tyldesley. 'Remember the name,' he said.

'Wayne Rooney!'

The even younger Rooney had been a season-ticket holder at Everton. In fact, his whole family were. And he'd been an Everton mascot – famously pictured before a Merseyside derby back in the days when I was a young reporter patrolling the Bellefield corridor. But sadly, Rooney lasted no longer in the Everton first team than Peter Beardsley did more than a decade before. After two seasons, he signed for Manchester United in a move which brought him into confrontation with Moyes and with large sections of the Everton support, who couldn't forgive what they saw as a betrayal. This, after all, was the young man who once scored in the Youth Cup only to lift his jersey and reveal a slogan on his under-shirt. 'Once a Blue, always a Blue', it said. Except it wasn't prophetic.

Still, Rooney wrote his name into the Everton story. In time, the bad feeling towards him would be tempered. And who knows, perhaps one day he will be an Everton player again. But the man who stayed throughout it all – to become one of Everton's longest-serving managers – was David Moyes. And he engineered a remarkable transformation in the team. Where we once fought relegation battles, we were now fighting European campaigns.

7, 17, 4, 11, 6, 5, 5, 8, 7

They're not lottery numbers. And there's been precious little luck about it. Apart from that 'second season syndrome' finish of 17th place, these are the final league positions of Everton in the first nine full seasons of David Moyes' leadership. Champions League qualification once. Other European qualification on three more occasions. This might not have been the team of the 1980s. Might not even have been *Nil Satis Nisi Optimum*. But this was a team which won. Which would carry on winning.

This was David Moyes' doing. In my new job, I was finally coming into contact with Peter Reid, a BBC pundit. He was now manager of Coventry and I'd chat to him on the phone about various appearances he might or might not make at Television Centre. In every conversation, we'd talk about Everton. In every conversation, we'd talk about the fine job Moyes was doing. It was like speaking to Alan Ball about Joe Royle. There was respect for a great manager from a great footballer. Doing a great job at the club they all loved.

Moyes himself hadn't been a great footballer. He'd had a journeyman career as a central defender, scratching enough appearances for a Scottish Premier League winners' medal with Celtic but plying the rest of his trade around the lower leagues in England before returning north of the border. Cambridge United, Bristol City, Shrewsbury Town, Dunfermline Athletic. Hamilton Academical. It was his move back to England, to Preston North End, which allowed him to see out his playing days at a club where he'd soon become manager. And the rest is history.

On 11 December 2004, Everton were rolling towards that fourth- place finish and Champions League qualification. The visitors to Goodison Park that day were Liverpool. And while I was working the day job at BBC Sport, dad was at the match. Lee Carsley scored the only goal of the game and Everton rode out a famous 1-0 win. Rode off to the home dressing room on the sound of 40,000 roars. My dad told me about it. David Moyes told me about it.

A few weeks earlier, Moyes had been to Television Centre for a Halloween night appearance on *Match Of The Day*. I missed him. But a colleague of mine got him to sign the show's runorder for me. And I still treasure it now.

To Neil.
All the best.
David Moyes.
EFC.

Simple words. But to me, they meant a lot. I wished I had been there to see him. To meet him. Although I was back in sports news, my professional associations with Everton were no longer such that I could just ring up the manager or rock up to Bellefield. Or spend my time driving around the country to meet some legends. Or hook up with the club's main playing idol for an exclusive interview or two. Now, I had to work a bit harder to combine my passion with my profession. So I resolved I'd do just that. I WOULD meet David Moyes. I would get him on to *Sunday Grandstand*.

It was brilliant. I rang the Everton press office. I reminded them of my former position on *The Evertonian*. They remembered me. They gave me the number for David Moyes' secretary at Bellefield. I rang her up. 'Hello love,' she said. 'I'm sure he'll come down. When do you want him again? I'll ask him. See ya. Ta ra!'

I could have been back at Bellefield. Back through those royal blue gates marshalled by Harry. Back down that long drive. Back alongside the sports hall to the left and those manicured lawns masquerading as football pitches to the right. Back towards that two-storey building at the end of the drive, with a simple, royal blue front door. Back in that corridor where the air is rich with the smell of fresh mud and the walls echo to the sound of clattering studs on polished floors.

I could have been talking to my own nanna, such was the familiarity of the tone on the other end of the phone line. And it wasn't long before I got a call back. David Moyes would come on the show. He would come to London. It would be on 12 December.

I waited for the day to come. But when the day came, I was ready. I'd hardly slept the night before but I got to Television Centre early. I waited for my guest at the stage door entrance. I waited there 20 minutes before his scheduled arrival time. But almost immediately, a big silver Mercedes drew up. And before the chauffeur we'd booked could even get out to help him, David Moyes was on his way towards me. Striding. Smiling.

He wore a grey suit. He was tall and slim. Ginger-haired. Something gently and affectionately mocked by the Everton supporters.

> He's got red hair but we don't care,
> Davie Davie Moyes.

He was holding a carrier bag bulging with every single Sunday newspaper. And he fixed me with his smile – and then his firm handshake. 'You must be Neil,' he said. 'How do you do. Did you enjoy that yesterday?'

David Moyes was still reliving the moment. His first derby victory over Liverpool had come less than 24 hours before. Now here he was, talking to me about it. Talking as if we were just two fans in the pub. 'Ahhh, it was absolutely amazing,' he said. 'It was unbelievable.

Our crowd. You should have heard our crowd. They were singing all down Goodison Road. Liverpool would have heard it in their dressing room. It was unbelievable.'

If you didn't know any better, you'd have thought this man was a born and bred Evertonian. A diehard. One of the fully signed-up members of the People's Club. And this seemed to confirm that he was. He'd found a natural home. For the next two hours, I sat with him in the green room at stage five of Television Centre. Moyes' fellow guest on the show was the *Daily Telegraph* writer Henry Winter. 'Ah, you two must be happy today,' said Henry when he arrived.

Moyes and I were sitting side-by-side, going through the match kick-by-kick. The Everton manager patted the couch space between us. 'This is our corner,' he said. 'This is the blue corner.'

We talked about Everton being fourth in the league. About how his players were constantly surprising him. About how hard-working Duncan Ferguson was. About players he might sign for Everton. About James Beattie, who he'd go on to buy the following month. About Robbie Keane, who he wanted to buy but never did.

'These players aren't fourth-placed players,' he told me, in assessment of his current squad. The same squad that had finished 17th the season before. 'What they're doing is amazing.'He deflected the credit. And yet it was clear the credit should be his. He gave me an insight into the coaching manual at that level. Into tactics. How he'd try to get more out of the players. How they were always seeking to get better-quality possession. 'That's the mark of a good team,' he said. 'It's about the quality of possession you get, and how high up the pitch you get it.'

We flicked through the papers. David Moyes had bought every single one. He'd probably wandered into a petrol station en route to the studios. Probably picked them all up and slammed them down onto the counter in front of him. Probably with the proudest of smiles. Probably wondering if the attendant recognised him. Except no, that wouldn't have been David Moyes' style. He was too unassuming for that.

All the papers carried the picture of the Everton players bundling on to Lee Carsley seconds after he'd scored the winner. Chief among them, taking centre stage, was that new Everton talisman Tim Cahill. Arm aloft in celebration. Looking for his manager to share the moment.

I didn't interview David Moyes. But I didn't need to. I sat with him for ages before his appearance and we chatted like pals. Never once did I feel like it was a chore for him. Never once did I feel like I'd imposed on him. He'd been early because he wanted to be early. He wanted to glory in the moment of that victory. I like to think he knew he was meeting an Evertonian, so there was someone to share it with that morning. That may be wrong, of course. But he was unwaveringly pleasant. Generous with his time and spirit. He was in the best of moods, as you would be after engineering your first win over Liverpool. I saw his piercing blue eyes and I could tell that this probably wasn't David Moyes' only demeanour. This probably wasn't the David Moyes you saw on the training ground or the David Moyes the players saw in the dressing room at half-time. Especially if they were losing. But this was precisely the David Moyes that I wanted to see. And it was a day to remember.

Never before had I asked a professional contact to sign something for me. But this time I couldn't resist. I already had my signed *Match Of The Day* runorder. But now I had met the man in person, I wanted the Everton manager to sign something in my presence. The dilemma had been what to take with me. But after the Merseyside derby, it seemed obvious. The day after Everton 1 Liverpool 0, I took my book *The Great Derbies: Everton v Liverpool*. It is now signed on the first page with the following:

> To Neil.
> Everton 1-0 Liverpool.
> Sunday morning after.
> All the best.
> David Moyes.

And I'll keep it forever. That same night, I broke my rule for a second time. A second time in 24 hours. I met Ian Botham at the Sports Personality show. I took a picture of me with him when I was 14 years old, when my dad had been despatched to interview him and I'd been allowed to bunk off school for the privilege of meeting the most swashbuckling hero in England's cricket history. I got the picture signed. And in one day, I'd met David Moyes. And as a bonus, I'd met Ian Botham.

Not long after that day, I met Kevin Ratcliffe. The man who lifted the first Everton trophy of my lifetime on that glorious day in May 1984. The man who captained us when we beat Watford at Wembley to win the FA Cup. The man who captained us through our best ever period. Kevin Ratcliffe. I met him at Heathrow Airport. Just bumped into him. Just said hi. Just shook hands. Just left it at that.

Botham, Moyes, Ratcliffe. Not forgetting Ball. Kendall. Young, Lineker ... and Ferguson. And countless others. But how could any of this be beaten? Who else could I possibly meet to match any of those illustrious names? Or even better them? Did such a person exist for me? Meeting David Moyes and Ian Botham in just a few hours at the BBC had been the sort of day that could only be topped by meeting a genuine icon. One of the faces of the 20th century. One of the most famous people on the planet.

A Beatle.

The Fireman

From the Electric Proms to Electric Arguments

For a long time, I didn't know why *With The Beatles*, the Beatles' second album, was actually called *Meet The Beatles* in America. And then it was explained to me. It was called *Meet The Beatles* because nobody in the States had ever heard of them before. *Please Please Me* hadn't only failed to register in America – it wasn't even released there. But then came *Meet The Beatles*. And with one press of that particular vinyl, Beatlemania swept across the Atlantic from these shores to theirs. *Meet The Beatles* was their introduction to the Fab Four. An introduction that prompted hysteria.

I try not to do hysteria any more. And at the age of 37, I'd done my level best to put it behind me. Everton defeats. Unsatisfying Macca records. I didn't need to leap into hysterics at the human flaws of my heroes. But the fervour which prompted those passions within me still burned. And much as I had largely given up, it was still a lifelong dream that one day I might meet Paul McCartney. That I might meet a Beatle. Meet 'the' Beatle.

Since 2005, I'd been working at ITN. Still in sports news but no longer with Auntie. Instead, I was now at the former home of Gordon Honeycombe, the man who co-wrote *The Golden Vision*. A man who I met in the newsroom one day, as part of the celebrations for ITN's 50th birthday. I chatted to him about *The Golden Vision*. I told him how much my father admired Alex Young. I told him how much my father admired the play about his hero. So much so that we'd run off our own DVD copies as soon as the film was dusted down from the BBC vaults, borrowed from the archives and played out one night on BBC4. Dad did the bootlegging. He even sent one copy to a very grateful Bill

Kenwright the film of the play not being available apart from dodgy copies on the black market, sometimes sold in the pubs around Goodison.

Gordon Honeycombe, that stalwart of nightly television news but long-since retired, was fascinated. 'Call your father,' he told me. 'Let me talk to him.' I did as he suggested. I put the receiver straight on to Gordon.

'Colin Roberts,' he said. 'This is Gordon Honeycombe. I believe you have a copy of *The Golden Vision*. I would very much like to get my hands on one.'

The two of them had a brief conversation. Coming out of the blue as it did, it was something of a shock to my father – but a fascinating one. Here he was, talking to Gordon Honeycombe, a man who he would watch on the television news in the sixties and seventies. In an era when television news was a focal point for the whole family. At a time when there were only two channels.

Gordon Honeycombe got his DVD ... posted to his new home in Australia. I got a postcard in return, by way of thanks for a copy of the long-lost BBC play. Working at ITN seemed to open up doors.

Some time later, I settled into a new relationship. Lizzie, my partner, was that rare thing in a girl. A beautiful girl. A feminine girl. But a girl who liked football. Result. Not only that, she'd come with me to Everton matches. She became an Evertonian. And she even let me indulge my musical passions. I'd bore her endlessly with Beatles anecdotes, old Lennon albums, old Harrison albums and old McCartney albums. But she put up with it. Tolerated it. Even seemed to embrace it.

In 2007, Paul McCartney played a BBC *Electric Proms* set at the Roundhouse in Camden. A small venue, perhaps holding some 3,000 people. Considering how hard it is to watch Macca when the venue holds 20,000 people, getting tickets for this seemed nigh on impossible. But I tried. And I succeeded. I called the ticket hotline from my desk at ITN. I held on the line for probably 40 minutes. And I finally got through ... and got two tickets. The gig itself was fantastic. He opened with 'Magical Mystery Tour' and finished with 'Get Back'. In between came a succession of smash hits. Some more familiar to non-Macca experts like Lizzie than others. But all of them expertly performed. And in the most intimate venue I was ever likely to see him in.

I didn't need my McCartney appetite whetting. But the gig did just that for Lizzie. And we promptly went into the ballot for tickets to Liverpool's European Capital Of Culture Celebrations the following summer. Again, we got lucky. Lizzie rang me to tell me we'd got tickets to see Paul McCartney. Great! Fantastic!

...

......

....

'At Anfield.'

....

......

....

Silence. Long pause. More silence.

'I'm not going,' I said, throwing my dummy out of the pram. 'There's no way I'm going to ruin my experience of watching Paul McCartney by spending the evening in that s***hole.'

'Can't you put it to one side just for once?' 'No.'

Here I was, having left all my hysteria behind me, picking up all my hysteria again.

As with any hysterical outburst, the dust eventually settled. And the toys eventually came back into the pram. I eventually calmed down. And I eventually (as I was always going to do) agreed that I would of course go to the gig with her. Seeing as she'd really like to go, you understand. But I had one condition. I'd be taking my Everton scarf with me. Otherwise I wouldn't be going AT ALL.

So the day came and we trudged through the streets around Anfield, queuing for what seemed like miles on our way to the concert. The streets, themselves, are far less salubrious than those around Goodison. There are lots of two-ups, two-downs with their own air conditioning. By virtue of not having a roof. And Anfield just has a much more downbeat feel about it than Kirkdale or Walton. At least as far as this admittedly biased Blue is concerned.

But I put up with the slow trek through war-torn Anfield and grimaced as we finally crossed the threshold on to the boarded-out pitch where Liverpool FC played their home games. We settled somewhere near the halfway line. And we faced towards the Anfield Road end, with the Kop to our backs. And then I remembered. Then I realised. I wasn't on alien turf at all. This had been Everton's home before Liverpool's. All right, we're talking about the Victorian era but we played there first. Not our fault the landlord put the rents up, forced us across Stanley Park and so the deformity that was Liverpool FC came to be born. No, I was okay here. It was Everton's ground first. And besides, I was wearing my George Harrison T-shirt and my trusty Everton scarf. The same scarf I'd had in the late 80s and early 90s; the scarf that I'd worn to the 4-4 draw at Goodison, and that I'd lent to Alex Young for the purposes of a picture. I was wearing my blue and white scarf. And I was here to see Paul McCartney. This was about music, not football. Nobody was going to bother me for being an Evertonian. Not tonight.

'Eh! Eh!' Some cheery Scouser began mocking me and prodding me. Pointing at the blue around my neck. 'Bit brave aren't ya? Wearing that scarf in here! Won't be many of you lot in here tonight!'

Momentarily, my heart sank. Momentarily, I felt isolated. Seconds later, my heart picked up. Seconds later, I felt a sense of belonging.

'Well I'm a Blue,' came a voice just feet from where I was stood. 'So am I,' said another.

'And so am I,' another still.

'You're surrounded!' said the first, teasing the loveable Red.

Here we were, a clutch of Blues, outnumbering a Red on his home turf. Outnumbering him while waiting for Paul McCartney to appear on stage. What could be better than this?

It was a truly memorable evening. I've been to some brilliant concerts, from Muse to Coldplay to U2 to REM to the Stereophonics and to the Rolling Stones and Bob Dylan. But seeing Paul McCartney in his home city would take some beating. Never before had 'Penny Lane' been so much 'in my ears and in my eyes'. And to top it all, the man on stage was an Evertonian.

A diplomatic Evertonian, who doesn't much care for football in truth. But an Evertonian nonetheless. One who went to the 1966 and 1968 FA Cup finals in Beatle boots and an overcoat even at the height of his fame with John, George and Ringo.

> Here's the deal. My father was born in Everton, my family are officially Evertonians – so if it comes down to a derby match or an FA Cup Final between the two, I would have to support Everton. But after a concert at Wembley Arena I got a bit of a friendship with Kenny Dalglish who had been to the gig. And I thought: 'You know what? I am just going to support them both because it's all Liverpool and I don't have that Catholic–Protestant thing. So I did have to get special dispensation from the Pope to do this but that's it, too bad, I support them both. They are both great teams. But if it comes to the crunch, I'm Evertonian.

These were Paul's quotes in the *Observer Sport Monthly*. And this was the evidence. Not so much of his Royal Blue credentials. More of his Royal Blue leanings. And a deference to Liverpool. Because actually, football has never been a passion for Paul McCartney. Everything he had went into his music. Not football. So he's a Blue but he likes the Reds a bit. In other words, he doesn't much care for football but his family are Evertonians and that's what he is if push comes to shove. The religious stuff is a misnomer. Everton have never been an official Catholic club. We were founded from St Domingo's church team – a bunch of Methodists. It was just that the Liverpool priests used to watch Everton before and after the last war, largely because of our Irish players – and our Irish superstars like the wingers Peter Farrell and Tommy Eglington. And besides, my mother and her family are Roman Catholics. My father and his were Protestants. I was brought up a Protestant. I'm still an Evertonian. And I didn't need to ask the Pope for his permission. But it all helped get me through that night at Anfield. Knowing that Paul McCartney, my idol, was actually much more Blue than Red.

Lizzie and I drove back south the next day, playing McCartney music in the car and talking about how great his Anglo-American band were. A really tight group. Master musicianship. First-rate performers. Americans Brian Ray and Rusty Anderson on guitars and Abe Laboriel Junior on drums. Plus Englishman Paul 'Wix'Wickens, Linda's old stage ally, on keyboards.

We pulled into Corley services on the M6. And as we lined up for a burger, I got a sharp dig in the ribs. 'That's Rusty,' said Lizzie, pointing across the room. 'And there's the drummer.'

True enough, McCartney's trio of American bandmates were queuing up for a spot of lunch. So we went to say hi. I made a beeline for Brian Ray. Lizzie chatted to Rusty Anderson. And she gave him the 62 pence he needed to complete his lunch order.

We sat down with them and spoke about the concert.

'It was cool,' said Abe, nodding slowly but enthusiastically and drawing out the final word in his best Californian drawl, dude.

'And it was a great party afterwards.'

'Yeah man,' said Brian. 'Yoko was there and Olivia [Harrison] was there. We just hung out with them and the Kaiser Chiefs [who also played]. It was super-cool.'

It was super-cool. Super-cool to just bump into them at the motorway services. And to meet such chilled-out, down-to-earth guys. Who just so happened to play in Paul McCartney's band. As we said goodbye, a father and son in Everton tracksuits recognised them also. The dad asked if it was okay if he got a picture. I thought he'd take a snap of his boy with the band. But none of it. He gave the camera to the kid. And he made sure he got plenty of photos with Paul's backing men.

Paul Wickens wasn't with them. Paul McCartney wasn't with them. Who knows where Macca was that day. Still in Liverpool? On a private jet somewhere? Already in the studio at Abbey Road? Perhaps. Because this was the time when McCartney was putting the finishing touches to his latest album.

Title: *Electric Arguments*
Artist: The Fireman

The Fireman had released two albums before. The first was called *Strawberries Oceans Ships Forest*. The second, more simply, was called *Rushes*. It was ambient dance music. Not revealed as the work of Paul McCartney. Not making any kind of dent on the pop charts, perhaps because of this. But it was brilliant. A brilliant tangent that McCartney had been following for years. A brilliant sideline to his mainstream work. Perhaps even better than his mainstream work. But because of Paul's desire for anonymity, for creative freedom and for the capacity to experiment, he kept his name off the records. They went out of print. They became collectors' items.

The Fireman was Paul McCartney produced by Youth, real name Martin Glover – the producer who gave Crowded House a distinctive sound and the man who started out as the bassist with the post-punk rock group Killing Joke. He was also the man who'd help Paul with that 'self-editing' problem he's sometimes described as having. Who helped bring his brilliance to the fore.

When *Electric Arguments* was released in November, Paul McCartney was finally revealed as the Fireman. The record still failed to make a major chart impact. But its grooves and rhythms, its alternative sounds and – this time – its vocals made it McCartney's best effort in years. It's also the record which finally allowed me to meet him.

A Day In The Life

Just before Christmas, I got the phone call which gave me the day of my life. Just a day in the life. But what a day in the life it was. Lizzie, who worked on the ITV regional news programme for London, had fixed up an interview with Paul McCartney for one of her reporters. He'd be signing copies of the Fireman album at HMV on Oxford Street. Would I like to tag along with the film crew so I could meet my idol?

It was an unbelievable offer.

'Yes! Fantastic! Of course! Thank you!'

....

......

....

Silence. Long pause. More silence.

....

......

....

My hysteria mechanism had kicked in. I was being spoilt. Again. But I knew I had the chance of a lifetime. And I was desperate to grab it.

'I'll do the interview.' 'What?'

'I'll do the interview. I don't want to be the muppet holding the mic. If I'm going to meet him, I want to meet him properly.'

Here I was being spoilt again. Toys out of the pram again. Calling the shots again. But thankfully, Lizzie humoured me. She put in the relevant request to her boss and he agreed that I could do the interview. He was hardly plumping for a television rookie because I'd reported on national television many times before. And I was known to the London team for work I'd done with them only recently. It's just that I was out of the fold. I was working in sports news, and now in production rather than on screen. I was not one of their 'family of faces'.

Even so, I got the nod. And the day came – 21 December 2008. Just before the winter solstice and the shortest day of the year. But one of the longest and most enriching of mine.

I was working a late shift at ITN that night, producing on the Setanta Sports News channel. The opportunity to interview McCartney was in the morning, after he'd signed everything for 300 fans who'd had to queue up overnight for wrist bands to allow them in. They queued up for hours and hours. But not for them the misery of queuing up for hours only to be disappointed. Not for them the misery I'd endured at Waterstone's on Piccadilly, six or seven years before. That said, the misery could still strike for me. I might still miss my chance. I was warned.

'He'll do it if he possibly can,'said the HMV manager running the event. 'Of course, it depends on his schedule and he likes to give as much time as possible to his fans. But I'm sure he'll do it for you. If he can. I'm sure he will.'

The words 'I'm sure' meant he wasn't sure. Paul McCartney had only agreed to two television interviews. Reuters and *London Tonight*. I had the second slot. And I'd just have to wait. Patiently. With fingers crossed. With everything crossed.

I got there in good time with Craig, my cameraman. Good enough time to set up where the fans were already queuing both inside and outside the closed store. It was a Sunday morning and the organisers hoped to have everybody out before opening the shop. We did some vox pops. I did a piece to camera. And the cameraman, lovely guy that he was, didn't bother telling me that my collar was skew-whiff. That the lasting image of me from that day would be of a scruff with a wonky collar. That if I did meet my idol, this is how I'd present myself to him. Oh well. It was a day in the life.

I did the piece to camera. We did a few more interviews. Tracks from *Electric Arguments* were playing in-store. And then the man arrived. I heard it before I saw it. From classical to folk. From easy listening to metal. From rock and pop to hip-hop. There was a huge cheer resonating around the empty aisles of CDs. McCartney arrived on stage. Did a huge thumbs-up. Thanked everyone for coming. And began a marathon session of signing and meeting-and-greeting. Pure McCartney charm.

We grabbed some of the lucky fans on their way out, proudly clutching their memorabilia. They told of how they were 'still shaking'. They spoke of lifelong dreams come true. Then we moved to the point where my lifelong dream might come true. Where I would shake. Where I might get an interview. Might get an interview if time allowed, that is. Downstairs in the store, somewhere tucked in by the jazz and blues CDs. Behind the Reuters crew already waiting.

The clock ticked. And ticked. And tocked. Upstairs, hundreds of McCartney fans were having their own day in the life. I was still on tenterhooks, hoping for mine. The danger would be if the store had to open. So I was told. If the store had to open, all bets might be off. If it got busy, he might not do it. It would all depend on how long the signings took.

One hour passed. Then two. Still no sign. Still no sign while the man was still signing. He'd gone way over time. And then the store opened.

My heart sank. I was destined not to meet him. So near and yet so far, I thought. Just like my experience at Waterstone's. Just like back in Bermuda when I was a kid. When John Lennon was hanging out on Elbow Beach. And for all I knew, I could have been riding my bike a couple of hundred yards away.

The customers began to trickle in. Craig and I were still waiting by the interview board. By a big, colourful sign that said 'Paul McCartney is the Fireman'. Reuters were waiting. I was waiting.

Two teenage girls arrived in the store, shopping for CDs. 'What's this?'said one to the other. 'Paul McCartney!?'Her voice was quaking. Not with excitement. With disdain. This wasn't Craig David – this was Paul McCartney. Who cared?

Then, within seconds, he appeared. 'Oh my god, it's him! It's him!'

They weren't my words. They might have been my thoughts but they weren't my words. They were the words of the teenage girl. The very same girl who seconds earlier couldn't have cared less. Who now seemed to be producing a pool of wee in all her excitement. Metaphorically, of course. But she seemed to be a one-girl tribute to Beatlemania, just 45 years too late.

This was it. This was my moment. Reuters would go first, but then I'd get my chance. I'd give my camera to Craig. I'd ask Paul to sign an album for me. I'd get to shake his hand. Get to talk to him. For five minutes, maximum. That was my given time limit. But I made the most of it.

I'd never ... ever ... been so nervous for a job of work. But when the moment came, I had to gather myself. Take a deep breath. Stop shaking, because the shaking had begun. And then begin for real.

Looking back at the tape now, I can tell in my voice that I was barely able to hold it together. It was ever-so-slightly quivering. As I was ever-so-slightly quaking in my boots. And as thrilled as I am to watch it back now, it still makes me nervous as those feelings come rushing back.

We shook hands. 'Hiya,' said Paul.

'Neil Roberts from *London Tonight*.' 'Hiya Neil.'

'Really pleased to meet you.' (That was me speaking to Paul, not Paul speaking to me.)

Craig moved the camera into place. Paul spotted someone in the background, lurking with a notepad.

'And who are you from, writing all the quotes down?' 'I'm from the Press Association.'

'Good.'

What followed was my own interview with Paul McCartney. His own undivided attention on my questions. An interview which I can still almost reel off word for word, even now. But not before I whispered in his ear ... would he be kind enough to sign my album at the end?

'Yeah, sure.' And so we began.

NR: Paul it's great to meet you. Erm. The Fireman 'rushes in'. Tell me where the name comes from.

Paul: The Fireman himself. I started making some kind of ambient dance records with a friend of mine, Youth. He did a mix for me and so we decided to go a little further and make an album. We just needed a name. And I like getting in the woods ... one of my hobbies is kind of making paths in the woods, you know, with my chainsaw. And I light a lot of fires. Erm. So I kind of, you know, thought of myself as the Fireman. And my dad was a fireman, when he was a young lad. So the combination, that's where we got the name from.

NR: And that's why the second album was *Rushes*, too, from 'Penny Lane'?

Paul: Yeah, that's why we quoted 'Penny Lane' there ... the fireman rushes in. And this one's called *Electric Arguments* for no particular reason other than I like the words and it's a quote from Allen Ginsberg, who's a very good American beat poet.

NR: Around the time of *Revolver* and *Sergeant Pepper* you were the creative force in the Beatles ... avant-garde, using that for all your experimental music. Why are you now using a sideline project for your experimental music?

Paul: Err, you know ... I ... I don't think of it like that. You know, I think of it like in the Beatles, erm, you know we were all quite experimental. I just happened to, err, you know, throw a few of the ideas in. But um, yeah ... err ... I kind of like hiding behind a pseudonym. It's actually just for fun. There's no particular reason. There's no significance. What it does is it frees you up a bit in the studio. You know you go in and instead of standing in front of the mic going, in your mind, you know, this is a Paul McCartney vocal ... *'Can't buy me love'* [singing] ... you kind of go in and you go: 'I'm not him, I'm some guy in a fictitious band'. So you ... it's just ... you think anything's possible. It just frees you up a little bit.

NR: Well you've had Johnny Ramone and you've had Percy Thrillington ...

Paul: Er, Paul Ramone, I was Paul Ramone. I was Percy Thrillington ... the Fireman ...

NR: Well why did you take so long before you officially put your name to the project?

Paul: To the Fireman ... erm. We did it just, err, as a fun thing. And we thought, well, we won't tell anyone, like I was never gonna tell anyone Percy Thrillington. But what happens is the deep fans find out. And they talk to each other, you know, nowadays on the Internet they all talk to each other. So it became obvious they all knew. So it was a little bit silly to go 'nooo, it's not us', you know, it was a bit coy. So we just thought, well, if they all know there's no point hiding any more. So the Fireman came out of the closet ... and found his voice.

NR: One final question then Paul and that's erm, obviously, there's an incredible following around you ... then and now. And that's, well, you know ... What's it like?

Paul: It's fantastic you know. I love it because I started off just because I was in love with music and that's the reason I still do it. But the great, err, side effect is that these other people like what you do too. And so it's great doing a thing like today, erm, at the record shop ... because they show up. And you get to meet them, you get to eyeball them you know. As I say, there was some girl there who'd just come in from New York ... through the snow ... she had to fly, go to Philadelphia, had to fly ... there's kids coming from Mexico ... I mean you know, I didn't even know I was gonna be here. But this, they, they know ... you know ... So it's just great, the um ... And you get to say thanks.

NR: Well Merry Christmas, Paul. Thanks very much.

Paul: Cheers, Merry Christmas. And to everybody out there, Happy Christmas.

NR: *London Tonight*, it's called.

Paul: *London Tonight*, Happy Christmas!

There was a trademark wink and a thumbs-up. And then I got my picture taken. I swear, as Paul put his arm around me, I began shaking again. My line of questioning had been nervous. Not very fluent. Awestruck. Starstruck. I know, it was hardly the most professional episode of my working life. I'd even forgotten that perhaps I should have called him 'Sir' Paul. But he didn't seem to mind. He spoke to me as if he was speaking to one of his mates. It was just a normal conversation. And if he could sense my nerves, he didn't show it. He seemed to warm to me. If it wasn't my most professional moment in journalism, it was my most memorable. A life's dream come true. I walked out pinching myself. Repeatedly pinching myself. Did this really happen?

I got straight on the phone to my father, now living in Thailand. And within minutes, half the expat community in Thailand knew my story. I'd met Paul McCartney. I'd had my picture taken with him. I'd got my copy of *Electric Arguments* signed by him.

Then, as he left, I told Paul's press guy that we'd had to sub Rusty's lunch at the service station. Paul was listening. 'Tell Rusty he owes my girlfriend 62 pence,' I said. Deliberately loud enough so Paul would hear. And he did hear. And he did laugh. And it made my day. My day in the life. One I'd remember forever. And all in the space of my five-minute limit. I'd achieved it all in four minutes and 43 seconds.

Imagine

Wembley twice

When you've met your hero, your true hero, there's a bit of a
come- down after the high. You're back to normal life. Perhaps
to a bit of humdrum. To the knowledge that you'll never again
be so excited to meet someone. That your senses won't be stirred
in quite the same way again. That you'll never reach the height
of those passions again.

And then Everton get drawn against Liverpool in the FA Cup.

In January 2009, my nanna had already been dead for almost
ten years. She'd passed away a few weeks after my return from
Bermuda. My one regret: that I didn't get a proper chance to say
goodbye. In January 2009, my father had already been living in
Thailand for two years. He was no longer a regular visitor to this
country. To my home. To Goodison. In January 2009, we played
Liverpool three times in a fortnight. And they didn't beat us once.

Tim Cahill was the hero in the league match at Anfield, a late
equaliser giving us a 1-all draw. I couldn't get a ticket. But when
we were back on their cabbage patch a few days later, I did have
one. I went with Lizzie and we watched 11 blue backs to the wall,
street- fighting their way to a replay at Goodison Park. Our key
midfielders, Mikel Arteta and Marouane Fellaini, were missing
from the team. Injured, suspended or a mixture of both – I can't
remember. But what we lacked in creativity, we made up for in
True Blue fighting spirit. Arteta, the jewel in Everton's crown.
Fellaini, the afro-headed record signing who'd come to embody
the hopes and the dreams of the supporters with his 6ft 4in
frame, his poise, his composure ... and his crazy hairdo.

There'd been a rumour sweeping the Everton section of the
crowd at Anfield that Arteta, our most gifted player, had had

a training ground bust-up with our right-back Tony Hibbert.
Now, I don't think it's doing Hibbo a disservice to say that of
the two, Arteta is the more gifted footballer. But Hibbo has blue
blood running through his veins. He'd give everything for the
cause, even if his crosses invariably end up in row Z. And if
Mikky was all style, Hibbo was all steel ... and not stainless. Still,
it's impossible to know if that training ground bust-up really
did materialise. But it gave me food for thought. And having
been taunted mercilessly by Liverpool fans when I went for a
pre-match drink at the Arkles, on the corner of Anfield Road, I
decided to put pen to paper about football in a serious way, for
pretty much the first time. So after the match, I sent an email
to my father.

Hello dad
How are things? Thought I'd drop you a quick line
seeing as my investment in Skype headphones has yet to
bear fruit! So the derby was interesting. It's such a shame
the atmosphere is so venomous now, compared to how it
used to be. But I'm certainly glad I'm on our side of the
fence and not theirs. I had a dream the other night that
you'd been lying to me all these years and really you were
a Liverpool fan. Your face metamorphosed into that of
the devil. It was a real nightmare!
The derby songs have changed somewhat. For the
last couple of years we've been singing 'The baby's not
yours' to Steven Gerrard. That's gotta hurt. But nowhere
near as much as 'ladyboy, ladyboy' at Fernando Torres.
You could see him going bright red as he turned away!
Oh well, poor lad. I can admit it to you (though not many
others) that I've always been secretly jealous of the Anfield atmosphere, the colour and (yes, though I HATE ad-
mitting it) that dreaded Gerry and the Pacemakers song.
But you know what? I've only realised recently that
Evertonians actually RELISH it. They relish the differ-
ences. They relish the fact that Blues don't go to the
match all decked out in kit, à la Celtic, Newcastle and
Liverpool. That the emphasis is on understatement with

a splash of colour ... we've much more of an irreverent crowd than Liverpool could ever have and Evertonians thrive on that. For instance, that berserk Pompey fan who dresses up like some kind of loon, all covered in Pompey tattoos and paraphernalia. Everton could NEVER have a supporter like that. Newcastle could. Liverpool could, and do.

We were very VERY noisy at Anfield. Liverpool, perhaps off the back of Monday night's league result, were very VERY quiet, until Gerrard scored and the whole place went crazy. (At that point, I thought we were goners). We'd been singing: 'Where's your famous atmosphere?' Guess what, they don't like that.

They've taken to singing: 'The elephant man. The elephant man. Joleon Lescott, the elephant man.'

And of course their favourite: 'The city's all ours. The city's all ours. Fuck off to Kirkby. The city's all ours.' (Incidentally, I've fallen out with the Arkles after listening to the pub full of Neanderthal Reds belting that out pre-match on Sunday.)

So imagine my unbridled joy when we all held our scarves aloft, midway through the second half, and started singing 'The city's all ours' at Anfield. The look of bemusement on their fans' faces ('what are they singing that for!?') was a joy to behold until they finally got the punchline: 'The city's all ours. The city's all ours. Fuck off to Norway. The city's all ours.' That was our little tribute to their healthy helping of Scandinavian fans.

Anyway, banter aside (and Martin's been giving me loads of stick), there aren't too many more of these derbies my heart can take. Monday's game (which I didn't go to) was even. On Sunday, they battered us. But we deserved the draw simply for the way we stood up to them, and given that they created about three chances despite 70%- plus possession. So it's with some trepidation, and probably a case full of valium, that I prepare for Wednesday night's replay at Goodison. The good news is I'm off that day and on lates the next, so I can go.

Plus Lee has just sorted my ticket (I think for the Upper Gwladys Street). We'll obviously be more adventurous, and hopefully have Mikky and Felli back. That in itself leads to problems though, doesn't it. A more open game means more chances for them. On Sunday, the chance count was Liverpool 3 Everton 1. On Wednesday, I reckon the chance count might be something like Everton 3 Liverpool 6 or 7. So I guess we throw the dice and just see what happens. We need to keep fingers crossed and pray for a famous night at Goodison.

And yes, let's just hope that Arteta is back. Incidentally, the rumour is that he got injured after a training ground bust-up with Hibbo. Apparently Tony went in late on him (like he does), and Mikky turned round to him and in his best Basque-Mersey accent called him a 'no mark'. Cue Tony to twat him one. Oh well – can't blame Tony, really, but I hope Mikky is back, that's for sure. What we desperately lacked on Sunday was someone to put their foot on the ball in the middle of the park.

So drop me a line when you can. (Did you email Lee, by the way?) And let's keep our fingers crossed for Wednesday. Maybe if you get over here soon, we could go to a match together. I'd like that.

Speak soon,

Neil

My dad replied that he liked the way I wrote about football. That I should write a book. That I should put my passions down on paper. So I did.

It would be a few more months before dad made a trip back to England and we were able to go to Everton together. But it would only be a few more days before Everton tasted a sweet victory over Liverpool. Arteta and Fellaini were back in the Everton starting line-up. And on that crisp, cold night, Goodison Park was only heated by the cauldron of noise it generated. No goals after 90 minutes. And with penalties beckoning, the ground erupted. Andy van der Meyde – a once-superstar Dutchman destined to become nothing more than a footnote in Everton's history –

produced a rare moment of magic. A whipping, curling cross. Dan Gosling, a teenage substitute, collected it. He turned inside the Liverpool defence. And he curled an exquisite shot past Pepe Reina in the Liverpool goal – with 118 minutes showing on the Park End scoreboard. The ground was shaken by a thunderclap of noise. The Everton players bundled on to Gosling on the Bullens Road touchline. Goodison Park, literally, went berserk, and the millions watching at home on ITV – Lizzie included – saw an advert for Tic Tacs instead. A transmission error meant the match coverage was switched to a commercial. When the output reverted back to the football, Gosling was engulfed – arms outstretched, fists clenched, team-mates mobbing him. And Liverpool fans had already left the stadium.

Tell me ma, me ma. We went to Wembley twice. This was Everton getting back to where they belonged. Not quite *Nil Satis Nisi Optimum*, perhaps. But getting there. We beat a young Manchester United side in the semi-final at Wembley. Scraped past them, in truth. On penalties. But that in itself was a remarkable triumph. Because Everton's record in penalty shoot-outs is only fractionally better than England's. But four superbly-struck penalties saw us through to the final. Another FA Cup Final for Everton. This time against Chelsea.

Between 2001 and 2006, Wembley was being redeveloped and FA Cup finals were played at the Millennium Stadium in Cardiff. During that period, Everton didn't get close to playing in English football's showpiece event at English football's showpiece stadium. But now, at the new Wembley, we were back at the top table. And we got there before Liverpool had managed it. The omens were good. We won the toss which allowed us to play in our home kit and forced Chelsea to wear their away strip. But when the big moment came, it was the Blues of Chelsea who seized it rather than the Blues of Everton. We blew it. For 35 glorious seconds, Everton had been the kings of the new Wembley. When Louis Saha lashed a venomous shot into the Chelsea net, many people still hadn't taken their seats. Sadly, the person next to Lizzie – reeking of alcohol – HAD taken his seat before the match. He puked all over the floor and barely missed her feet. And then he retired under the stands somewhere, presumably to lower his head over a sink. He appeared briefly towards the end of the first half. He didn't return after half-time. There were 35 seconds of joy as Everton took the lead over Chelsea in the FA Cup Final. And this lad missed it. Idiot.

The rest of the match was all too predictable from an Everton perspective. Didier Drogba equalised midway through the first half. And even though Everton just about managed to hang on to the Chelsea coat-tails, in the end we just couldn't keep a tight enough grip. Tony Hibbert couldn't cope with Florent Malouda. Our midfield couldn't cope with theirs. Our defence creaked every time the pressure was turned up a notch. Frank Lampard scored the winner. John Terry lifted the cup. Everton lost. Everton were runners-up. The pre-match optimism had gone. And I left the stadium early, rather than watching Chelsea parading with the trophy.

The Everton family

The pain of losing a cup final doesn't get any easier. Losing to Liverpool in 1989, a month after Hillsborough, hurt. A lot. Losing to Chelsea, with precious little rivalry between the sides compared to the great Mersey divide, still hurt. A lot. Yet this is what football does to you. It's a passion. It's pride. But it's pain too. How could I want so much to pass this on to my son? How could I inflict on George this lifetime of misery? This lifetime of dashed dreams? This torment and torture – that made me turn to poetry as the only catharsis after being knocked out of the cup by Tranmere Rovers? How could I?

I wanted to do it – because I could. Because I could remember well the pride I felt at my own Everton connections. I could sense a stronger common bond between us if we shared our football. Like I did with my dad. Because I could imagine celebrating derby victories with George. I could envisage happy times. I could dare to hope. And dream. And share those dreams with him. I could put last week's defeat to one side. And think about next week's victory. I could return to that optimism. And I could share it with my son. That optimism. That euphoria that only football can bring.

In 1980, my first Everton match was a 3-1 home win over Bolton. Almost 20 years later we were playing the same opposition at Goodison Park. Bolton Wanderers. That team of a former girlfriend. That team who'd dumped us out of the cup when they were in the third tier of English football. That team who we'd pipped in avoiding relegation in 1998 by the width of a goal line – erroneously. That team which played Everton in my first match. Well, this was to be George's first match. And he had a three-year head-start on me. Where I was eight, George was only five. This would be his debut match.

It's lucky that Lizzie and I can break the journey to Goodison by stopping over at her parents' house in Staffordshire. It's not that I need a break on the round trip from Hertfordshire. After all, I've done it from Kent before and that's at least another 50 miles each way. But it's lucky for George. It meant it was less of a trek. It made his first ever match that much more 'doable'.

But on the Saturday morning, when we were about to leave Burton- on-Trent, George had other things on his mind.

'I don't want to go, daddy.' 'What.'

'I don't want to go. I want to stay here and watch films. We can go another time.'

Even as I write this now, I can sense the steam coming out of my ears. We were going and that was that. So I dragged him into the car. Not literally, you understand. And in truth, not kicking and screaming either. But with George's hang-dog expression. With his glum gob. With his five-year-old tantrum, this could turn into a nightmare day all round.

Still,we got to Goodison and parked up. We walked down to County Road. We had a slap-up lunch in the County Café. We wandered slowly around the ground and mingled with the other fans. It was a fine day. And so far, so good. We had seats in the Bullens Road End so with about 15 minutes to go, we walked up to the ground. I gave George and Lizzie their tickets. Lizzie went in. Then I realised. In front of me. Steel bars. A seven-foot turnstile. Electronically operated. How to get round this one? Momentarily, George froze. Where was his daddy taking him? What was on the other side of these steel bars? But the ticket went in the slot and the barcode registered a bleep. I shepherded George through. I followed him in. We were safe. And he was unfazed.

Next, to the seats. Good seats. Lizzie to the left. Me to the right. George in the middle. Level with the goal line at the Gwladys Street End but pretty much an unobstructed view of the pitch. Not too bad for Goodison Park, but a long way from the Park End goal. George got up and started walking.

'Where are you going?'

'Over there,' he said. 'I want to sit over there.'

He pointed to his left, towards the halfway line. Towards a more central view. Where the crowd was thickening. Where it'd be impossible to sit.

'We can't, George. These are the seats we paid for.'

Thankfully, he accepted this. He took his seat. He sprang up again. He said he wanted to stand so he could see better. And this he did for the full match.

I'll never forget the look on his face when the first bars of the theme from Z-Cars on the public address system were greeted with a great roar around the ground. Seasoned Everton-watchers know that the Z-Cars theme tune signals the entry of the teams on to the pitch. But George was no seasoned Everton-watcher. Not yet at least. So the roar of welcome from the Everton fans – and then the arrival of the teams – left him wide-eyed in wonder.

The game began. And it's fair to say it wasn't a classic. George followed every kick. Every tackle. Every header. Every throw. But no goals. Half-time. No score. A sense of frustration. From the crowd. From me. From George. Lizzie and I swapped seats, hoping for a change of luck. The Park End clock ticked down. Still no score.

'Daddy, this is rubbish! Nobody is going to score!'

'Well that happens sometimes, George. Sometimes there aren't any goals.'

Then, with 20 minutes left, Everton won a free kick. Arteta picked the ball up. Checked the ref wasn't looking. Walked forward about six paces. And put the ball down in a much better position. There was a blast of the referee's whistle. Arteta stood behind the ball. Focusing on it. Then he began his run. He hit the ball. And it flew into the back of the net. 'Yessssssssssssssssss sssssssssssssssssssss!' 'Yessssssssssssssssssssssssssssssssssssssss!'

Not just from the crowd. Not just from me. Not just from Lizzie. But from George too. I held him aloft so he could see the players celebrating, grouping around Arteta in front of the Gwladys Street End. And if George was losing his early football faith when we were struggling to score, he'd found it again instantly.

It was the cue for some free-flowing football from Everton. With a minute to go, we'd doubled the lead when Steven Pienaar finished off a fine move. George was once again aloft in the Bullens Road crowd. Celebrating with me. Kissing me. Cheering from the rafters. At the final whistle, I asked him if he'd like to come again.

'Definitely now,' he said. 'Definitely now.' And I couldn't have been prouder.

From Goodison Park to Hyde Park

When we got back to Lizzie's parents' house that night, I flicked through the Everton matchday programme and there – on page 35 – was a picture of Edgar Chadwick. The man who, most probably, was absolutely no relation of mine. But the man who, according to family folklore, really could have been. Might have been my great- grandfather. My dad's grandad. Except he wasn't. He wasn't part of my family. At least, I don't believe he was. But here was a family connection to Everton. Here was a story to pass down the line. As my grandfather spoke to my father about him, so my father spoke to me about him. And so I would speak to George about him. About Edgar Chadwick. About how he really probably wasn't Charles Roberts. But about how he was the first football superstar. I could tell George about Dixie Dean. About Alan Ball. About Alex Young, Howard Kendall, Gary Lineker and Duncan Ferguson. About Paul McCartney. About my heroes. About the people I had met.

There was only one thing for it. George's football initiation was complete. Now for his musical initiation. By the time of that Everton–Bolton match, George had become as obsessed with my Paul McCartney DVDs as he had become about Marouane Fellaini. The only thing missing from that Everton–Bolton match was an appearance by Fellaini. George's footballing hero. Where

I'd once admired Andy King, George now admired Fellaini. A boyhood hero. A young lad's very own Roy Of The Rovers. More for his hair than for any other reason. But he didn't play in that game against Bolton; a nasty challenge at Liverpool had left him out of action for the rest of the season. So George had to content himself with looking for

Fellaini in the crowd rather than on the pitch.

But while Fellaini may be a legend to a five-year-old, he's not quite got the status of Sir Paul McCartney. And that was the other man George was desperate to see in action. Around Christmas time, he acquainted himself with my Paul McCartney concert DVDs. So much so that he learned 'Drive My Car' off by heart. That he'd sing along to all the big tracks. That he'd sit there transfixed. Forget *Star Wars*. Forget Indiana Jones. Even forget Doctor Who, his fictional hero. George LOVED Paul McCartney. And I didn't even have to try to encourage him. All I had to do was put on a few CDs.

In the December, McCartney played a gig at the Millennium Dome but try as I might, I couldn't get tickets. George didn't know I'd tried and failed. But even so, I was disappointed. And he was disappointed.

'Daddy, how many times have you seen Paul McCartney?'

'Four.'

'When can you take me?'

'Ah. I'm not sure. He's getting on a bit now. And he doesn't tour that often. Maybe when you're a bit older.'

'Oh. Can't we go next week?'

'Sadly not, George. I think he's in America at the moment. I just don't know when he'll next be doing a concert.'

'Oh.'

He was disappointed. I was, too. It might never be possible. I'd waited years before I got to see Paul McCartney in concert. Because of the generation gap, George might never get to see him. But then, as if some kind of instant karma had landed in my lap, Paul McCartney announced he'd be playing at Hyde Park. And I got us tickets.

Months later, when the day finally came around, the World Cup in South Africa was in full swing. England had barely scraped into the knockout stages, having stumbled past the might of the USA, Algeria and Slovenia with two dire draws and one ugly, narrow victory.

Their reward was to finish second in the group behind the Americans. And that meant a last-16 match against old foes Germany instead of Ghana. Perhaps they shouldn't have dropped Everton's Leighton Baines from the squad before the finals. Mind you, perhaps they were just rubbish.

Now George and I didn't touch red. Except where England were concerned. So we put on our England tops. We went round to my mate's house in London. And we watched England get thumped 4-1 by Germany. Thankfully, this wasn't Everton. Thankfully, this meant George was more interested in his Doctor Who computer game than the football. And thankfully, I'd packed my *Band On The Run* T-shirt to change in to for that night's McCartney concert.

Even so, I had to go through it again. 'I don't want to go, daddy.'

'What.'

'I don't want to go. I want to stay here and play my Doctor Who game.'

Steam.

Anyway, George forgot about Doctor Who. And we all forgot about England. We packed up our gear and we crossed London. Crosby, Stills and Nash were still playing when we got there. But just like at Goodison, we arrived as late as we dared so as to avoid too much build-up ... and too much boredom. After all, as Paul had turned 68 just a few days earlier, George had only turned six on the same day.

We sat right at the back. Laying out our blanket, observing on the very fringes. Taking the safest option. But when Paul finally came out, they may as well have played the *Z-Cars* music to herald his arrival. There was excitement of the same magnitude. And when the intro to 'Jet' rang out across Hyde Park, George – on my shoulders – shouted: 'Oh, I love this one!'

I knew I was on to a winner. It may have been a long night. It may have required a lot of attention. It may even have been a school night. But George rocked with the best of them. To 'Hey

Jude'. To 'Get Back'. To 'Live And Let Die'. 'How many times have you seen Paul now, daddy? Is it five? Can we go again?'

When the encore came, Lizzie suggested we got nearer. Little did I know, but George had been badgering her for a closer view. So we moved forwards through the crowd. George on my shoulders, blowing kisses to Paul. Telling him he loved him. Telling him he was brilliant. Shouting: 'More! More!'

At the end of the gig, George shouted up to the stage.

'Paul, I'm going to love you forever! I could never not love you!'And afterwards, he asked me if Paul might let him join his band. Paul had signed my album but this might be too big an ask. Rusty Anderson did owe us 62 pence. But giving up his place as McCartney's lead guitarist might just be too big a price, for the sake of a sandwich at Corley services.

Maybe George will never get to jam with Paul McCartney. Maybe he'll never even see Everton become champions of England again. But some things are meant to be. And nothing is perfect. As Fellaini was missing for that Everton–Bolton match, so Paul didn't play 'Drive My Car' in his set list. It wasn't lost on George. But it spoiled absolutely nothing. He was buzzing all the way back to the car. He'd seen his hero in concert. He'd spent the night blowing kisses at him. He'd spent the night rocking to his music. This little Evertonian loved my football team. Loved HIS football team. And loved Paul McCartney's music.

And I couldn't have been prouder.

Epilogue

I had every intention of buying George a Fellaini wig ahead of Saturday's cup match with Chelsea – only his second ever trip to Goodison Park. But Bill Kenwright's secretary rang me on Friday to ask us if we'd like to watch the match from the directors' box as the chairman's guests. So we did. It meant no wig for George. But Bill did give him a brand new Everton coat. And he made him feel special. A part of the Everton family.

Among the other guests were Howard Kendall, Dave Hickson, Frank Lampard Snr and England's assistant manager Franco Baldini. Even Sammy Lee was there. And I had to tell George not to tap him on the shoulder to tease him about his Liverpool allegiances. We had magnificent seats. We had magnificent hospitality. Shame about the Chelsea equaliser. But for us, it was five-star football.

The chairman's generosity to us, which came from an email I sent him about this book, underlined to me what a special club Everton is. A family club. A club which I embraced from an early age, just like my father did. And just like my son is now doing. George will be an Evertonian for life. And that is my proudest achievement of all.

The hard winter of 2009 was followed by an even harder one in 2010 – and a harder one still in 2011. But as I look out of my window this early afternoon, there is glorious sunshine. And a glorious sky. A blue sky.

I've been to another 19 Everton matches since I started writing this book almost two years ago. George has been to three of them.

And now he's been in the directors' box and shaken hands with Howard Kendall.

Today he is at school. Probably exhausted. But probably thrilled. Showing off the new Everton coat given to him by Everton's chairman. Showing off the Marouane Fellaini picture I bought him from the

Everton megastore. Proudly doing his 'Show And Tell'.

For George, it's probably the same story as a few months back. The night when we got home at 12.15am. From the Paul McCartney concert. The concert that he was still talking about the next morning. He took the tickets to school with him the day after that, too, so he could show his teacher and his friends.

When I read *John Lennon: The Life*, by Philip Norman, I cried. I cried even though I knew that he was orphaned when his mother was run over. Even though I knew how the story would end. Halfway through writing this book, a nation was crying over the (mis)fortunes of the England football team after yet another World Cup failure. When will they ever learn? When will we ever learn? When will I ever learn?

I've been through it with Everton. Been through the ups. Been through the downs. And it sometimes seems as though there are far more downs than ups. But it's the good times that you remember. And even in recent seasons, Everton have given me plenty of good times. A 3-0 win over Liverpool. That Dan Gosling goal which knocked the Reds out of the cup. Taking Lizzie for the first time – and watching Everton destroy Newcastle, her ex-boyfriend's team, 3-0. So trivial stuff. And tremendous stuff. Back-to-back wins at Tottenham. Going to Nuremberg to watch Everton win in the Uefa Cup. And going to Wembley twice. Again.

But the best times of all have come recently. And they will come in the future. Because I am now sharing my team with my son. The Bolton match at home. Taking him to Blackpool away, just me and him. Our one-off trip to the directors' box for the Chelsea match, just me and him. And Bill Kenwright and Howard Kendall. What a special football club Everton is.

Everton have given me ups. They've given me downs. It's a reflection of life, of my life. Of the ups and downs. But you keep on believing. You keep believing that there will be more ups in the end. That your love life will work out. That you'll be happy.

That your children will be safe. That Everton will win trophies. That Paul McCartney will keep making records. And that George will always want to go to the football with me.

What is life without football and music? Without something to be proud of? Without something to believe in? Without people to admire and without people to give you hope? Without people to give you dreams? Because when you have a son to share those dreams with you, they automatically come true.

Liam

On Wednesday 9 February 2011, Liam James Roberts was born. Unlike George, he didn't share his birthday with Paul McCartney, or any other Beatle for that matter. But you could say he was born exactly half a century after the Beatles themselves were born.

Liam's first day in the world was the 50th anniversary of the Beatles' first ever performance at the Cavern Club on Mathew Street in Liverpool. I can only imagine what it was like on that day, in that sweaty underground club which forged their sound, their identity and their following. The Cavern crowd had seen the Quarrymen before. But on 9 February 1961, they'd never seen the Beatles. The lunchtime set which they played earned the band just £5 – split five ways between John Lennon, Paul McCartney, George Harrison and those early Beatles Stuart Sutcliffe and Pete Best. I'm sure it was the rawest of performances, back in the winter of 1961. Little did those watching know that they were watching history in the making. Because that's what February the 9th was. It was a date which made history. And 50 years later, 9 February 2011, was a date which made history in my own life.

February the 9th was also the date of the Beatles' groundbreaking debut on the *Ed Sullivan Show* in America, when 73 million people watched them perform live in 1964. So while George shares a birthday with Paul McCartney, Liam's birthday has its own historic Beatles connections. And his birthday has an Everton association, too. Edgar Chadwick's final goal in Everton's first ever season of professional league football was scored on 9 February. The man who we once believed was, in fact, a Roberts scored Everton's goal in a 2-1 home defeat to Wolves, at Anfield, in 1889 – 122 years before Liam's entrance into the world.

Most importantly of all though, 9 February was the date that Liam became my second beautiful boy, a brother to George and, of course, the world's newest Evertonian. He came into the world little more than a week after George and I had our own dream date in the directors' box at Goodison Park. And when George met his little brother, one of the first things he did was show him his Everton scarf and sing: 'It's a Grand Old Team to play for ...'

So now it's two sons to share my dreams with. Two sons to share my passions with. Two sons, in time, to take to watch Everton. It's a little early to be taking Liam to the match or to be talking to him about the Beatles' back catalogue. Or that debut performance at the Cavern. Or that landmark appearance with Ed Sullivan on American TV. But one day I'll tell him. One day I'll tell him how I met Paul McCartney. One day I'll take him to watch Everton, at Goodison Park or wherever we may play in the future. One day I'll tell Liam how George met Howard Kendall. And if Liam should become envious, I'll tell him that one day he will have his own special experiences with the club and hopefully he will meet his own heroes. And one day so will George – whatever those experiences may be, whoever he should be lucky enough to meet.

I have lots of experiences to tell my two sons about. Many dreams fulfilled. Many dreams unfulfilled. But what amazing experiences I've had. In time, George and Liam will be able to read about them in this book. About how I lived my life through those dreams. About how I met my heroes. They say you should never meet your heroes. Let me tell you, they are wrong. And I hope George and Liam meet theirs.

Acknowledgements

At the risk of sounding like some diva giving a speech at the Oscars, I do need to thank many people for helping me write this book. The process of becoming an author involves so much more than just committing pen to paper, or rather tapping away at the keyboard of your computer. The mammoth task of writing a book is actually only half the job. The rest of it involves finding a publisher, working with a publisher, a designer, an editor and various other very clever people involved in turning your work into an actual book. Not only that, but there's a painstaking process to go through to clear various copyrights, including your own interviews!

At this point I must stress that I have endeavoured to leave no stone unturned when it comes to seeking the correct permissions to reproduce various pictures and texts within this book. And hopefully I have contacted everybody it is feasibly possible to contact. If I haven't achieved this anywhere, please accept my most sincere apologies as I have tried so hard to act in the best of faith throughout this process. As any good Evertonian would, of course!

Firstly I would like to thank Chris Walker and Tony Hall from the Liverpool Daily Post & Echo for allowing me to reproduce my interviews and various photographs. I always knew that the Post & Echo were great employers. They've been great friends to me throughout this project, too. Thanks also to Max Dunbar of the Everton Collection Charitable Trust for opening my eyes to their wonderful work. I think they have the world's largest single collection of football memorabilia and it is a real treasure chest for any football fan, not just an Evertonian.

ACKNOWLEDGEMENTS

Thanks must also go to Ben Smith, from News International, for permission to reproduce a section from Ed Bottomley's article on the 50 Greatest Everton Players which appeared in *The Times* in March 2009. And, at the risk of de-personalising these very sincere thank yous, I am grateful to the BBC for consent to include the quotes from Kevin Ratcliffe on Brian Labone and Brian Labone on Liverpudlians, taken from BBC News at bbc. co.uk/news. I have no idea which individual at the Beeb helped me out, as I received an email from 'newswebsitepermissions'. But thank you to you, whoever you are.

Helen Wilson from Guardian Newspapers was very kind in allowing me to reproduce Sir Paul McCartney's quotes on his football allegiances, given in an interview to *Observer Sport Monthly* (copyright Guardian News & Media Ltd 2008). And so too was John Hillier. Captain John Hillier, in fact, who deserves special mention for his rank in the Royal Marines, that great body of men who once counted my great-grandfather and my wonderful grandad among their number. As editor of the *Globe & Laurel*, I have Capt. Hillier to thank for the reproductions of the photograph and match report of the 1904 Army Cup Final, in which great-grandfather Charles Roberts played such a significant role.

When I worked at ITN, John Battle frequently steered me on to the right path in terms of media law so I ought to be doubly grateful to him. Firstly for that. Secondly for allowing me to reproduce in full the interview given to me by Sir Paul McCartney for ITN/ITV *London Tonight*.

And there are various photographers, also family friends, who I need to thank. Bob Vickers, Tony Cordeiro and Mike Green were all particularly helpful. But I'd like to extend my thanks also to Paul Fender and Craig Doyle for taking memorable pictures of me with Sir Ian Botham and the man himself, Sir Paul McCartney.

A friend and former colleague of mine from my days in Bermuda, Nigel Henderson, gave sound advice and pointed me towards Pitch Publishing, who did a great job in producing the book. So thanks too to the main man there, Paul Camillin, but also to Jane Camillin for various pieces of very sound advice.

Duncan Olner from Brilliant Orange also produced a fabulous cover design for *Blues & Beatles*. A sterling job was also done by Dean Rockett, who edited the book. If I'm an Evertonian with a soft spot for Portsmouth, he's the reverse: a Pompey fan with a soft spot for the Toffees! Aside from Dean, thanks also to Andrew Searle for his painstaking and diligent work in the typesetting process.

There are many other people, both directly and indirectly, who helped contribute to this book. And perhaps some of them didn't know it. Thanks to Stuart Bell, who helped arrange my interview with Sir Paul McCartney and also to Nancy Griffiths who works in his New York office. Closer to home, Bill Kenwright CBE was an absolute gentleman and made my son George (and me) feel very special indeed in the directors' box at Goodison Park. Thanks also to his PA Emily Dallas. And of course thanks to all those who are quoted in the book and who gave me such fabulous interviews – and helped make my dreams come true.

Most of all I need to thank those closest to me. To Dawn, for sharing so much with me and for providing me with my wonderful son George. To Lizzie, for offering me the greatest love and for being the greatest support I could wish for ... and for providing me with my beautiful little son Liam. To my mother, for her unconditional love, in spite of the fact that she never was an Evertonian! To my sister Caroline, the best sister in the world. And of course to my brother Matthew.

Last, but by no means least, thank you to my late nanna and my late grandad, who I loved very, very much. And thank you to my father. Without Colin Roberts, I would never have had the truly amazing experiences I describe in this book. Thank God he didn't steer me to the dark side, but he showed me the light. And finally to George, who gave me the inspiration for this book. And to Liam, who came along just in time to get his name in print. To both of you: may all your dreams come true.

Neil Roberts, 2011